SUPERMARKETER TO THE WORLD

Books by E. J. Kahn, Jr.

Year of Change: More About *The New Yorker* and Me
The Problem Solvers
The Staffs of Life
Jock: The Life and Times of John Hay Whitney
Far-flung and Footloose: Pieces from *The New Yorker*, 1937–1978
About *The New Yorker* and Me
Georgia: From Rabun Gap to Tybee Light
The American People
The China Hands
Fraud
The Boston Underground Gourmet (*with Joseph P. Kahn*)
The First Decade
Harvard: Through Change and Through Storm
The Separated People
A Reporter in Micronesia
The World of Swope
The Stragglers
A Reporter Here and There
The Big Drink
The Merry Partners
The Peculiar War
Who, Me?
The Voice
McNair: Educator of an Army
G. I. Jungle
The Army Life

THE STORY OF DWAYNE ANDREAS
CEO OF ARCHER DANIELS MIDLAND

SUPERMARKETER TO THE WORLD

E. J. KAHN, JR.

WARNER BOOKS

A Time Warner Company

Portions of this book appeared, in considerably different form, in *The New Yorker.*

Copyright © 1984, 1985, 1991 by E. J. Kahn, Jr.
All rights reserved.
Warner Books, Inc., 666 Fifth Avenue, New York, NY 10103
A Time Warner Company

Printed in the United States of America

First Printing: September 1991

10 9 8 7 6 5 4 3 2 1

Library of Congress Cataloging-in-Publication Data

Kahn, E. J. (Ely Jacques), 1916–
    Supermarketer to the World / E. J. Kahn, Jr.
        p.   cm.
    Includes index.
    ISBN 0-446-51495-0
    1. Andreas, Dwayne, 1918–   . 2. Businessmen—United States—
Biography. 3. Soybean industry—United States. 4. Food industry
and trade—United States. 5. Archer Daniels Midland Company.
I. Title.
HD9235.S6A545   1990
338. 1'75655'092—dc20
    [B]   90-50535
                                                            CIP

Book design: H. Roberts

AUTHOR'S NOTE

It is hard to write definitively about a living person, especially one whose ongoing activity belies his chronology. This, then, does not purport to be a full-fledged biography of a busy man bestriding his seventy-third year, nor is it a fully authorized one. Dwayne Andreas—like his family and friends and business associates—has been cooperative in the assembling of material, but the winnowing of that and its presentation is wholly my responsibility.

Hundreds of people, some of course far more than others, have helped in my research. I apologize to those whom I may inadvertently have omitted, and who would otherwise have gratefully been listed here along with Boris P. Alekseyev, Gary K. Anderson, G. Allen Andreas, Jr., Inez Andreas, Lowell W. Andreas, Martin L. Andreas, Michael Andreas, Terry Andreas, Charles P. Archer, Shreve M. Archer, Jr., Martin E. Ashkenazi,

William T. Atkinson, Thomas H. Atwood, Kenneth L. Bader, William Barnes III, J. M. Barturen, Charles T. Bayless, Alexander T. Bonkowski, Dan Brennan, Richard E. Burket, George Burns, Ernest Callenbach, Mike Carr, Barbara Charnes, Charles Conrad, Ingrid Cravens, John H. Daniels, Gordon Ellison, Roy L. Erickson, Peter Fitch, Raymond Floyd, Thomas E. Frankel, David G. Gartner, James H. Giffen, Jean Godbey, John C. Goodchild, Ishmail Habib, H. D. Hale, Marcy V. Hargan, Sheldon J. Hauck, James O. Hey, Christian Holmes, Judy Inman, F. Ross Johnson, William Kent, J. Roger Kilburn, Walter C. Klein, Burnell D. Kraft, Ann Landers, Hobart Lewis, Willard C. Lighter, Victor F. Lishchenko, Richard J. Lutovsky, Claudia Madding, Sandra A. McMurtrie, Clare Morganthaler, Sister Jeanne O'Laughlin, Thomas P. O'Neill, John Phipps, Donald P. Poboisk, Raymond Price, Robert Raclin, James R. Randall, Benjamin H. Read, John G. Reed, A. Daniel Reuwee, David Rockefeller, Happy Rockefeller, Preston W. Schellbach, Sue Shellenbarger, William Shurtleff, Otto A. Silha, Martin Sorkin, Morton I. Sosland, James E. Stewart, Ellen Stoutenberg, James W. Stowell, Robert S. Strauss, John K. Vanier, Donald B. Walker, Grace K. Warnecke, Herbert J. Waters, Steven Young, Juliet Zavon—

and last, but emphatically not least, Dwayne Orville Andreas.

EJK

Truro, Massachusetts
November 1990

PROLOGUE

An Easterner on a business trip to Decatur, Illinois, was awakened at four A.M. by a fierce storm—a barrage of thunder and lightning, torrents of rain beating against his window. The outlander was depressed. He wanted to go home. It was still raining, and the sky was an inhospitable dark gray, when he dragged himself off to a seven A.M. appointment at the Hotel Ambassador restaurant.

It was the time and place for Decatur power breakfasts. The mayor was on hand, and the head of the Chamber of Commerce, and, scattered around the scene, local eminences in real estate, banking, engineering, and insurance; practically the entire board of directors of the Macon County Economic Development Council; and last, but by no means least, the vice president in charge of community relations for Archer Daniels Midland, the world's largest processor of agricultural products and Decatur's very own.

To the Easterner's surprise, the indigenes, to a man, were bubbling over. They seemed as happy, if also as wet, as clams. The corn, one of them explained, had just started to sprout, and it would soon be soybean-planting time. Last night's downpour, accordingly, was providential. "A million-dollar rain!" one of them said.

A few miles away, in bed at his home overlooking Lake Decatur, Dwayne Andreas, the urbane farm-born-and-raised CEO of ADM, who once said of his corporate domain, the fifty-seventh on *Fortune*'s 1990 list of its Big 500 and as such bigger than Borden and Heinz and Campbell Soup, "Basically, my business consists of Midwesterners teaching Easterners —most of whom know very little about where their food comes from—about the facts of life," had also been roused by the storm.

"It got me thinking about nitrogen," he said to a lunch companion later. "Are you aware that a single thunderclap releases one million tons of nitrogen into the air? Very few people stop to think that our crops are dependent on the nitrogen let loose by thunderclaps like that. What a splendid storm that was! I listened to it for a bit, and then I rolled over and purred like a kitten."

1

Except for nuclear war, world hunger is the world's biggest threat to peace.

—DWAYNE O. ANDREAS

WHEN the general secretary of the Communist Party of the Soviet Union had the president of the United States to dinner in the Kremlin on May 30, 1988, the host allowed his guest to bring along thirteen additional Americans. (It was protocolary tit for tat; the same number of lower-ranking Russians had been asked to break bread with Ronald Reagan at a White House banquet for Mikhail Gorbachev the previous December.) Eleven of the favored few were in President Reagan's official party: his wife, Secretary of State and Mrs. George Shultz, U.S. Ambassador to the USSR and Mrs. Jack Matlock, Secretary of Defense Frank Carlucci, White House Chief of Staff Howard Baker, National Security Adviser Lieutenant General Colin Powell, Assistant Secretary of State for European and Canadian Affairs Rozanne Ridgway, and two high-level members of the White House staff—Kenneth Duberstein and Thomas Griscom.

Of the two remaining Americans, one was Armand Hammer, then ninety, who first went to Moscow in 1921, at twenty-three, as a physician during a typhus epidemic. His family had a pharmaceutical business, and he brought along an ambulance loaded with supplies. From their sales he hoped to help out his temporarily embarrassed father, in prison for having performed an abortion on a woman who soon thereafter died. The younger Hammer met Lenin then and would soon be acknowledged as the foreigner—the foreign capitalist, after he went into business—on best terms with a succession of Soviet leaders.

The second remaining American was another businessman, seventy years old, dark haired and hazel eyed, who over the past few years had increasingly been referred to, and not without reason, as "the new Armand Hammer." According to the *Wall Street Journal*, he was on track to becoming "Moscow's favorite American businessman." Indeed, in one of the first biographies of Gorbachev distributed in the Western world, there were more references to him than to Hammer.

This was Dwayne Andreas, among whose published sobriquets—because he stood, jockeylike, only five feet four inches and weighed 137, "Little Giant" was one—the best known was "the Soybean King." A monarch with five residences, a golf handicap of twenty-six, a stretch Rolls-Royce, and a host of extremely well-placed friends, Andreas was perhaps particularly noteworthy because of his stubborn lifelong belief that it was possible, given the abundant resources of the planet he inhabited, for none of its other billions of people ever to have to go hungry.

More prosaically, Andreas had since 1971 been the chief executive officer of an agricultural complex, Archer Daniels Midland, that under his guidance had become a huge processor of soybeans, corn, and wheat (not to mention peanuts, cottonseed, oats, rice, et al.), with annual revenues of over $8 billion and a net income of close to $500 million. In 1989 in the United States alone, ADM, as it is informally known, had more than nine thousand employees in 118 processing plants in twenty-nine states, and they marketed, managed, stored, and moved around more than 75 million tons, of fifty commodities, a year. (ADM had one of the highest sales-per-employee ratings on record: about $750,000 annually apiece.) Every day of the year, ten thousand trucks, ten thousand railroad tank cars, two thousand barges, and one hundred ocean-going ships were in transit somewhere or other sporting the ADM colors—orange, gray, and black, when they are visible. So many trains chugged in and out of the company's Decatur, Illinois, base of operations that in 1988 it had to dig a tunnel under the tracks to enable emergency vehicles to get through and its employees to drive unhindered to and from work.

It is one of Andreas's few regrets, in a career otherwise brimful of satisfactions, that in 1990 ADM was marketing only a thousand tons a day—only!—of ingredients for ready-to-eat soy products. That constituted less than one-half of one percent of the company's sales. ADM, which day in and out routinely bought 5 million bushels of grains and oilseeds, had four principal areas of operation: oilseed processing, which included its soybean, peanut, and cottonseed divisions; corn milling (ethanol and biodegradable plastics fell under that); wheat milling; and a catch-all embracing its cane-sugar, pasta, barley-malting (five plants devoted exclusively to *that*), and hydroponics activities. Its grain elevators at last count had a storage capacity of some 200 million bushels. It may have been that grandiose statistic that inspired the *Washington Times*, in the winter of 1990, to confer on Andreas yet another lofty honorific—that of "Grain King."

One of ADM's slogans goes, "We put our money where your mouth is." In some of its advertisements, the company calls itself "supermarket to the world." Nowhere on earth are any edibles sold at retail bearing an ADM label, which explains why the company, for all its size, is relatively unknown to the general public. A catalogue devoted exclusively to products containing ADM-processed soybeans, however, has a two-page center spread illustrated with more than a hundred supermarket staples—to name only a few, Mr. Goodbar,

Lipton Cup-a-Soup, Chilli Man Chilli, Quaker Instant Grits, A&P German-Style Potato Salad, Nabisco Onion Tuna Twist, Hormel Burritos, Chef Boyardee Spaghetti Dinner with Meat Sauce, Birds Eye Swiss-Style Vegetables, and Handy Andy Hot Dog Buns.

Another ADM brochure that covers a wider spectrum of food ingredients lists 102 of these made by sixteen subsidiary companies under its broad corporate umbrella: acid salt, brown rice, Danish-pastry mix, canola oil, wheat nuggets, yeast foods, six varieties of cornstarch, six icing and glaze stabilizers, thirteen refined vegetable oils, eighteen refined *packaged* vegetable oils, and twenty-one kinds of corn syrup, ranging from high viscosity, bland flavor, and low sweetness to high sweetness and high fermentability. ADM's soybean-oil production lines, for their part, account for twenty-nine different grades under 478 labels belonging to its customers. "We regard ourselves as a place where other big food people buy their groceries," one ADM executive says. "It is nearly impossible for a major food company *not* to do business with us."

Andreas was well acquainted with both Gorbachev and Reagan before joining them that evening at the Kremlin. He grew up on a sixty-acre farm just north of Lisbon, Iowa, then a town of about seven hundred. (When it comes his turn to contribute to a down-to-earth locker-room symposium, Andreas is apt to say that when he was a boy, Lisbon was so small a community that the town whore remained a virgin for two years.) Dwayne often visited relatives at nearby Dixon, Illinois. Its park had a swimming pool, and the pool had a lifeguard. For several years, in the 1920s, this sentinel, because of the haircut he then affected, was known as Dutch. A longer name was Ronald Reagan.

Many years later, during a small dinner in the upstairs family quarters of the White House, Andreas was invited to say a few words about the incumbent paterfamilias. So he reminisced about Dixon and the lifeguard and how Dwayne's mother or an aunt, for five straight years, would drive him and a cousin or two to the pool. The women would never leave until Dutch had waved to them. What the wave meant, Andreas told the Washington assemblage, was "Everything's okay; I'm in charge here."

Well, Andreas went on, he'd been curious to see how the two world leaders would relate to one another while they were all dining in the *Granovitovava Palata*—Faceted Palace— of the Kremlin, a many-splendored hall, with a vaulted ceiling, massive chandeliers, and a floor of agate jasper, that Ivan the Great had built in 1491. "When Gorbachev used phrases like 'God willing,' that clearly pleased the president," Andreas recalled, "and when the then general secretary said, 'We are praying for a good result,' Reagan looked over at me and flicked one eye. Soon he got up and said to Gorbachev, 'God bless *you* for the things you are trying to do,' and then he made the same little waving gesture Dutch had made back at the pool and the feeling came over me of 'I'm in charge here' —the same 'I'm in charge' feeling from sixty years ago."

In 1969, ADM moved its headquarters from Minneapolis to Decatur. In Andreas's spacious office there, along with a replica of a Grant Wood depiction of a dozen or so threshers sitting down to eat and a plastic-framed steel screwdriver bearing the name of Dwayne's father's Lisbon feed firm, there are photographs of Reagan, Gorbachev, and a third contemporary acquaintance—Pope John Paul II.

Decatur, which lies roughly halfway between Springfield (state capital) and Champaign-Urbana (state university), is close to being the center of the country's corn- and soybean-growing acreage. (Illinois's more than 9 million acres planted to soybeans outranks all other states, and Decatur's Mayor Gary Anderson was inducted in 1989 as an honorary member of the Illinois Corn Growers Association.) "The real knowledge, the real sophisticated people in this line of business— who understand crops and how to buy them, how to sell them, and how to process them—are all Midwestern people," Andreas told the *Decatur Herald & Review* in a 1981 interview. "It's a culture, that's what it really is.... It's a culture and it sure has to be based where the crops are."

For many years, more soybeans were processed at Decatur—at the peak, five thousand tons of them every working day—than anywhere else on earth. The city called itself the Soybean Capital of the World, and within it were the Soy Capital Bank & Trust Company, the Soy City Motel, the Soy City Towing Company, Soy City Electric Supply, and Soy City Tire & Tread. Its convention bureau called it "a comfortably sized Midwestern city full of pleasant surprises." One surprise falls short of pleasantness—a sickly sweet odor that sometimes pervades the town when the atmosphere is especially hot and humid. "Sometimes when you're out on the golf course," one power-breakfast regular told a visitor, "the damn odor nearly knocks you out." The smell—some call it a stench—is the result of the large-scale drying of corn gluten feed and the toasting of soymeal. ADM, which is justifiably proud of having one of the best environmental attitudes and performances of any American corporation, tends in this instance to be a bit defensive. "Akron has the same trouble with its tire plants," one of Andreas's henchmen told a visitor.

Notwithstanding a billboard along one approach to Soy City that proclaims "Decatur—Pride of the Prairie," the community is by and large a blue-collar, smokestack one. Along with ADM, there are other substantial industries—Caterpillar, Firestone, Pittsburgh Plate Glass. But the place is never referred to as Tractor City or Plate Glass City, and when the residents fiddle around with their radio dials, they often hit WSOY or WSOY-FM. (More corn is processed at Decatur nowadays than soy, but nobody has yet dubbed the place Corn City, either.) When the Bureau of the Census last paid it a formal call, in 1980, the city's population, slightly down from previous counts, stood at 90,360. Of the 42,816 members of the civilian labor force, Dwayne Andreas was probably the most consequential, but he was by no means the biggest hometown celebrity. That honor was generally conceded to belong to major-league baseball's Bill Madlock.

Decatur is the kind of place where from May to September there are free band concerts every Sunday evening in the city square. It is also the site of Millikin University, a

Presbyterian school with a coeducational enrollment of fifteen hundred, which was founded in 1901 and named after a nineteenth-century banker and philanthropist who in 1876 built himself a home so big it could for a spell be readily converted into a hospital. (The city itself, now Illinois's fifth largest, was first settled in 1829.) Just southeast of the Millikin homestead stands a nine-foot-high effigy of Stephen Decatur, commemorating the commodore's 1804 Battle of Tripoli against the Barbary pirates.

Today Millikin, thanks in part to Dwayne and Inez Andreas—she, his wife of more than forty years and in every real sense a helpmeet, is one of its trustees—like many another institution or enterprise they have taken to heart and to purse, is in robust financial health. Similarly, when in 1987 Dwayne's old hometown of Lisbon was trying to raise, from all imaginable sources, $60,000 for a community center, somebody sent him a fund-raising brochure, and although he hadn't set foot there for about fifteen years, he at once mailed back a check for $10,000.

Andreas gave the commencement address at Millikin in 1982 and, as is usual in such circumstances, received an honorary degree. It was his first degree of any sort; he never finished college. He seized the occasion, as he often has at other times and in other settings, to inform his listeners that world hunger could be alleviated, if only anybody cared enough, for less than $100 billion a year, or about one-eighth of the annual global outlay for armaments. Corporation executives not infrequently deliver themselves of pious declarations, sometimes self-written, about this or that burning issue. Andreas's concern about feeding humanity began on the farm and has never faltered during his climb to the boardroom. "Except for nuclear war," he told his Millikin audience, and he wrote it and meant it, "world hunger is the world's biggest threat to peace. A billion people on our planet go to bed hungry every night. The anger of these hungry people ... is potentially the most explosive force in the world today next, perhaps, to the atomic bomb itself. I wish you

could see what I have seen—little children with swollen
bellies, listless adults without the energy to do a day's work
...these sights are burning within my mind."

He went on to say that "there is no place I would rather
deliver this message than right here in Decatur...a city
that processes more grain and oilseed into food and feed than
any other city on earth...here in Millikin University, right
here"—he knows a lot of politicians and was beginning for a
moment to sound like one—"in Illinois, the greatest of our
fifty states."

I'm a strong believer
that trade is the greatest
promoter of peace and
goodwill on earth.

—DOA, 1989

ROBABLY few Americans outside the farm belt know or
care much about Decatur. Ronald Reagan was not
among them. Like many Washingtonians, the television programs to which the president was most addicted
were the Sunday-morning talk-and-interview shows, "decisionmakers" some people called them: *Meet the Press, This Week
with David Brinkley,* and the like.

Some of ADM's scattered subsidiaries, in their advertising, lean toward the hard sell. ADM Milling, in the weekly
Milling & Banking News, is apt to show a couple of characters in graduation gowns under the catch line "Magna Corn
Laude," and that offshoot sends its customers musical cassettes featuring something called the Grain Group, composed
in part of Bagel on the bugle, Pasta on the piano, and Corn on

the horn. "Get smart," intones an announcer. "Feed the brain grain."

The parent company, with no consumer goods to hawk through television or any other medium, occasionally verges in its ads on the conventionally self-serving ("The soybean's role as food must grow") but in the main concentrates on bringing loftier issues to the Sunday shows, in accordance with Andreas's conviction that the people he believes watch them—the movers and shakers in the realms of investment and banking along with politics—are those he most wants to reach with the messages he thinks they need to hear.

Like most big national businesses, ADM has an advertising agency (a farm-belt-oriented one, in Minneapolis), but perhaps few big businessmen get as personally involved in their commercials as does Andreas in his. (Lee Iacocca, of course, who at times seems unable to drag himself out of camera range, is sui generis.) No word or picture is released without his imprimatur. Along with soil conservation, hunger is a much-stressed favorite theme. There was one TV commercial in 1989 that moved along visually from a dot to many dots to a human eye to the face of a young Asiatic woman, while the voice-over reminded viewers, echoing an oft-uttered Andreas lament, that the world has plenty of resources with which to feed its hungry millions, but that "it won't happen as long as we continue to look the other way."

"That ad is supposed to be a response to frustration," Andreas explained to an inquiring acquaintance. "I'm always running into frustrated businessmen—like builders or real estate people who all say they can't understand why there have to be any homeless Americans. 'Why can't a president come along someday,' they say, 'and say, "Let's build!"' It's the same in the food business, when you see food all around you and also people starving wherever you look. I say, 'Let's build better structures for getting it to them!'"

Back in 1830, the Thomas Lincolns spent a year in a just-spawned Decatur cabin. Thirty-one years later, their son Abraham passed through en route to his Washington inauguration. But aside from a Harry Truman whistle-stop during his 1948 campaign, Decatur has not figured as a regular port of call for the country's chief executives. So when President Reagan decided to stop by on August 20, 1984, on his way to Dallas for renomination, the city was understandably elated.

So was Andreas, who was serving at the time as chairman of a Presidential Task Force on International Private Enterprise, which was supposed to help stimulate trade among poorer nations. (Later, Reagan would dub him chairman of the Foundation for the US Constitution, in whose magazine ADM placed an ad showing ten peas on a plate, with an accompanying caption that went, "Contrary to what your mother told you, cleaning your plate won't feed the hungry people of the world.") The Soybean King was especially pleased when Reagan said he'd been motivated to come by watching ADM commercials on the Sunday Brinkley show. "I called David and told him," Andreas says, "and he was one happy man."

Brinkley, a wintertime Florida neighbor of Andreas's, later once visited Decatur himself, to address a Chamber of Commerce gathering. When he said he was staying at a friend's house and that he hoped the city appreciated the guy, the audience broke into applause that the local press rated spontaneous. The Decatur Hall of Fame has rules not unlike those of major-league baseball. Andreas will not be eligible until he's been five years retired, and inasmuch as he has never shown the slightest interest in retiring, although he is a shoo-in for election—along with, no doubt, Bill Madlock— he may only make it posthumously.

"Decatur Greets the President" was the headline that swept across page one of the *Herald & Review* the day Reagan materialized. Among the ten thousand spectators who flocked to the airport to greet him were a well-scrubbed bunch of 4-H clubbers, a few catcallers (conceivably wanting to remind the visitor that his was a two-party country), and the Archer Daniels Midland world-champion men's fast-pitch softball team. Some of the grandstand seats from its home field were carted over to the airport to accommodate the welcomers.

Introducing the guest of honor to some ADM employees, their CEO, showing he was acquainted with other TV sponsors' lingo, said, "Mr. President, the farmers make money the old-fashioned way," and then veered from the script with, "They work with God."

From 1980 on, ADM had been looking seriously into hydroponic agriculture, and out of one ten-acre indoor garden, it was, by then, harvesting three tons of lettuce, or thirty thousand heads, every twenty-four hours. The president obligingly posed holding one.

Every day, ADM's Decatur corn plant grinds ten thousand tons—about five hundred truckloads. Reagan watched a couple of trucks being unloaded and flatteringly compared the sight to the seven wonders of the world.

The president also remembered his politics and where he was and said, "The federal government has an important role to play as a partner of the farm community...to help farmers do what they can't always do on their own...seek out new markets."

He seemed most interested, all in all, in a large bag of jelly beans included in an array of products made at least in part from regional corn (you can't make jelly beans from soybeans), among them five gallons of ethanol—a supposedly less environmentally polluting motor fuel that has also been featured on ADM TV commercials—and three dressed chickens. Andreas thinks about chickens a lot. "Are you aware," he is apt to interject when a conversation about almost anything seems to be lagging, "that we have reached a point in history where we can realize one pound of chicken from only one point eight pounds of chicken feed? Why, as recently as fifteen years ago, it took four pounds of feed, and even then the chickens came out scrawny."

The jelly beans were not the only special treat the host had arranged that day. The Dixon house in which Reagan was raised has been converted into a sort of shrine, and one of the Dixonians who made that possible—a onetime charge of

Dutch-the-lifeguard who was also a member of the town's delegation to the first Reagan inauguration—was James Orville Hey, Dwayne Orville Andreas's first cousin. (Both were named after their uncle James Orville Duffey, a Moody Bible Institute evangelist.) Dwayne had phoned Cousin Jimmy, who'd also gone into the food business—Hey Brothers, Makers of Fine Ice Cream—and urged him to come around for President's Day.

"Mr. President," Andreas said, pointing, "you remember Jimmy Hey, over there in the audience, from the old days."

With a "Hey, Jimmy!" Reagan, possibly to the consternation of the Secret Service, scrambled over to shake his former fellow-townsman's hand.

"I thought, there's a great politician," Andreas said afterward.

Politicians of all stripes have learned over the years that no matter how much Andreas may admire their tactical astuteness, they had better not expect him to kowtow to them. Toward the end of 1984, for instance, the task force on private enterprise that Reagan had asked him to chair had its findings ready to present. They were voluminous. Their main recommendation was that an Economic Security (later "Policy") Council be set up in the White House as an equivalent, in nonmilitary matters, of the existing National Security Council. Its purpose would have been to, among other high-minded objectives, promote private enterprise in developing countries—to link, as the Bush administration would eventually get around to espousing, aid and trade. (One idea Andreas has long cherished, though he did not spell it out at that particular time, is to put American funds at the disposal of Israeli agricultural experts, who could apply their proven technology to barren tracts—ten thousand acres apiece struck Andreas as a manageable dimension—of crop-short Africa. David Ben-Gurion, when Andreas was staying with him at a kibbutz one time, thought that was a capital notion. But aside from François Mitterrand, Andreas has never been able to get any other international personage with any clout even to endorse his proposition.)

When Andreas, a longtime nonmincer of words, delivered

the report to the president, at a Cabinet Room ceremony, he took occasion to inform Mr. Reagan matter-of-factly—while such concerned onlookers as Donald Regan, Edwin Meese III, James Baker, and George Bush appeared to wince—that whatever his aides might have told him about a mere $50 billion American trade deficit was poppycock, and that the deficit—as it indeed turned out to be—would be at least twice that.

There are no statues of Lincoln or Truman in Decatur. Not long after the Reagan stopover there, Andreas thought it would be nice to commemorate the occasion by commissioning a Reagan statue to be enshrined near the spot of his historic confrontation with the ADM jelly beans—in front of the principal entrance to the corporate headquarters building.

The outcome was a bronze by the sculptor Stan Efron, a Minneapolitan specializing in portraits of athletes and wildfowl, who at Andreas's behest had earlier done a head of Dwayne's close friend Hubert Humphrey.

The Reagan statue, not quite as towering as Stephen Decatur's but a respectable enough seven feet tall, was mounted on a two-ton granite base, around the sides of which were carved other excerpts from the president's remarks that memorable August day; among them:

> If people want to see the country at her best, if they want to see the bright light of adventure and innovation, let them come here to the heartland.

and

> From corn and soybean processing that produce food products to feed a hungry world to your pioneer work in ethanol that increases demand for farm products, you create new jobs and lead to greater energy security for our country.

Enough people paid the statue enough compliments for Andreas to be persuaded to have a duplicate cast and presented, in Jimmy Hey's name, to the citizens of Dixon. Showing the president a photograph taken the day the bronze at Decatur was unveiled, Andreas said, "You know, I want to give one of these to Jimmy Hey to put in front of your old Dixon house, but I'm having a long delay in getting approval."

From just whom? the president demanded.

"From your staff and your legal counsel," Andreas said.

"You've got it," said the president, and Ronald Reagan II was unveiled a week before Christmas in 1988.

It was later the same year, 1984, in which Reagan favored Decatur with his solidly remembered presence, that Andreas, by now the chairman of the US-USSR Trade and Economic Council—a nongovernmental, private-sector group—was invited to meet Gorbachev. Andreas brought along some snapshots taken during the president's descent upon Archer Daniels Midland. Gorbachev wondered whatever could have prompted Reagan to go there. Why, replied Andreas, to get a firsthand view of the largest agribusiness complex on earth. "If I came, would you show me what you showed the president?" Gorbachev asked. Andreas promised he would. He came close in the spring of 1990, but when the Soviet president elected to make a Midwestern pit stop during his American visit, he picked Minneapolis instead.

Several years after meeting Gorbachev, by which time the Reagan memorial was in situ and Gorbachev had been installed as general secretary, Andreas amplified his proposition. He told Gorbachev that if he ever made it to Decatur, he'd get a statue, too.

By the time of this first encounter with Gorbachev, Andreas had often been to the Soviet Union. His first trip there was in April 1952, when he had just turned thirty-four and was a vice president and salesman for the big commodities firm of Cargill, Inc. His Moscow mission was to interest the rest of the world in buying American vegetable oils. Andreas believes he was one of a very few Americans—maybe the first—to be granted a visa in those Stalinist days specifically for the purpose of engaging in trade in the Soviet Union; he had the status of an unofficial delegate to a fifty-one-nation international trade conference that was about to get under way. The Korean War was on, and the Cold War was at its iciest; a number of Russians at the gathering complained to him in dead earnest about some grasshoppers that the American Army was supposed to have infected with cholera and shipped to Korea to launch an epidemic.

Nearly any American, especially one identifiable as a businessman, was a fairly rare sight in Moscow then. When, with advance notice, Andreas arrived at the Sovietska Hotel, where he was booked, a crowd was waiting to see what he looked like. One girl of about ten tugged at his sleeve and seemed to express doubt (according to an interpreter assigned to him) that he was either an American or a capitalist. He said he was indeed both. "No," the girl replied, "you're not old enough and you're not fat enough."

The most consequential Soviet official Andreas met that time around, during a brief encounter at the conference, was Minister of Trade Anastas Mikoyan. At the Sovietska, however, Andreas did have, he thought, a longer get-together with another foreign guest, Chou En-lai, representing the Chinese Ministry of Trade. They had a good talk about growing and processing wheat in their respective climes.

A couple of decades later, when Andreas mentioned that acquaintance to a Chinese diplomat in Washington, the man said Chou hadn't been in Moscow at that time. Whatever doubts that may have raised in Andreas's mind, there was no disputing the fact that shortly after his chat with the person he took to be Chou an emissary delivered two silk tapestries to his hotel room. They now hang in a Fifth Avenue Andreas apartment in New York City.

Andreas was surprised, when he flew into Moscow from Helsinki via Aeroflot, to discover that whoever handled accommodations at the Sovietska had assigned him to what he recalls as an eight-room suite. It was affordable—the equivalent in rubles of twenty American dollars a day, all meals included. He was further surprised to see how few soldiers were visible on the streets and how—naturally a matter of special interest to someone in his line of work—the markets he inspected seemed to be adequately stocked with such staples as potatoes, vegetables, and bread. How much barer their shelves would sometimes seem to be on later trips!

Andreas didn't negotiate any binding business deals that time, but he was beguiled when one Russian official told him privately that if hostile Washington would ever approve any such transaction, Moscow might be interested in buying 150,000 tons of soybean oil, and what was more, paying for it in gold.

In the course of many subsequent trips to the USSR, all business-oriented, Andreas grew aware, as others had before him, that when it came to getting along with Americans, the Communist satraps seemed to feel most at ease with those who more often than not were dyed-in-the-wool, hard-core, unapologetic capitalists. One had only to reflect on a roster of distinguished names. There was the first-edition Armand Hammer, of course, probably the leader of the rich and powerful pack. And right on his heels were such other wealthy influential eminences as W. Averell Harriman, Joseph E. Davies, Cyrus Eaton, David Rockefeller, and Donald Kendall. "He got criticized a lot," Andreas says of Hammer, the man often said to be his prototype, "but I think he did great work, in many areas. I don't care what they say about him—he was a nice guy. He was important. There've been half a dozen times when he was the thread that kept things going between the two governments. A great man. I try to stick to my knitting. My role with the Russians is strictly one of trade and business, and that's enough for me. I'm a strong believer that trade is the greatest promoter of peace and goodwill on earth. I feel pretty patriotic doing what I'm doing."

Andreas, who has consorted, on comfortable and companionable terms, with all those worthies save Davies, has his own explanation for the Russians' acceptance and even embracing of the species. "It's a strange phenomenon," he says, "which few Americans seem to understand. People who gravitate to the top in the USSR are economic conservatives. The job of these government people is to manage industry. In Russia, that's done by businessmen. The Russians have brought twenty-five hundred captains of industry to Moscow to run their government. Businessmen everywhere talk the same language and find it easy to get along. But the United States tends to send mostly lawyers and professors over there. 'We love them, all right,' the Russians say, 'but our job is to provide goods and services and to make the economy grow, and with all due respect to the lawyers and professors, we like to talk to people who know how to do that.'" Considering the state of the Soviet economy over the years, of course, some observers of that scene have perforce had to wonder if, while the Russians were talking to people who could tell them how to provide, they did not somehow sometimes fail to listen or to perform.

David Rockefeller, a cofounder of the US-USSR Council in 1974 and since 1984 its sole director emeritus, does not disagree with Andreas, but he has his own viewpoint. "The reason the Russians look favorably on people like Dwayne and me," he says, "is that their leaders have become convinced by their own propaganda that the USA is run by a handful of capitalists, and that therefore if you want to get anything accomplished, these are the people to deal with." After one visit to the Soviet Union with her father, Rockefeller's so aptly named daughter Neva told Joseph Finder, whose book *Red Carpet* treated the Communist-capitalist entente at significant length, "Just as Khrushchev represented the interests of the Russian people, he thought David Rockefeller represented the interests of Americans."

When the Soviet ambassador to the United Nations rose to utter a few testimonial words at a seventieth-birthday party given for Andreas by Rockefeller's sister-in-law Happy (among the guests was yet another American conservative— Henry Kissinger), he toasted "a wonderful image of a capitalist."

3

The Russians are not just another grain
buyer. They've bought billions and billions
of dollars' worth over the years and have
never defaulted. You get your impressions
of people like them from what you experience,
not from what you dream.

—DOA

In 1983, the year before his introduction to Gorbachev,
Andreas had once again traveled to Moscow. The
purpose this time was to attend, in October, a long-
scheduled trade fair called Agribusiness USA. There was a
hitch. Less than two months before, the South Korean airlin-
er 007 had exploded over Soviet waters, and relations between the US and the USSR were at a dismal ebb. Some
Americans, including those at the White House and the State
Department, seemed to be backing off from the show as fast
as they could. Washington let it be known that its ambassador to the Soviet Union, Arthur Hartman, would be temporarily recalled so that he wouldn't have to either attend or be
known to be in the vicinity and pointedly absent.

But there was another hitch. Although ADM was to be
only a small-scale exhibitor—some soy milk and some soy-

meal isolate intended for use as a meat substitute—Andreas had been tapped to head up the American delegation to the exposition. The heads of the huge commodities industries— Cargill, Continental, Louis Dreyfus, Bunge, and ADM—do not customarily fraternize. Leery of being accused of restraint of trade or price-fixing, they tend to shun even the appearance of being in cahoots. Andreas was determined not to let the 007 tragedy undermine both the intensive preparations made by more than a hundred American companies and the progress toward bilateral trade that had so painstakingly been achieved over so many years. In this instance, accordingly, seeking to present a show of strength in at least his own industry, he phoned Walter Klein, the then president and CEO of Bunge. Although they generally moved in quite different off-duty circles (Andreas played golf, Klein collected stamps), they had been friends for more than forty years. And they had considerable respect for one another, in part because both, before they'd climbed toward the top of the economic heap, had after a fashion begun toward the bottom—Andreas doing farm chores, Klein (hiding the fact that he was a Harvard graduate) unloading freight cars.

On the phone, Andreas said, "We shouldn't let this fair go down the tube." ("The Russians are not just another grain buyer," Andreas says. "They've bought billions and billions of dollars' worth over the years and have never defaulted. You get your impressions of people like them from what you experience, not from what you dream.") Klein agreed to accompany him to Moscow and share the heat, or whatever awaited them. Klein had perhaps less reason than some to be concerned about the feelings of the United States government; Bunge is an Argentine-based and -controlled enterprise, and like all its major competitors, ADM notably excepted, is privately owned and unbeholden to any public shareholders. Klein headed for Paris, where Andreas and his Falcon 900 jet were waiting to whisk them to Moscow. "As soon as we got there," Klein recalled, "Dwayne said, 'Let's go over to the embassy and see what's happening.' We were surprised to find that Arthur Hartman had come back. He said, 'Well, boys, what are you going to do?'

" 'I don't think you really want to know,' Dwayne said, 'inasmuch as the government isn't involved in this anymore.'

"But Hartman was good enough to show up anyway, and after Dwayne's opening remarks, to say a few welcoming words himself. Even so, it was evident to all present that Dwayne had taken charge. That day he *was* the US ambassador."

Among Andreas's plenipotentiary remarks were these:

> Our exhibits represent a small part of the great arsenal of peace, an arsenal composed of industrial and agricultural products for sale. They represent the power of trade, a power that draws nations together instead of driving them apart, a power that satisfies human needs rather than inspiring human fears.
>
> Our fair takes place in the shadow of the tragedy that befell the South Korean airliner and the escalation of tensions between the US and the USSR that followed. If we look back in history, we will find countless examples of nations going to war over incidents far less serious. . . . It is a tribute to the good sense of Mr. Reagan and of Mr. Andropov that this incident has not been allowed to bring about such an unthinkable result. It is a mark of mankind's growing maturity that war as an instrument of national policy is no longer considered a feasible option by great nations, no matter how angry at each other they may be.
>
> Trade is a tool for peace. It can thaw the ice in relations between states. It can bring the citizens of those states together in harmony and partnership.

By 1984, Andreas had become acquainted with quite a few high-ranking Russians (though he had not made much linguistic communion),* and since 1982 he had been

---

*Never much of a linguist to begin with, Andreas knew from experience the pitfalls of trying to speak in foreign tongues. At a dinner he gave at the Waldorf one night for some visiting Russians, one of them wanted to toast the host in English, and after a whispered colloquy with his interpreter, he raised his glass and smilingly intoned, "Up your bottom!" Not long afterward, to avoid confusion on a more consequential level, Andreas instructed his staff to have ADM's annual report printed, in its entirety, in Russian—and while they were at it, in Chinese, too.

serving as cochairman of the eight-year-old US-USSR Council, which was formed by the chief executive officers of twenty-six American companies plus the heads of the National Association of Manufacturers and the U.S. Chamber of Commerce and an equal number of ministers, deputy ministers, and senior officials of Soviet trade-related organizations.

The Council was started, during the Nixon administration, at a time when, not counting grain, trade between the two big nations was minuscule—at $16 million a year, it was less than that between the United States and Trinidad and Tobago. (Andreas likes to remind people of a 1973 prediction that came true—the conjecture by the anointed heads of General Motors, General Electric, and Citicorp that within a decade Russia's trade with the West would hit the $50 billion mark—except that it wasn't the United States that was in the partnership but Western Europe.) In any event, there couldn't have been too much bilateral trade because of the existence of the Jackson-Vanik Act, which specifically excluded the Soviet Union from most-favored-nation status and made any change contingent on a liberalization of that country's rules about emigration.

The governmental signatories to the 1974 establishment of the Council were George Shultz, then President Nixon's chief economic advisor, and Foreign Trade Minister Nikolai Patolichev. Donald Kendall, the Pepsi-Cola man, was the first cochairman for the American side, and he was succeeded by C. William Verity, the ARMCO CEO, and later President Reagan's secretary of commerce. After Andreas took over—he was a logical enough choice, what with the only substantial trade being in grain—he had the impression that some of Shultz's confrères at State were less sanguine about the Council than was their boss. "George once supposedly said to a Soviet counterpart," Andreas says, " 'You negotiate with my department about things like defense and culture and education and fisheries, but when it comes to business, you treat with Andreas.' From then on, I became a kind of supersecretary of commerce." When he learned that a couple of State Department functionaries tentatively scheduled to speak at a Council session had elected to beg off, Andreas recruited ex-president Nixon in their stead.

Eventually, nearly 300 American companies and more than 130 Soviet foreign-trade-related bodies would join the Council. Each nation had thirty directors on its board (almost all but a few of the American ones were CEOs), and resident binational staffs were recruited in both places. "We have a thousand times as many contacts with the Russian business sector as the American government has," Andreas liked to say. He has long believed that United States trading, or nontrading, with Communists was until just recently characterized by extraordinary shortsightedness. "Every president from Harry Truman on has said to me, 'We want to have more business with the Russians,'" Andreas says. "But the rest of the government was usually split down the middle, half of it helping you and half fighting you."

Of all the movers and shakers high in the Soviet hierarchy, Andreas was on especially good terms with Anatoly Dobrynin, who for many years served as ambassador to Washington. Dwayne's wide circle of friends also included a man no less lofty in the ranks of the *Reader's Digest*, Hobart Lewis, its editor-in-chief. With Lewis's concurrence, he tried to sell Dobrynin on the idea of a Russian-language edition of the magazine. "We Midwesterners always thought the *Digest* was our kind of magazine—simple," Andreas told a friend. "So I thought it might be good for Russian farmers. But Dobrynin was unenthusiastic, though not negative."

In September 1988, Andreas sent Hobart Lewis the draft of a speech he'd made before the Chicago Council on Foreign Relations, on "Developments Relating to Reagan-Gorbachev Accommodations." A few excerpts were:

> Now, with Gorbachev's revolution, I've had a front-row seat at one of the most remarkable policy transformations in history.

Mikhail Gorbachev approached political issues with the sensibilities of a businessman. His country's politicians and ideologues have made a mess of the Soviet economy, and he knows that only perestroika and glasnost—restructuring and opening—can save it.

Can we trust him? That's the question I'm most often asked. But it may be the wrong question. Instead, we should ask if it is in our national interest to wind down the cold war. If so, we can go down the road one step at a time with him, just as we would with any business partner—testing intentions and verifying agreements along the way. Trust is not a necessary prerequisite for such a procedure.

Lewis, in whose day the *Digest* had been markedly less conservative than it was to become after his retirement, gave Andreas's thoughts high marks and sent the text of his draft speech along to Kenneth Gilmore, the magazine's incumbent editor, accompanied by a long letter suggesting that a number of articles might well be derived from it. "I came away from reading it feeling the way I twice did in my years at *Reader's Digest*," Lewis wrote. "Once, when Jim Michener came to lunch, and second, when Richard Nixon came to lunch. Both of those visits led to a series of articles and to a long and good relationship."

It took Gilmore more than a month to reply. When he did, it was to express a lack of enthusiasm that made Dobrynin's resemble a paean. The contemporary *Digest*'s attitude toward the USSR, Gilmore said, was far removed from Andreas's and was much better exemplified by that of William E. Simon, the archconservative former secretary of the treasury during the Ford administration. As it happened, during the very same month in which Andreas had spoken in Chicago, Simon had been represented in the *Digest* by an article titled "Should We Bail Out Gorbachev?" His answer was, in effect, no way.

Simon, as it happened, had been one of the progenitors of the Council in 1971, and in the spring of 1974, when United States relations with the Soviet Union were far from warm, he had chaired a commission that recommended the signing of a ten-year bilateral pact "to facilitate economic, industrial, and technical cooperation." In the light of that, Andreas was puzzled. "Now that there is a new man with a 180-degree different attitude toward us," he wrote a mutual friend, "[Simon] had done a turnaround which I suppose is a measure of his desire to please the *Digest*." But Andreas was fond enough of Simon as a person and was inclined to give him benefit of doubt about the article. "When I read it," Dwayne said, "two thoughts crossed my mind. One, Bill Simon couldn't possibly have written it. And second, most likely he didn't even read it or he wouldn't have signed it."

Andreas and Dobrynin had kept in touch after the envoy returned to Moscow, in 1987, as a sort of éminence grise and elder-statesman/adviser to the secretary general. Packing his things prior to one Moscow journey in the spring of 1989, Andreas included, to help Dobrynin and his family keep in touch with cultural life back in the United States, cassettes of a few recent movie releases, among them *Moonstruck, Punchline, Big Bus,* and *The Mob.* Andreas told a friend that inasmuch as Dobrynin's Kremlin office was just down the hall from Gorbachev's, maybe the former would let the latter borrow the films for the edification and entertainment of *his* family.

Early in December 1984, Andreas had been on the verge of winding up still another business jaunt to Moscow—some Council affairs and discussions about a putative sale of a couple of hundred thousand tons of soybeans or corn or whatever. He was in a hurry to board his corporate jet and fly home. There was a fund-raising dinner at which he was expected, and he himself expected, to be the most generous patron. But something unexpected intervened. When he stopped by the office of Mikoyan's successor as minister of trade, Nikolai Patolichev, an octogenarian of, within the context of communism, conservative stripe, the old-timer begged him to stay over one extra day.

There was a relatively youthful colleague of his in the

government, the minister said, who like Andreas was much involved with agriculture, and whom, he felt, it would in the long run prove highly useful and profitable for the American to get to know. The man's name, one Andreas could not recall ever having heard before, was Mikhail Gorbachev. (That was three months before Gorbachev's widely heralded catapult to power.) "This young man is going to be very important," Andreas recalls Patolichev telling him. "My group is counting on him to reorganize our economy. We're all in our eighties, you know. You must get to know him and you must know that eight of us Stalinist ministers are supporting him." And, he went on, Andreas would further recollect, "Dwayne, if you don't meet this man, when you get back here, you won't even know this country. That is how many changes he is going to make."

Andreas stayed over, reflecting resignedly that by skipping the fund-raising affair he'd probably end up having to double his contemplated in-person pledge. He spent an hour and forty minutes with Gorbachev over at Central Committee headquarters. He brought along James H. Giffen, a New York merchant banker who was his colleague at the Trade and Economic Council and, on the American side, its chief day-in-and-day-out man.

An attorney who'd worked for William Verity at ARMCO, Giffen had been a student of Soviet foreign policy since the early 1960s. He was the author of *The Legal and Practical Aspects of Trade with the Soviet Union,* and ever since the formation of the Council he had been all but commuting between New York and Moscow. He was well versed in pitfalls. On Christmas Eve in 1979, on behalf of the Council, he had signed a $350 million trade contract with the Russians so complicated that it took up eight thousand pages in twenty-three volumes. (There had even been negotiations about which documents pertaining to negotiations he was allowed to carry back and forth.) But that was the very night that the USSR moved into Afghanistan, and thus in less than twenty-four hours there had instantly gone for naught—Giffen kept careful track, as a good merchant banker probably should—

three years, eight months, and one day's worth of intricate negotiations.

There were a number of things about Gorbachev that appealed to Andreas straight off. For one, he hailed from a family of peasants and as a boy had taken his turn in the fields harvesting grain. For another, the Russian reminded the American of his mother's sister's husband—a Methodist minister back in Lisbon who had the same kind of mild voice and conversational style, a blend, as Andreas saw it, of articulateness and persuasiveness. "Mr. Gorbachev is inquisitive, pragmatic, and very knowledgeable," Andreas told the *Journal of Commerce* in April 1987. "He lights up when he's talking about agribusiness." For yet another, it quickly became apparent that Gorbachev, like Andreas, enjoyed thinking big. Andreas, for instance, would tell people back home how in one of their dialogues Gorbachev said that if ADM would build a soybean-processing plant in the USSR, the Soviets could raise their annual production of chickens from 500 million to 3 billion, and Andreas had ventured that perhaps a mere eight million tons of soymeal could turn *that* trick. (Andreas has an impressive grasp of statistics. Asked once in a general way how sales of soybeans to Russia were faring, he replied, "One million eight hundred thousand tons up to noon yesterday.")

At one point in their conversation, Gorbachev wondered how he, a Soviet leader, could make United States conservatives, historically the most anti-Communist and pro-strong-defense of Americans, feel comfortable about the idea of mutual disarmament. "I told him that both our countries needed to start cutting down on military expenses to put an end to our deficits," Andreas recalled. "We were both overextended, while the Japanese and the Germans were striding ahead. We both needed savings, and neither of us could get them without the cooperation of the other. I assured him that the best appeal to conservatives about anything was a financial appeal."

After his introductory session with Gorbachev in 1984, Andreas appraised the new acquaintance as "a remarkably educated, sophisticated man." ("I perceived him right then and there," Andreas says, years later, "to be an *extremist:* that is, a man in possession of *extreme common sense*. A pragmatic and practical gentleman.") In some notes the American took at the time of the meeting, he said ("talking as one businessman to another") that "he wanted to talk about... how to provide incentives to farmers. He wanted to talk about why the Soviet Union wanted to restore *freedom* to farm and *freedom to worship*. [The underlining was Andreas's.] And why the Soviet Union needed to unleash the forces of supply and demand and unleash the forces of public opinion, *glasnost*. He asked a lot of questions about getting cooperatives and small businesses to inject competition into the system. And he focused on what works, not on what is sanctioned by dogma. No ideology."

"This guy Gorbachev was fired up with ideas that not long before you could have gone to jail for," Andreas told an inquiring friend early in 1990. "Here was a fellow who was obviously disgusted with the Soviet standard of living. Journalists have since said, 'This guy battled his way to the top.' Nonsense. He got there because his colleagues pushed him up. People also like to predict that he'll be thrown out, like Khrushchev. That's baloney, too." That was in 1990.

In 1989, reflecting on that first encounter, Andreas said in a speech:

> It was clear to me that this gifted man was determined to make socialism work better by adapting the economy to market forces. So when he became general secretary six months after our meeting, I had the gratifying experience of seeing him put these bold ideas into practice with the program of reforms the world has come to know as "perestroika."

> These days, there is a lot of discussion here in the US about whether perestroika will succeed and whether the

Soviet economy will take its place in an integrated world economy.

To me, the answers are clear. I believe the policy of perestroika will succeed. And I believe it must succeed. Success might not be obvious for a few years. But in the meantime, since man does not live by bread alone, the spiritual awakening resulting from glasnost is a powerful life-support system.

Appearing on the Brinkley Sunday TV show one time not as a sponsor but as a speaker, Andreas further characterized the secretary general as "open-minded, reasonable, pragmatic," and "a man honestly in search of truth and improvement, and one"—here was icing on the cake—"who knows his agribusiness." Andreas would tell the *Wall Street Journal* that whereas he could talk to Gorbachev for hours about farming, "Dr. Hammer is a great man, but he couldn't do that."

There is less available evidence, aside from his continuing willingness for them to get together and share ideas, of Gorbachev's opinion of Andreas. The author of *Perestroika*—in which, incidentally, there is no mention of the "new Armand Hammer" while the old one is flatteringly credited with having done "much to promote understanding and friendly contacts between our two countries"—did inscribe a gift copy of the English-language version of his book, as the recipient had it translated, "To Mr. D. Andreas—With friendly feelings. M. Gorbachev." Later, he would sometimes call him Dwayne. Andreas stuck to, in turn, "Mr. Chairman" and "Mr. President."

It is known that one time, at the general secretary's request, Andreas sent him a memorandum outlining his own views about—and as it turned out, against—a superagricultural agency Gorbachev had recently installed, and which, not long after hearing from the American, he disbanded. Andreas's longtime crony Robert Strauss, the Texas-spawned Washington lawyer and man-about-politics, has a penchant for hyperbole, but even so he is an astute observer of the high-level international scene and thus perhaps deserves to be listened to when he says, as he does say, "Whenever Gorbachev sees Dwayne, his eyes kind of light up." The new Andreas connection did not go unnoticed in other circles. "When Reagan found out that I knew Gorbachev," Andreas says, "somehow after that I was often around the White House."

Andreas has never been a slave to the written word. (Like every other uncommonly successful man, he has had his detractors, one of whom was once heard to mutter something to the effect of "What you don't put down on paper can't hurt you.") After another long talk with Gorbachev, though, this one at the Kremlin in 1985, Andreas wrote up an account of the conversation for the benefit of Reagan's secretary of agriculture, John Block:*

GORBACHEV: Andreas, after we talked a year ago, I reported the contents of our conversation to the Politburo, whereupon we decided to make a study of the efficiency of our meat production [feeding] program. We came to some startling conclusions. Do you want to hear them?

ANDREAS: Yes—eager to hear them.

GORBACHEV: We found by comparing the United States program to ours that you get approximately 20 percent more meat from a pound of feed and a unit of input than we do. In searching for the reason, although there are many, by far the most important reason appears to be a very simple one. Your country uses one part of protein to six parts of grain. We use only one part of protein to twenty-four parts grain. I simply cannot understand why our people, who have to import both, have been importing feed grains when it would be far more profitable to import protein. We need, theoretically, 17 million tons of soymeal per year to balance the grain that is available to us....Furthermore, I want a

---

*There was another elaborate dinner at the Kremlin this time around, during which a good deal of talk dwelt on a recent Soviet purchase of seven hundred thousand tons of American soybeans—but not, as it happened, from Archer Daniels Midland. When one of those present commiserated with Andreas, he shrugged and said, "We had our chance, but we weren't the lowest bidder."

program to produce, as much as practical, our own protein, by growing and processing soybeans and other oilseeds in the Soviet Union. I am treating this as an urgent matter because, by correcting this huge error in our feeding system, I estimate we can produce 20 percent more meat at no extra cost. Mr. Andreas, I want to know what can be done about this problem.

ANDREAS: Mr. Secretary, your calculations are absolutely correct. As you know, my company is a major processor of oilseeds and producer of protein. Together, with others, we can go a long way toward solving your problem. First, my company and others have excess oilseed-processing capacity in Europe. It is at your disposal. We can sell you any part, or all, of the production, or you may buy soybeans anywhere in the world that fits your purposes—Brazil, China, the United States, Argentina—and ship the soybeans to crushing plants in Europe. The beans can arrive in your own ships, and we can load the resulting protein into your ships of all sizes to move regularly into all of your ports. In addition, we can process soybeans in the United States. We, together with our competitors, could provide you with 10 million tons available for export. In addition, our German affiliate [Toepfer, in Hamburg] and other trading companies could coordinate all of that with 5 million tons or more from Brazil and Argentina.

GORBACHEV: Our people say that it is difficult to handle soybean meal in the ports and railroads because it blows in the wind and leaks out of cars.

ANDREAS: The solution is very simple: Buy it in pellets. Processors can deliver all of it in pellet form with a minimum amount of dust, saving you 15 percent transportation cost and probably 1 percent in shrinkage from dust. Mr. Secretary, you should also take note of another important fact. You are buying corn, which averages 9 percent protein, whereas we export 4 million tons of gluten feed, which is 20 percent protein. It is 20 percent protein because we have converted the starch in the corn into sugar, ethanol, starch, and other products. Gluten feed, made entirely from corn, is what is left. The gluten feed is eagerly bought by the

European Common Market, frequently for less than the price of corn. Since the Soviet Union needs protein and not starch, you would save hundreds of millions of dollars by buying gluten feed instead of corn. In addition, Mr. Secretary, if we were participating in this kind of long-range program with you, we would be willing to exchange team agronomists with you for the purpose of developing a soybean crop in the Soviet Union. They would come from US processors and the University of Illinois and Purdue University. Your potential for producing soybeans is limited, but there are several places in the Far East and perhaps in the Southwest where significant quantities can be produced. It would take time—several years. In these ten or twelve localities we would like to build for you regional 100,000- to 300,000-ton plants to serve the local regional communities. Oilseeds would be trucked in, protein meal trucked out, and cooking oil bottled for distribution. This program would require the cooperation of our government, who could adjust our farming program to permit an acceleration over the next three to five years of the switch of acreage from corn to soybeans. I would urge you in the interest of efficiency and economy to enlist Brazil and Argentina also in this effort. I could help you with such an effort.

GORBACHEV: I am eager to get on with this.... Since this program envisions continued heavy imports for an economy short of dollars, could you help it along by buying something from the Soviet Union?

ANDREAS: Well, for one thing, I also have a substantial interest in a very large cement company. [Lone Star Industries, of which he was a director as well as a large stockholder.] We could use over a million tons of cement and bring it to the United States as a ballast in empty soybean-meal ships. Do you have it to sell?

GORBACHEV: Yes.

That was as far as that scheme got. But when Andreas was in Moscow in the spring of 1989, some Latvian entrepreneurs, having heard somehow that Lone Star was proclaiming a new kind of quick-hardening cement that when dry resembled marble, flew over to express an interest in a joint venture in their Socialist Republic. In the three years subsequent to that dialogue, Soviet imports of soybean meal rose from seven hundred thousand to 3 million tons a year.

Did you know that filet mignon is thirty percent tallow and the curse of the rich?

—DOA

Two of the most pressing worldwide concerns of the past half century have been keeping the peace, which for all practical purposes has mainly meant keeping the US and the USSR from becoming implacably inimical, and feeding the hungry. (The first concern has been far better dealt with, on the whole, than the second.) Andreas has been much involved with both. So has Gorbachev, who in the summer of 1988 referred to food as "probably the most painful and the most acute problem in the life of our society." This despite the fact, oddly, that the Soviet Union has never seen fit to assume membership in the UN's Food and Agriculture Organization, the very purpose of which, after all, is supposed to be to eradicate, or at least alleviate, hunger. When a friend mentioned the Russians' aloofness to Andreas and wondered if he had ever suggested to Gorbachev that his country make its peace with the FAO, he said, "If I did, he would join. I think I'll send a note to Dobrynin, and he'll pass it along to Gorbachev." (Russia stayed out; maybe the message never got transmitted.) Andreas's enthusiasm for that sometimes perplexing Roman enclave began to wane—as indeed did that of the United States government—when its powers-that-be decided that the Palestine Liberation Organization should be considered a full-fledged self-governing state.

Early in 1989, Andreas was pleased to be told by another high-level Soviet friend—Prime Minister Nikolai Ryzhkov— that his country's number one priority should be food. Andreas, doffing for the moment his Soybean King's crown, and donning his Grain King's mantle, urged Ryzhkov to concentrate on wheat. (It was not long afterward that President Bush, whose position theretofore had been against subsidies for American farmers, authorized subsidized sales to the Soviet Union of a million and a half metric tons of the grain.) While he was on the subject, Andreas suggested to Ryzhkov that it might be helpful if his Soviet friends applied themselves also to better handling of the grains at their disposal, some 40 percent of which, the American felt obliged to inform the prime minister, became useless—as is lamentably the case more or less worldwide—somewhere between harvesting and consumption. Andreas has long maintained—as, of course, have others who share his concerns—that there has never been an actual shortage of foodstuffs on earth, but rather, a lack of means of getting them, insect-free, rodent-free, and spoilage-free, to the people who need them the most.

Why, Andreas is eager to point out whenever he can find an audience, the United States alone grows enough soybeans so that, if proper distribution were ever achievable, they could be processed into the equivalent in nourishment of one hamburger a day for every human being. (Advocates of soy-based foods and other nonmeat diets are fond of reminding all and sundry that the end product of every twenty-five square feet of irreplaceable Brazilian rain forest leveled to provide grazing space for beef cattle is a single two-ounce hamburger.) One ADM publication touting the nutritive virtues of the soybean declares, "Malthus said it would take a miracle to feed the world. Here it is." And one ADM television commercial has declared, "The newest development in nutrition is actually one of the oldest foods known to man." (The text of that message also included the phrase "That's using the old bean.") Andreas himself says, "You could feed the whole world with soy if people would just learn to eat it." He has also said, "There is no question in my mind but that the soybean is the fundamental future of the planet."

Andreas's ADM marketing executives are glad that their livelihood does not depend on such statements. "Edible soy is a very hard sell," one of them says. "One problem is that when our people go out, they keep being told, 'What is this that you are proposing we eat—dog food?' " Dog- and cat-food trailer trucks, as it happens, can frequently be found in ADM parking lots, waiting to be loaded up with a soybean derivative that is a substantial ingredient of Alpo beef and Alpo chicken and Alpo lamb and Alpo rib of veal. (Alpo is forever bragging in television commercials about how its cat foods are "loaded with meat, fish, poultry, and"—how it makes Andreas wince that so many people find "soy" so hard to utter!—"grain sources.") "My dog eats better than I do," Andreas says. To one woman who wrote him wondering why, if so much of so many kinds of dog food stemmed from soybeans, companies didn't come right out with full-fledged vegetarian meals for animals, he responded that he didn't think there'd be much of a market for such concoctions, and that purveyors of dog food had to have at least enough meat in their wares to justify mentioning it on their labels. "That is because buyers love their pets and want the feeling that they are feeding them real meat," he wrote.

Andreas's dog's master has idiosyncratic eating habits of his own. Now and then he disconcerts a hostess or a maître d' by, when presented with some special treat, reaching into a pocket and sprinkling the delicacy with bran flakes. He won't touch chocolate cake. Every morning, he ingests, stirred into water, a packet of the fibrous powder Metamucil, for regularity— orange flavor preferred. When he is in Decatur—his house there has a swimming pool incorporating a Jacuzzi with extrapowerful jets, against which he is often found hurling himself at five A.M.—one member of his staff sees to it that there is an apple on his desk every morning. He did not succumb to the oat-bran craze that swept the country in the 1980s, and unlike a couple of its big rivals, ADM did not build any new plants to process the once-lowly hulls of oats. "It's true that by eating fiber you reduce your appetite for fats," Andreas says, "but it doesn't make much difference what kind you eat—oat bran or any other kind of bran. Rice bran may turn out to be a better bran, when it comes to that, than oat. But let's face it—fiber is fiber. And whatever the television commercials say about it, it's basically nothing but wood—just plain wood."

For the last fifty years, moreover, he has been faithful to a daily dose of lecithin (ADM makes it, wrestling a single ounce from a hundred pounds of soybeans), which he credits with keeping his cholesterol down to a gratifyingly spartan 120. It also keeps the oil and water constituents of margarine from separating, keeps chocolate candy creamy (though that is for others than Andreas to worry about), serves as a handy gun grease, and, he is convinced, enhances memory. Whatever has been responsible, he has a good one. He is not much of a meat-eater, and when touting soybeans, he is apt to startle a listener with some such challenging statement as "Did you know that filet mignon is thirty percent tallow and the curse of the rich?"

Over the years, Andreas has hobnobbed with many politicians. Of all his friends in and out of public affairs, perhaps the closest have been a pair of presidential nominees who at first glance would seem to have had little else in common— Hubert H. Humphrey and Thomas E. Dewey. Had either been elected, Andreas would unquestionably have been offered a cabinet post, which he would more likely than not have declined. During Dewey's governorship of New York, from 1943 to 1954, he decreed that soybeans be included in the bread baked at state prisons. Humphrey made sure that in

America's Food for Peace program soybeans played a prominent pacifying role.

Later, two more close friends of Andreas's also came
from opposite ends of the political spectrum—Senator Robert
Dole and Representative Thomas P. ("Tip") O'Neill. Andreas
was in charge of the arrangements for a testimonial dinner
for O'Neill at the Washington Hilton when the speaker of the
house retired in 1986. It attracted, at a thousand dollars a
plate for those who paid, two thousand well-wishers, not
counting the flock of Secret Service operatives who attended
President Reagan when he showed up. The next day's *Washington Post* dutifully listed some of the other notables present—Gerald Ford, Bob Hope, Edward Kennedy, just about
everybody anybody had ever heard of—but made no mention
of the man who had put the whole bash together, and whom
the guest of honor extolled as "one of the most brilliant and
successful people in America...one of the most brilliant
people I've ever met in my life." (The first time they met,
back in 1960, O'Neill said to Andreas, "You and I have
climbed pretty far. Let's remember never to pull up the
ladder against people behind us.") Nor did any orator that
evening choose to recall that when the speaker was introduced to Mikhail Gorbachev, the future general secretary and
president said, pleasantly, "Oh, yes, Dwayne Andreas told me
about you. He says you're a nice fellow and the leader of the
opposition." O'Neill would also later recall that when he told
Gorbachev that Andreas had told *him* that Gorbachev would
be the USSR's next general secretary, the Soviet leader had
responded, "Russia is a big country. There are many places to
hide."

One knowledgeable Washingtonian said, at about the
time of the O'Neill testimonial, "I would guess that five to
eight percent of the people who run this town would know
the name of, say, Malcolm Forbes.* In Dwayne's case, it

---

*Observers of the end-of-the-twentieth-century social scene noted with interest that
in the fall of 1989, when such as Henry Kissinger scrambled to attend the seventieth-
birthday party that Forbes gave himself at his Tangier motorcycle service station,
Andreas was among the invitees who stayed home.

would probably be less than one-tenth of one percent—which would be exactly the way he would want it. It's not so much whom he knows. It's that he knows whom in government to know, and in terms of being able to accomplish things where government plays a role, his success rate must be phenomenal. He has an uncanny instinct about who or what is important. Also, he's a nice guy."

One evening in 1985, Andreas gave an off-the-cuff address (he had left the prepared text on his plane) to the White Burkett Miller Center of Public Affairs at the University of Virginia, of which he and also Cyrus Vance, Walter Cronkite, and a couple of dozen other such luminaries were "national associates." (By the time President and Mrs. Bush came to the Center's twentieth-anniversary dinner in March 1989, Andreas was vice chairman of its board.) Waiting to go on, Andreas remarked to a companion, "It occurred to me while I was sitting here that I'm about the only person in the room that I had never heard of before."

Despite his acceptance, as a successful adult, by a variety of clubs—among them, the Links and the Knickerbocker in New York City; the Blind Brook in Westchester County; the Union League in Chicago; the Minikahda in Minneapolis; and the Decatur in Decatur, the only one of them all at which he has his own parking space—there remains in him something of a farm boy's conventional diffidence. Some of these establishments normally take time to get into. Treating an out-of-towner to breakfast at the Knick not long ago (comparable CEOs often prefer to hold working breakfasts at the Regency or "21," so they can be seen inside and so their limousines can tie up traffic outside), Andreas remarked that he had just recently been admitted. On being asked if that had been a tedious procedure to go through, he said, "All I know is that Laurance Rockefeller had me over here for a drink one day, and the next thing I knew somebody told me I was a member."

Andreas may well be the only member ever to show up

there, as he had that morning, toting a shopping bag full of comestibles that he wanted his companion to take away— samples of two food supplements for Third World children: a soy-protein-enriched cereal called Protinia and a soy-based milk substitute called Nutri-Bev. "Nutri-Bev isn't sold," Andreas said, a trace of passion infusing his usually gentle manner. "It comes in six flavors, and it's given away. ADM has been doing research on it for twenty-five years, and now we're improving it even more, with fructose, because mouthfeel is very important. Its cost is a tenth that of milk, and it's nutritionally better. After all, some millions of people can't tolerate cow's milk. We've been frustrated every time we've tried to push this product. Do you realize that for a mere twenty-five billion dollars you could give a quart of this drink every day of the year to five hundred million people, and—presto!—you'd have the end of hunger? And there are enough soybeans in United States government storage right now to do the job. This is the most exciting long-range product we have. It's to milk what margarine turned out to be to butter. I draw some comfort from reminding myself that it took margarine twenty-five years to get off the ground."

As late as 1940, Andreas likes to remind anyone who will listen, Americans consumed nine times as much butter as margarine, in part because the powerful dairy lobby saw to it that the latter could only be marketed white, on the well-established premise that housewives believed that if something looked like lard it would probably taste like lard. (As late as the 1970s, residents of Wisconsin expecting visitors from other states would beg them to bring along coloring matter.) Once margarine was allowed to look like butter, that ratio began to be reversed.

Because of his high corporate status, Andreas tends by and large to consort less with Democrats than with Republicans. Some of the latter do not know quite what to make of him. How can one of their crowd go around, they wonder, recommending to friends and acquaintances and even passing out copies of Nick Kotz's book *Let Them Eat Promises—The*

Politics of Hunger in America, which has an introduction by *George McGovern!* (It was principally McGovern who, while in the Senate, brought into being that body's Select Committee on Nutrition and Human Needs.) What might some of these golfing cronies not think if they knew that Andreas had scribbled in his copy an "Excellent!" alongside McGovern's "Our president wants to lavish $7 billion to protect the missile sites with dubious military hardware. We can purchase with half that an end to hunger in America"?

Andreas modestly left unannotated his obvious approval of Kotz's endorsement of soybeans; the author proposed that the federal government should, with respect to *Glycine max,* "require enrichment and fortification of basic food products such as milk and flour, and encourage the development and marketing of more low-cost, highly fortified foods."

The *Decatur Herald & Review* has had a hard time, over the years, getting its probably most influential reader to sit down for an on-the-record interview. When it did catch up with Andreas one day in 1984, among the sentiments he expressed was, "Without any question, the easiest thing to do is put up food plants instead of defense plants, but it is impossible to get any government to do it, due to political impediments. Starving people have no constituency."

And in what was more or less an interview with himself, after one meeting with Mikhail Gorbachev, Andreas jotted down on the back of an envelope:

> Food for thought on world hunger. If the cost of feeding the world's hungry was in the defense budgets of the world's countries it would be viewed as a small amount; we could equate the cost of fueling the world's hungry bodies to fueling the world's tanks and planes.... Estimates for providing the basic nutritional requirements to the world's 500 million needy range from $15 billion to $20 billion annually.... The world produces food for 7 billion but only feeds 4.6—pets and rodents waste. Twenty-one children starve to death every minute.... Fulfilling the nutritional needs of the world's hungry would not be an expensive

program. It could be done cheaply because you would use otherwise idle land, idle farmers, idle processing plants, and idle transportation networks.... The food is available; only the political will is lacking.... Bankers panicked to get fuel for inessential automobiles but have ignored for centuries fuel for hungry bodies.

5

Food is fuel. You can't run a tractor
without fuel, and you can't run a human
being without it, either. Food is the
absolute beginning. It may not be the end,
but it sure as hell is the beginning.

—DOA

WHEN Ronald Reagan's secretary of defense, Caspar Weinberger, asked Andreas to join a dozen or so other CEOs for dinner at the Pentagon, so they could get a special explanation of his department's goings-on, the host was reported to be a mite taken aback when Andreas piped up and said some of the inflated budget over which Weinberger had jurisdiction might be much better diverted to what his friend Hubert Humphrey had long ago proposed: to take unemployed and perhaps unemployable young people out of the nation's cities and pay them to terrace productive farmland that was being irreparably lost to erosion.

Andreas often traveled abroad with Humphrey. A vice-presidential swing around part of Africa, in 1965, took them to eight countries. Calling on President Nasser in Cairo, Humphrey and Andreas asked him what he thought was best and worst about the existing American foreign-aid programs. Nasser said he was hesitant to answer because what he believed was best involved the smallest amount of money. The free meals provided in a school-lunch program, he explained, constituted the most effective bait he knew of to entice children, and their parents, to a spot where they could be introduced to such concomitant essentials of a better life as literacy, vaccinations, and birth control.

Both Humphrey and Andreas took copious notes on most of their travels together, sometimes in the form of a dialogue—an interview, say, with Andreas the questioner and Humphrey the respondent. "When we got back home from a vice-presidential trip, we would normally make recommendations to President Johnson," Andreas said.

With respect to that African trip, the recommendations had to be gloomy. Wherever we went, the national leaders seemed to have been educated in Europe and influenced by the Socialist leanings of the London School of Economics. They all wanted to industrialize when what they should have been doing was increasing the production of food. They were trying to nationalize industries that hadn't yet come into being.

I urged them, while I was there, to wait fifty years and then take over, but nobody was listening. So they were all going for an office building and an airline and a steel mill when what they needed was a food program, to get the level of diet raised, and at the same time, a crash program in agricultural technology. We could set those up for them, I told them, in collaboration with the Israelis. We could assure them one good hot meal including soy protein and grain per day for fifty cents per capita, which would increase IQs by one-third and would make people four to five inches taller and twenty to twenty-five pounds heavier, and thus capable of more sustained work. A Norwegian cement company that built a plant in Ghana did provide its workers with such a meal and got them up an average of thirty pounds in eighteen months. When people can gain that much, you know that previously they were starved. Food is fuel. You can't run a tractor without fuel, and you can't run a human being without it, either. Food is the absolute beginning. It may not be the end, but it sure as hell is the beginning.

Like most corporate executives, Andreas has taken on many *pro bono publico* jobs. He spent eighteen months working—much more than titularly—as chairman of a Presidential Task Force on International Private Enterprise set up during the first Reagan administration. The full-time executive director of the task force, Christian Holmes, told a friend after its recommendations had been submitted in 1984:

> It doesn't matter how much technology, wealth, and food we have to meet world hunger if we don't have the leaders to package those assets. I know this firsthand, having worked as the deputy director of the Office of U.S. Foreign Disaster Assistance and as the principal deputy assistant secretary of state for refugee programs. The leadership has to come from not just government and the voluntary agencies; it also has to come from leaders of major corporations who are willing to use their political and economic power to help the hungry here and abroad. Dwayne is one of those corporate leaders who has used his power to help the poor.

In adult life, Andreas, raised as a Mennonite, has never been much of a churchgoer, but he has been attracted to, and been found attractive by, a whole flock of men and women of the cloth. Priests and ministers and rabbis know that he is rich, of course (although the October 1987 stock-market crash caused him to be dropped for a year from *Fortune*'s list of the five hundred wealthiest Americans), but they are also aware that he has time and again expressed concerns about the least well-to-do in anybody's flock. He has been notably close to and generous toward Jewish groups, among them the Anti-Defamation League of B'nai B'rith. (In 1990, he was given B'nai B'rith International's Distinguished Achievement Award.) Several of the older men in the agricultural-processing field to whom he turned for counsel in his youthful days happened to be Jewish, and while learning the tricks of their trade he also became privy to their nonbusiness concerns. "I guess I just sort of naturally got involved in Jewish affairs," he would say years later, "and I've managed to help Jewish organizations with a few things, especially after Humphrey grew important. I became sort of a link between Hubert and them. Anyway, coming from a rural and Mennonite background, you were very definitely, like the Jews, not part of the establishment. Like them, you were looked at as being different. I suppose in my subconscious mind, too, I have a natural inclination to be friendly to the forces of all religions."

Curiously, one of Andreas's friends and beneficiaries, if not exactly his idea of the consummate statesman, has been the Reverend Pat Robertson. When that rather special clergyman and his wife, Dede, were newly married, they were for a while so hard-pressed that, she has recalled, "we either ate soybeans or we didn't eat." The reverend included a "Thank God for Soybeans" chapter in one of his exhortatory books. Mrs. Robertson and a collaborator, for their literary part, gave *Glycine max* an entire volume. They started right off with: "At one level this is a book about soybeans. At another level it is a book about God's protection. The two are directly related." Later on (Andreas's own proselytizing has always been markedly more restrained): "Throughout, the story of God's provision and the tale of our encounters with the soybean are one and the same story. The Lord has taught me so much about Himself through the humble little bean!"

Mrs. Robertson introduced every chapter with a recipe. Among the soy dishes she espoused were Love Waffles, Gentleness Beans, Patience Beans, Self-control Chili, Goodness Meat Loaf, Meekness Bits, Joyous Beans, Peace Buttons (a TV snack, with sugar and pecans), and Faith Hamburgers, of which she observed, "Some people prefer this dish to the all-beef variety." Andreas recalls that during the Depression his household was glad to come across a similar, if less elegantly phrased, recipe book. "We took it into the kitchen and Mother played around," he says.*

Andreas was not displeased when he first learned that soybeans had two such prominent buffs as the Robertsons, and he was pleased to be twice invited to make a guest appearance—once being booked on the same day with some models promoting Born Again Fashions—on the reverend's syndicated *700 Club* television show. Echoing his host's helpmeet's appraisal of hamburgers, Andreas asserted the first time around, in 1981, that "bacon made from soy really tastes more like bacon than bacon." He has gone less flat out about a pseudobacon dog food whose proprietors contend—without citing the sources of their research—that pets cannot differentiate it from genuine bacon.

Back on the *700 Club* in 1984, Andreas confessed (any of his ADM directors or employees who happened to be tuned in that morning must have been startled) that he watched the program nearly every day and that in a way he and its master of ceremonies were pursuing parallel courses, both of them trying to enrich lives—on Andreas's part, by contributing to the elimination of starvation. The Robertsons operate some soup kitchens, and ADM has stocked them, by now, with hundreds of thousands of dollars' worth of soy foods.

The religious personage who has probably benefited more than any other from Andreas's largesse, however, is Mother Teresa. He is, all in all, not superstitious, but when he flies into the Soviet Union—since early 1989, his private jet has been allowed to fly into Moscow unescorted, a privilege up to then generally thought to be Armand Hammer's alone—he likes to make sure that tucked in one of his pockets is a rosary she gave him.

---

*At one ADM board meeting in 1990, Andreas presented each of his directors with a copy of a much fancier cookbook, published in England, Linda McCartney's *Home Cooking* (written with Peter Cox), from which a reader could perhaps deduce that the Beatles kept up their strength by subsisting *chez leur* on soy-based burgers served variously à la king, with fried onions, with parsley butter, or with sour cream and red wine.

Andreas got to know Mother Teresa through a daughter of his, Sandra McMurtrie, who went to India in 1981 with a friend who worked for Catholic Relief Services. In Calcutta, they met the celebrated nun. Ever since, Mrs. McMurtrie has been one of her most steadfast disciples and coworkers. When cabdrivers in Washington, D.C., take to their garages in sleet storms, Mrs. McMurtrie can sometimes be spotted fearlessly driving a vanload of nuns—conceivably they feel protected from misadventure by a higher power—around the capital's glassy streets. By 1988, when a son of Sandra's graduated from an inner-city Jesuit high school in Washington—where Sandra was devoting four days a week to Mother Teresa's Gift of Peace home for the indigent dying and for AIDS victims—the relationship had become so close that Mother Teresa delivered the commencement address.

Once his daughter got involved with Mother Teresa's hospices and soup kitchens, Andreas got involved, too—giving money, food, and the kind of assistance people with his connections can furnish. When Congress legislated the country's Food for Peace program in 1954, the distribution of edibles to the dying was, because quantities were thought to be limited, ludicrously prohibited. But the dying, of course, have from the outset been among Mother Teresa's principal charges. Andreas persuaded Humphrey, then a senator, to have that restriction lifted.

At a meeting one day in the mid-1980s with Mrs. McMurtrie and her father, Mother Teresa said to them, "I would like to make a gift of my sisters to Cuba." Fidel Castro, who at first wasn't especially happy about the notion, agreed to let Mother Teresa open two homes during a two-hour get-together with her and Sandra McMurtrie after Andreas had them flown down in his plane. The nun's presence wasn't widely publicized, but word got around, and when one church held a mass in her honor, the place was mobbed.

The next time Andreas saw Mother Teresa, she said, "I would like to make a gift of my sisters to Moscow." Andreas explored that possibility first with Anatoly Dobrynin, who told him, "We're not great on religion over here, you know.

But when and if the pope comes to Moscow, we'll issue her a visa, too."

Andreas demurred. "No good," he said. "She'd draw attention away from the pope."

Dobrynin said he'd take up the matter with Gorbachev. Just before the Soviet leader left the United States in December 1987, after his summit conference with President Reagan, he summoned Andreas and James Giffen into an anteroom for a farewell glass of champagne and told them he'd decided to grant the nun a visa.

Not long afterward Mother Teresa, who had a hospice under way in Moscow, again had Andreas's ear. "I must have a house for my sisters in Albania before I die," she told him.

There were limits to what even he could do on her behalf (indeed, since she was born in Albania, he suggested to her that she handle that one herself), but during the cocktail hour (fruit juices only) that preceded the May 1988 summit-conference dinner at the Kremlin, Andreas did manage to orchestrate a three-way conversation—Reagan, Gorbachev, and himself—in which he talked the other two into agreeing to try to collaborate in helping Mother Teresa get some relief food into northern Ethiopia. "When I told Mother about it afterward," Andreas says, "she was one happy woman."

In December 1986, Andreas had said:

It is true that India has achieved self-sufficiency in wheat and rice production. The item lacking in a balanced diet is protein. Per-capita protein intake has actually declined in India. That is why the extraordinarily effective work of Mother Teresa in feeding people is so important. She has told me about her methods of achieving successful results. I learned that her method is fundamentally based on the use of soy protein mixed with grains and vegetables. Her people gather together local vegetables and even grain. They stew it in a large kettle and add pieces of soy protein [this supplied by the speaker] that tastes and chews like meat. The physical response has been so dramatic as to defy verbal description. This dedicated woman is utilizing the

world's surplus low-cost protein resources as a global dem-
onstration project. I salute this great humanitarian!

After she recovered from an illness in 1990, Mother
Teresa wanted Andreas to know that soy milk had helped
restore her strength.

6

At heart, I'm just a Mennonite
farm boy.

—DOA

On May 2, 1918, Secretary of Agriculture David F.
Houston issued a First World War circular titled
"Use Soy-Bean Flour to Save Wheat, Meat, and
Fat." There were recipes for—by Mrs. Pat Robertson's standards, rather uninspiringly named—Soy-Bean Meat Loaf,
Soy-Bean Mush Croquettes, and Victory Bread. Andreas—who
would come to agree wholeheartedly, in time of peace no less
than of war, with the secretary's espousal of soybeans as a
substitute for wheat in biscuits and for corn flour in griddle
cakes—could not then read that manifesto; he was not quite
two months old. But although seventy years later the United
States would be deriving a larger dollar volume from soybean
exports than from those of, for instance, jet aircraft (by then,
too, the New York Times would have long since dubbed
Andreas "the nation's grain trader nonpareil"), there were not

then many soybeans on hand to serve that patriotic end—imports being negligible and the country's acreage devoted to them a trifling three hundred thousand. By 1990, the corresponding figure would be 60 million acres, and that was down by 8 million from a 1985 peak. They produced almost 2 billion bushels—55 million tons' worth of beans.

Soybeans, of course, were much better known in Asia—as far back, it is believed, as 2800 B.C. when they were mentioned in the writings of the Chinese emperor Shen-nung, sometimes known as the father of Chinese agriculture. By A.D. 1918 (meanwhile, the Chinese, Japanese, and Russians had thought highly enough of soybeans to fight a couple of wars over them), Manchuria was exporting 612,000 tons of whole beans, 151,316 tons of soybean oil, and 1,055,000 tons of soy cake. Americans can move fast when they have a mind to. By 1942, the United States would be outproducing Manchuria.

Wheat is a single item on the Chicago Board of Trade, and so is corn. The soybean is traded, vigorously, as itself, as its oil, and as its meal. The University of Illinois plant geneticist Theodore Hymowitz, who pursued soybeans all over the planet and was so obsessed with them that he once read through every one of Benjamin Franklin's extant letters hoping to find a single mention of them (he finally spotted just one), acclaimed his favorite plant as "the most important grain legume crop in the world in terms of total production and international trade."

His country's serious involvement with soybeans has, as it happens, just about coincided with Andreas's life span. He was two when the American Soybean Association was founded, and four when the state of Illinois's first processing plant opened for business. (That was a year after Armand Hammer met Lenin.) Even before Andreas's birth, in 1917, an Indianan who'd experimented with raising soybeans had written in the *Orange Judd Weekly Farmer* that "after the requirements are well understood soy beans should prove considerably more profitable to the careful farmer than oats, and should run a very close second to corn and wheat."

However, like most farmers at Worthington, Minnesota (where much of their produce annually went to sustain the community's claim to be Turkey Capital of the United States), the Andreases in residence there were still trafficking exclusively in conventional grains.

In the summer of 1876, just short of his seventy-fifth birthday, Johann Andreas, for many years the elder of the Elbing-Allerwald Mennonite Church in West Prussia, immigrated to the United States and settled, with his family and a handful of followers, at Mount Pleasant, Iowa. He didn't live there long—only five months. It was not so much the move that caused his death, probably, as the stress of having for the nine previous years defied the Prussian authorities and a cabinet order they'd issued decreeing that Mennonites—against their deepest-seated convictions—be drafted into the army like everybody else for seven years, or perform some alternative service. Johann Andreas, whose kinship to Dwayne is uncertain but who was probably a not-too-distant cousin, chose the harsh alternative of expatriation.

There had been Andreases of the Mennonite faith in West Prussia (the name was sometimes recorded as Andres, Andries, Androes, or Andresen) at least as far back as 1638. They moved out in many directions, some ending up, responding with coreligionists to an invitation from Catherine the Great, in South Russia, where they shortly established an Andreasfeld Mennonite Brethren Church. The empress had offered varied inducements for their eastward trek, including exemption not only from military service but also from taxes. Czar Alexander II nullified all that, though, and the Mennonites in his realm, like their Prussian brethren, began looking elsewhere for a promised land.

It was a wonder that any of them existed anywhere. Their sixteenth-century forebears, like other Anabaptists, had suffered grievously during the Protestant Reformation: Andries Claessen broken on the wheel and beheaded in the

Dutch province of Friesland, for instance; Andries Jacobsz burned at the stake in Antwerp, while his fiancée was obliged to look on.

The first Mennonites to reach Minnesota—and to bring with them, of enormous importance to Dwayne Andreas and others of their descendants, their unbending commitment to social justice and social harmony—arrived in 1873 from the Crimea and settled at the village of Mountain Lake, forty miles from Worthington. In December of that year a member of the Minnesota Board of Immigration said of them in a report to the governor of the state:

> There can be no doubt that this chapter will form a bright leaf in the history of the development of our State, since by their scrutinizing and careful observation of all the Western States, not only will their compatriots in Russia and Prussia look favorably and act intelligently in watching the growth of the seed thus limitedly auspiciously sown, but the men of other colonies and organizations scattered without number over Europe will receive an impetus to immigrate, which must feel to them like a welcome, ere they have learned to know us.
>
> I congratulate Minnesota on the present acquisition, for of such people are great States made.

The Mennonites, wherever they put down roots, led a no-nonsense life. They abjured gambling, dancing, bright-colored clothing, and jewelry. They tithed. (They were sometimes considered detrimental to a community because they spent so much less on consumer goods than did their neighbors.) At work in their fields, they preferred horses to tractors, which, Andreas is fond of pointing out today, is not at all a bad way to farm at any time; you don't have to buy fuel for horses, and they furnish you with fertilizer. The Bible was the Mennonites' favorite book, and on Sundays all other reading matter was proscribed.

At the time of Andreas's birth, however, the Mennonites were not left, as they stoutly wished to be, to their own simple devices. As Ian Frazier has recounted in *The Great Plains:*

> After America entered the First World War, in 1917, Congress passed the first universal conscription act since the Civil War. This act contained a clause exempting from combatant service "members of any well-organized religious sect or organization at present organized and existing" whose beliefs did not allow them to participate in war. The act said that such people would be given noncombatant service, but did not spell out what that service would be. About half the Mennonites who were drafted agreed to perform noncombatant service. The other half said that any service at all that aided the conduct of war was wrong. ...Mobs painted their meetinghouses yellow or burned them down. Several Mennonites were tarred and feathered. Teddy Roosevelt said the Mennonites were not fit to live in America. Eventually, seventy-six Mennonites, the grandsons of men who had left Russia rather than serve in the Czar's Army, were court-martialled, given terms of from ten to thirty years, and sent to the Army prison in Fort Leavenworth.

Dwayne's father had four children by the time the United States went to war and was routinely deferred.

In 1954, a year in which Andreas, by then comfortably a millionaire, joined his friend Hubert Humphrey, the chairman of the Middle East Subcommittee of the Senate's Foreign Relations Committee, on a fifteen-day jaunt to Spain, Italy, Egypt, Greece, Lebanon, and Israel, Dwayne told the *Minneapolis Star,* "At heart, I'm just a Mennonite farm boy." Unadorned his clothing might have had to be back on the farm, but he was to become a dapper dresser, sometimes accoutering himself for golf in an all-lavender outfit and usually topping off his more formal ensembles with a pearl stickpin. In further defiance of the Mennonite canon, he came to enjoy dancing; one astute observer of the social scene, his friend Ann Landers, after telling a mutual acquaintance that Dwayne was "an absolutely terrific ballroom dancer," added, in a phrase she thought apt, "He's never heavy furniture."

As a man of Anabaptist blood, Andreas has enjoyed talking to such friends as Nelson and Laurance Rockefeller about their Baptist upbringing, which included total immersions at youthful christenings. Dwayne was bemused by Laurance's assertion that he had found his childhood dunking so unsettling that as an adult, having a swimming pool constructed, he insisted it be no more than four feet deep, so he wouldn't be tempted to dive into it and once again find his head underwater.

In 1965, when the Department of Agriculture was behind a pending bill to cut back on agricultural production, Andreas, who was then executive vice president of a St. Paul, Minnesota, cooperative called the Farmers Union Grain Terminal Association (its scattered terminals had a total storage capacity of some 40 million bushels), made a speech describing the project as "a sordid chapter in American history" and using no-holds-barred phrases such as "ignoble goals" and "crop-cutting orgy." He went on: "When our leaders overrule the men of little vision dedicated to crop-cutting and plan for more feeding instead of shooting"—the Vietnam War was on full-scale—"more production instead of cutbacks, then we will be able to stand before the world as a mature and sophisticated civilization."

Sending a copy of his remarks to Humphrey, by now vice president, Andreas wrote, "I was born and raised as a Mennonite, and although I am not much of a religious person, there is no way that I could support massive destruction of food production, even if I thought I ought to for my own good. We were taught that it is criminal to destroy food."

In Moscow, in 1989, by which time Andreas was known the world over as someone who had Mikhail Gorbachev's ear, a mutual acquaintance sought to ascertain from Professor Victor Lishchenko, the head of the Food and Agriculture Department of the USA and Canada Academy of Sciences of the USSR, just what it was about this particular American that made the Soviet leaders listen attentively to what he had to say. "Maybe because of his religious beliefs," Lishchenko said.

Dwayne's father and mother, Reuben Peter Andreas and Lydia Barbara Stoltz, were both born in 1882 to strict Mennonite families, a couple of months apart and in Illinois towns—he in Milledgeville, she in Sterling—a few miles apart. They were married in Sterling on November 27, 1902, and not long afterward moved to Minnesota. She was a compulsive worker and small in stature. The tallest of her five sons stood at five feet eight inches. (Dwayne Andreas, though never noticeably self-conscious about his diminutive stature, has referred to Mikhail Gorbachev, who is indisputably taller, as "one smart little fellow.") While raising the boys and a single girl—Dwayne, born on March 4, 1918, was next to the last of the lot—like other farmwives of her time, along with all the housework, she took care of butchering.

When Lydia Andreas died in 1938, on Mother's Day, one newspaper obituary said: "Many a youth will long remember her as a beautiful fairy that in time of need was present and when little hills of difficulty came in the way, she almost miraculously appeared and lifted them over." (Soon after her death, Reuben married her divorced sister, Pauline Hummel.)

When Dwayne was four, his parents learned of a sixty-acre Iowa farm that was available fairly cheap outside Lisbon, and the family moved again. They were not well-to-do, but as Mennonites they had frugal habits to begin with, and in any event they could quite satisfactorily manage on what they raised and grew. "Some people would say we were poor, but we didn't think so," Andreas said years later. "We canned our own vegetables, grew oats for our horses, hay for our cows, corn for our chickens and pigs." At their table, nobody ever ate a morsel until grace had been said.

In later life, Dwayne seemed to find it difficult to comment on just about anything without alluding to his boyhood on the farm. Thus, in his seventies, reflecting on his country's trillion-dollar deficit, he would say, "I don't know how the United States will even dig itself out of this hole. I know what my father taught me when I was about five. He said,

'When you're in a hole, stop digging.'" Asked one time if he wasn't worried about the Russians' gaining access to American computer know-how, he retorted that trying to stop transfers of technological information was akin to shoveling smoke. Or, addressing an assemblage of polished investment bankers: "These days, if you don't recognize that you're living in a socialist society and have to get along with the government whether you like it or not, you're going to get rolled over, as if you were a pig in a manger with its mother sow. When she rolls over, either you get a teat in your mouth or you get squashed."

And when asked on his return from one trip to the Soviet Union what its people most needed, he replied, casting his mind back half a century as he spoke:

They say they want high-tech plants to process corn and wheat, but that's not what they most need. They need storage capacity for sixty million tons on farms because now they waste one-third of their crop. They need three million trucks—which they could make in their tank factories without too much redesign—and four hundred thousand rail cars, which they could build in other defense plants. They could use their bomb factories for making dairy equipment. But what they need above all, for their farmers, are fertilizer and a distribution system, and that means roads and phones and electricity.

It's like what we went through on the farm in the thirties. Hell, I was living right through the time when we finally got farm-to-market roads, and under the New Deal—while the Republicans were screaming "Waste!"—rural electrification. What the Russians have to do is to make people on the farm feel comfortable, so they can phone a doctor. Oh, they'll get some high-tech, though not as much as they want, but the big thing for them is to be able to call a doctor.

You know, somebody once asked me how I would differentiate myself from other CEOs. Well, maybe it's that I've come up to wherever I am with my own body and my own hands. Coming up from the skunk works is the most important part of running any business. Some administrators who emerge from business schools are put in charge of businesses without understanding them. If you're going to be in the dairy business, there's no substitute for a cow's teats. You'd better also have ridden a horse and plowed some ground and seen some dust blow in a drought. Wherever you go, first you've got to have been there.

In 1927, Reuben Andreas, who had aspirations beyond self-sufficiency, heard of an opportunity to take over a bankrupt grain-coal-and-seed business in Lisbon. With a mortgage loan from the Lisbon National Bank (which like others of that day printed its own money), the Lisbon Elevator was soon operated by R. P. Andreas & Son. (By 1934 it would be "& Sons.") Its telephone number was an easy-to-remember "4." In 1927, Reuben—known to his neighbors as R. P.—began selling feeds to cattlemen and others, mixing all the ingredients—corn, soymeal, oats, alfalfa, molasses—by hand, as he and his sons shoveled them from a garage floor into bins.

Dwayne, at nine, was deemed quite old enough to pitch in. "I've been doing the same thing all my life," he reflected more than half a century later, "that I began doing as a boy: helping to store and process and transport plants in order to get them into the food chain." Some of his former neighbors recall that while ready and willing enough to assume his share of the family burdens, as a teenager he seemed often to be found hanging around R. P.'s office, chewing the fat with the salesmen who stopped by, and every now and then dipping into his father's till—scrupulously leaving an IOU—for some petty cash, on the accumulation of sufficient amounts whereof, Lisbonites widely believed, he would invest—with success enough to replenish the exchequer—in the stock market. "I owe a lot to Lisbon," Dwayne would tell the local paper, the *Sun*, in 1987, "for that's where I got my education at a very good school...and that's where I learned the business in a country elevator."

The school and the Andreases had especially close ties. Reuben went on the school board soon after arriving on the scene and in due course became its president. Basketball players didn't have to be outsize freaks back then, and Dwayne is remembered as a pretty good ball handler. He was also an outspoken one. When the basketball coach got fired, for reasons that are now obscure, Dwayne went on strike. He was suspended and sent home. When he got there, the president of the board gave him a licking, not so much for his defiance as for falling behind in his studies by the couple of classes he'd missed.

The grain elevator had other-than-business uses. The Andreas boys and their cousins would ride up and down a hand-raised rope inside it. "Right now I remember it as about a thousand feet, but I'm sure it was under a hundred," Jimmy Hey recalled many years afterward. "In the elevator were large storage bins for corn. Across each corner was an angled support placed probably four feet apart. We would climb up to two or three supports and then jump. A constant challenge for who had the nerve to jump from the highest support. One day my older brother Dean jumped from five up and that ended the competition for a while."

The Andreases called their output, logically enough, Andy's Feeds. There would be echoes of this nomenclatural device years afterward, when Dwayne would be running Archer Daniels Midland and sanctioned the name Uncle Archie's Vegetable Protein Entrées for an experimental line of packaged soy-based meat-substitute dishes, which came in Pepper Steak Style, Chicken Almondine Style, or Sweet-n-Sour Pork Style. It was ADM's only contemplated foray into the retail market under its own name, or nickname. Samples were sent to other food-processing companies, but there was never a wholehearted attempt at bulk distribution, and eventually Uncle Archie's went the way of all nonflesh. "We moved too fast too soon," one ADM executive lamented. "It was like the Chrysler Airflow."

In his prime, Andreas more often than not arose at 5 A.M. This was no strain because as a boy on the farm he was usually up at four, to feed the pigs and shovel the corn and do other assorted routine chores before heading to school. More than half a century after all that, when at a gathering of corporate executives someone asked him how he contrived to run such a huge enterprise with such seemingly little effort, Andreas said, "Hell, what I do now is easy compared to when I was a kid." After school, once he had mastered enough arithmetic, he would help balance the company books. "I knew the basics of running a business by the time I was twelve," he says.

Self-effacement is a part of Andreas's adult stock-in-trade. At an ADM corporate presentation in September 1989, before a lunch meeting of the New York Society of Security Analysts, Chairman Andreas told a tale about a chap who went into a pet store looking for a parrot. The price tag on a beautifully plumaged one that could speak French and German was $10,000. What else? the customer inquired. For a less colorful one conversant in Chinese and Japanese, $20,000. Too much. For a scruffy one with no apparent redeeming skills, $25,000. How come? "The other two address him as 'Mr. Chairman.'" The security analysts laughed, as did Mikhail Gorbachev when Andreas recounted the story at a Moscow function.* Andreas had them in hand. He switched instantly into a dead-serious commentary on Third World hunger.

When Dwayne was about seven, he shared the responsibility for a household cow with an older brother, who milked it. Dwayne watered and fed it. What nobody had got around to telling him, he insists to this day (he was big enough, as maturity was measured in those circles, to carry two pails), was that if you give a cow enough food, it will keep on eating until it dies. Dwayne stuffed his bovine charge with lethal helpings of bran. When he came to learn more about farm animals and their habits, he never was able to comprehend the origin of the phrase "eating like a pig," inasmuch as the hogs he remembered not only wouldn't stuff themselves to death but would even seem to regulate their intake of rations— so many carbohydrates, so much protein, selectivity all the way. (Andreas is a compulsive doodler, and a collector of his works would end up with a barnyard's worth of swine. He

---

*So often did Andreas spin that psittacine yarn that his wife eventually bought him a handsome, bright green parrot, which Inez christened, inevitably, "Mr. Chairman."

himself collects miniature pigs. "Dwayne accumulates pigs," says longtime ADM vice president Richard Burket, "the way political-party partisans collect elephants and donkeys.") In that respect at least, he came to conclude, they were a good deal smarter than a good many two-legged creatures whose paths he crossed.

7

Most people don't understand about
interest. I do. You've got to know
about compound interest because otherwise
you can't even think about business.

—DOA

I N the Lisbon years, there was time to play. Many of
Dwayne's playmates were cousins, and much of the
socializing the Andreases took part in was at family
reunions across the Illinois state line—at Joliet or Maywood
or Dixon or De Kalb. But work, even for the children, always
came first. Dwayne's after-school chores for a time included
delivering the *Des Moines Register* and selling subscriptions
to the magazine *Household*.

Even after his own worth was estimated at more than
$200 million, Andreas retained a door-to-door commission-
salesman's approach to making money. Sitting in his Fifth
Avenue apartment in New York, awaiting a corporate executive wanting to add to his wealth to the extent of a quick
$24-million profit on a stock sale, Andreas got to reflecting
on the city's Upper East Side multiple-leashed dog walkers.

When a companion remarked that by exercising a dozen or so dogs for a couple of hours a morning, a walker could probably earn five or six hundred dollars a week, Andreas shook his head in awe and admiration. "That's *real* money," he said.

As an adult, Andreas was fond of harking back to something his father had taught him about money, extracurricularly, when he was in the fourth grade. "Most people don't understand about interest," Andreas *fils* would say.

I do. You've got to know about compound interest because otherwise you can't even think about business. Here's the way he taught me to go about it. You can take any interest rate and divide it into seventy-two and find out how long it would take you to double the cost of your borrowing or, if you're the lender, your return. If you have twelve percent interest it goes into seventy-two six times; that means with compound interest at twelve percent it takes six years to double your money. If you have a six-percent interest rate, it takes twelve years. This little formula always works. It saved me a lot of trouble in my arithmetic lessons, and in business in later life.

But the widespread lack of knowledge about interest the world over causes problems. Ninety percent of the time when the government lends people money, they go busted. And the government thinks it's doing them a favor! The whole capitalistic system is exploding because the educational system is so weak in this area. Why, I spoke to a bunch of high-powered businessmen in Miami once, and in the question-and-answer period it was apparent that they didn't know this fundamental thing about business.

Bankers know it, of course, and like to keep it their secret, because lending money is the most profitable business on earth, with the interest piling up days and nights and Sundays and holidays, too. The lack of knowledge about interest is behind this whole takeover thing. I wonder if anybody around Henry Kravis's place knows that if you borrow twenty-four billion at twelve percent at the end of six years you'll be paying back forty-eight billion. The whole takeover field is one big black hole.

Stock analysts often call attention to Archer Daniels

Midland's uncommonly low ratio of debt to assets; the *Wall Street Journal* noted admiringly in the winter of 1989 that Andreas "keeps ADM's balance sheet sloshing with surplus cash."

Another lesson from his father that Andreas was happy to share in later life had to do with buying and selling. "Trade teaches us that both sides of a transaction are winners," he told his listeners at the 1983 Moscow trade fair. "The seller finds a market for his wares; the buyer gets the goods he wants." He continued:

> I think I can best illustrate that by a story my father told me when I was a boy.
>
> We were farmers and he got to trading in horses. And to explain this to me one day he said: "Let me tell you how it works, son. Here is a farmer over here with three horses and no cows. The first horse is worth six hundred dollars because it does all the work. The second horse is worth three hundred dollars because it works about half the time. And the third horse is worth nothing to him because it eats oats and doesn't work.
>
> "Now over here on the other side is the farmer with three cows and no horses. The first cow is worth six hundred dollars because the milk feeds the children. The second is worth three hundred dollars because he can sell the milk to his neighbors. But the third cow is worth nothing because there is no way for him to market the milk.
>
> "Now I as a trader get these two farmers together. The farmer with three cows trades his worthless cow to the farmer with three horses, who gives his worthless horse to the farmer with three cows. Now the farmer has two horses and a six-hundred-dollar cow because it is his first cow. The other farmer is ahead by the fact that he has a six-hundred-dollar horse because it is his first horse. Now each farmer is six hundred dollars richer and I hope I make fifty dollars in the trade."
>
> I always remember that story and I have found that almost every business transaction I know of turns out just like that.

The Lisbon public school was a conventional, no-nonsense academy. Once when Andreas was assigned, as a high-schooler, to submit a book report, he turned one in on *Brave New World*. For reasons not made clear to him (in later life, he'd have insisted that they were), it was considered so unbecoming a choice that he was suspended for a week. Nonetheless, he finished high school in three years. He never did quite get the hang, though, of correctly spelling proper names, as the notes he has scribbled to himself after meeting important global figures have attested. He would omit the first "a" from "Reagan." It was perhaps his orthographic good fortune that the Soviet leader he came to know best was not Khrushchev.

Among other big events in 1934, along with Dwayne's graduation from Lisbon High, were the purchases by R. P. Andreas & Sons of a corn-sugar molasses company and of a feed-mixing machine that could handle ten tons of ingredients an hour and the Chicago World's Fair. At that spectacle, Henry Ford, whose romance with soybeans was legendary— he cultivated them on three continents, modeled a suit made of a soy-based fabric, and had an automobile chassis molded out of a soy-based plastic—treated thirty apprehensive guests to a sixteen-course soy dinner, from soup to nuts and coffee substitute. (A year later, he could have thrown in the result of a short-lived attempt to use soybean flakes—they were supposed to produce a creamier and longer-lasting head—as a substitute for malt in brewing beer.)

Visitors to ADM's headquarters at Decatur are often invited to sit down to a similar repast. Among the items derived in whole or in part from soybeans at one lunch over which Andreas presided were a chocolate beverage, taco dip, salami rolls, spareribs with barbecue sauce, stir-fried chicken, beef and snow peas, bread, margarine, and an all-vegetable frozen dessert. When Tofutti, the mock-ice-cream soybean hit of the eighties, made its imitative mark, it sometimes also made the ADM carte du jour. A partaker of one such single-minded repast, proferred a strawberry for dessert, wondered warily whether it was real. "Maybe in the twenty-first century we'll make strawberries out of soybeans,"

Andreas said reassuringly, "but that's still far down the list."

Entertaining at a year-round apartment he has had at the Waldorf Towers in New York since 1961, Andreas has been apt to supplement what room service proffers with soy-milk drinks of various flavors and other soy-based comestibles. When he was pushing his Uncle Archie's line, Uncle Dwayne would tell a visitor heading toward a Waldorf elevator—often as burdened as if the leavetaker had been to a supermarket— that ADM's chicken almondine was all but indistinguishable in taste from, and incomparably superior in nutrition to, chicken almondine made from real chicken.

Some years ago on a David Susskind show (it was easy to get booked; Susskind's step-daughter was married at the time to Andreas's son), Dwayne even personally prepared what may have been the first all-soy meal—"pepper steak," soybean salad with "bacon" chips, soy-and-corn bread—ever to be sampled on television. Andreas has dispatched ADM's chef de soy cuisine, a pioneering lady named Joan Godbey, to the Soviet Union, India, Mexico, and Des Moines to impart some of the secrets of preparing her delicacies to Mother Teresa, the Pat Robertsons, and other interested parties. At home, Ms. Godbey has catered in her special fashion to, among other transient eminences, the chief of the United States bureau of the New China News Agency and a correspondent from *Pravda*, who after spending three fact-gathering days at Decatur in the spring of 1988 reported:

> At lunch in the company cafeteria we were served dishes made from the company's own products. The salad made from hydroponic vegetables was probably the only natural dish, so to speak, the only one that looked like what it was. Everything else was made of soy, which in one instance looked for all the world like a tuna fillet, and in another was indistinguishable from fried chicken. "A practically unlimited number of the most varied dishes right up to ice cream can be made from our products," was the response to my surprise of the ADM workers who were dining with me.

When a national softball championship was held at Decatur in the fall of 1983 and hot-dog and hamburger stands were set up to accommodate the spectators, there was also a stand that sold sloppy joes and tacos made of a soybean extract called textured vegetable protein, or TVP. William Atkinson, who helped produce soy-based clothing and other oddities for Henry Ford, was also instrumental in developing TVP, which has approximately the chewability—or as ADM executives like to put it, "mouthfeel"—of meat.

The stand at the ball game was presided over by the proprietor of a local breakfast-and-lunch establishment called Just Around the Corner. The sloppy joes and tacos were so popular that Andreas offered to provide the eating place with just about all the raw materials it needed if it would stay open for dinner, too, for a six-month test and would serve soy-constituted equivalents of chicken à la king, chop suey, lasagna, and other dishes. All hands involved in the enterprise were aware of the widespread misgivings about eating soy foods; the word "soy" nowhere appeared on the menu.

Andreas was one of the steadier patrons and said he liked the mouthfeel of all the offerings except the lasagna. That surprised the proprietor because the lasagna was one of the more popular dishes with everybody else. The venture proved unrewarding though, and not long afterward the restaurant folded.

As a concession to his devout mother, who kept hoping, in vain, that at least one of her five boys would enter the ministry, in 1935 Dwayne matriculated at Wheaton College, in Illinois, which prepared many students for that line of work and a few years later demonstrated its mettle by graduating Billy Graham. Andreas dropped out, though, toward the end of his sophomore year ("I just didn't respond"), and that concluded his formal education. One further reason for quitting school was that he got married, when he was eighteen and she three years older, to Bertha Benedict, whom he met at Wheaton. That youthful union was short-lived and ended in divorce, but it did produce daughter Sandra, later McMurtrie and Mother Teresa's faithful acolyte.

Another and ultimately far more consequential reason was going into business with his father. One of the five Andreas boys, Albert, had since 1927 been Reuben's "& Son." Now, in the mid-1930s, toward the dawn of what some people began calling the agrindustrial age, the paterfamilias took three more sons, Osborn, Glenn, and Dwayne, into the fold. (Lowell, the youngest, would soon come aboard, but he was then still in high school.) Dwayne, not yet twenty, was put in charge of sales promotion, and when annual sales shortly reached the million-dollar mark (one eight-thousandth of ADM's later total), the milestone was acclaimed by the regional press.

Dwayne was also allowed to buy a $1,500 stake in the enterprise. He had no trouble borrowing the sum at 4 percent—the Andreases were the solidest of citizens, with Reuben on the bank board and running the school board—from Willard Stuckslager at the Lisbon National.

The loan was paid off in two years and Dwayne had his equity free and clear. That $1,500, the only cash he has ever put into the food-processing business, would proliferate giddily, step by rewarding step, into Archer Daniels Midland stock worth a couple of hundred million—a rate of return on the investment of roughly 130,000 percent.

In 1936, the Andreases changed the name of their business to the Honeymead Products Company and moved it to Cedar Rapids, where Dwayne came under the tutelary spell of one of his Jewish mentors, Joseph Sinaiko, a leading soybean processor. "A very classy guy," Andreas would say years afterward, "and the best soybean processor of that era." Lowell Andreas ran the processing end of their business; Dwayne handled sales and transportation. (That was also the year in which the Pennsylvania Railroad, anticipating a rise in soybean activity and concomitant freight traffic, dispatched a soybean-exhibit car—among its presentations were samples of paint, varnish, and plywood made in part from the versatile plant—on a seventeen-thousand-mile tour through eighteen states. The departure point was New Brunswick, New

Jersey, because it was at the Rutgers University agricultural-extension station there that James Neilson was credited with having grown, in 1878, the first commercial crop of soybeans in America.)

Honeymead Products would soon have its own claim to trailblazing. A plant it built in 1938 was the first soybean-oil processing mill in the country. It was also, according to the *Chemurgic Digest,* "the world's largest deodorizer, designed to deodorize ten-tank carloads of soybean oil per day." (Nobody has yet come up with a design for thoroughly deodorizing Decatur.) For the feed side of the burgeoning business, there was an old Cedar Rapids storehouse that could accommodate one hundred freight-car loads. Soon Honeymead would install three machines for the manufacture of hard-pellet feeds, in different sizes. Even the tiniest of the lot, made for poultry, were robust enough not to be swept about, as were powdered feeds, by gusts of wind. Also, feed in the shape of pellets was supposed to enhance digestion.

The pellet production line was practically a gourmet operation, with ingredients imported from hither and yon: peanuts from Georgia, for instance, and fish meal from California. By this time, Honeymead, with Dwayne its most aggressive salesman, boasted a fleet of forty-five cars and trucks to deliver its goods to customers as far off as Omaha and Chicago; and not even counting Andreases, it had eighty-eight employees.

In August 1937, when the company's net worth was appraised at $24,200, the Iowa Securities Commission had authorized a public stock offering. One man who bought $800 worth of shares early on sold his holdings a while later for $23,000. The Andreases, who in the natural order of things kept most of the stock for themselves, did all right, too.

A while after the move to Cedar Rapids, Andreas, so he could expand his sales territory and diminish the time it took to cover it, got himself a pilot's license and bought an Ercoupe. "I remember one of his visits to my farm in his airplane in 1937," said his Lisbon neighbor Gordon Ellison. "I was plowing corn with a team of horses, and he landed the plane in the field and asked me to go for a ride with him. I tied the horses to a fence and boarded the plane. We flew around the Lisbon-Mount Vernon area along with Cedar Rapids. On the way back to the farm we noticed my uncle in the field on his tractor. I told Dwayne to fly in back of him to the side, about fifty feet away, and then gun the motor when he got near him. He did and it scared the hell out of my uncle. He told Dwayne later that if he had had a gun with him, he would have shot him down."

Riding with Dwayne made Cousin Jimmy Hey nervous, too. (Dwayne was flying solo when, on a sales mission, he ran into some newly strung telephone wires, which caught him like a net and dropped him, more or less gently, to the ground. He was thereupon persuaded to retire his wings.) During the Second World War, Hey, too, would become a pilot. He flew B-24s with the Eighth Air Force in Europe. During a postwar visit to Cedar Rapids, the cousins rented a small plane together for a friendly spin.

"Have you ever looped?" Jimmy asked.

Dwayne confessed that he had not.

"I said, 'Fasten your belt tight,'" Hey recollected. "We really wrang the old bus out. I had completed requirements early in flying school, so I learned to get proficient in acrobatics in the spare time allotted. I'm sure that is one ride that is still vivid in Dwayne's mind."

In December 1987, in the course of conferring on Andreas a regional award called the Order of Lincoln, Governor James R. Thompson of Illinois hailed him as "the Soybean King." However unexceptionable that might have been to most of the world, it was a bit too much for Decatur, Illinois, in the heart of the egalitarian, populist, anti-Royalist Midwest. The *Herald & Review* observed that August Eugene Staley had started his soybean-pioneering A. E. Staley Manufacturing Company there in 1922, when Andreas was four; and an aide to the governor, backtracking fast on Thompson's embarrassed behalf, said, "Most certainly the soybean spotlight shines not only on Dwayne Andreas, but on A. E. Staley and dozens of scientists, researchers, marketers and farmers." Andreas has tried ever since not to seem to be Decatur's most spotlighted resident. In 1989, for instance, reluctant to be seen tooling around a town with a substantial unemployment rate in a fancy limousine, he elected to be chauffeured in a plain-looking Ford van—albeit, to be sure, one with a splendidly fitted-out interior.

A turning point for Andreas, and for soybeans, had occurred in 1938, when he was not quite twenty-one and for the first time went to Decatur, two hundred miles by road from Cedar Rapids. His destination—thanks largely to Staley—was already known as Soy City. As steel was sold F.O.B. Pittsburgh, so was soy F.O.B. Decatur.

Dwayne's mission was to buy eight thousand tons of ground soymeal. A booklet put out by the Decatur Convention and Visitors Bureau describes the place as "a comfortably sized Midwestern city full of pleasant surprises." Young Andreas got one when he'd finished his business with a Staley henchman and was about to head home. He was intercepted by Mr. Staley, who invited him to lunch.

"I felt like I was in the presence of God," the emphatically still-far-from-enthroned Soybean King said afterward.

During their conversation, Staley remarked that it looked as though Iowa farmers were going to be cultivating more and more soybeans in the years immediately ahead. Somebody would have to crush them. Staley had no plans to move beyond Illinois. Honeymead was already in Iowa. Why didn't the Andreases build a plant of their own where the beans would be grown?

Andreas said his family didn't have access to the kind of money that that would surely require. Staley advised him to go to the Allis-Chalmers people, in Milwaukee, and borrow it. The twenty-year-old drove back at, he would claim after he could vote, eighty miles an hour, talked to his father and brothers, and having donned a hat to look more mature, roared off to Wisconsin. He got the loan.

After ADM became part of the Decatur scene itself, in 1969, Staley was its principal competitor, but on the whole the two were friendly rivals. Right off, when Mr. Staley heard that the Andreases were on their way, he persuaded the governors of the Country Club of Decatur, which had a waiting list for prospective members, to add twenty new places, at the head of the line, for the newcomers' foursomes.

In 1985, Archer Daniels Midland, which by then had access to untold sums, would be taking over the operation of five Staley soybean plants—Staley itself was fated to be taken over by a British firm, Tate & Lyle—worth $74 million.* And today one is likely to see, in Decatur, behind an Illinois Central engine, ADM and Staley freight cars hooked up in tandem and waiting, like paired golfers on a tee, to start moving along their prescribed course.

---

*ADM's financial people determined that it would be fiscally advantageous to lease the plants rather than buy them outright. For leasing, a third party was required. So Andreas and a bunch of other ADM executives borrowed $80 million from a bank and created an entity, called Independent Soy Processors, that consisted of themselves.

Don't make the mistake of assuming
governments are rational.

—DOA

B Y the time the Second World War started, Andreas,
not quite twenty-three, was a father. So he was draft-
deferred. Moreover, he was in a sense involved in the
war effort, inasmuch as the production of soy-based products
rated fairly high among all the major participants. The Germans, for instance, had made hospital bread out of soybeans
one war earlier, and they now proceeded to convert 2 million
tons into much more widely distributed foodstuffs. I. G.
Farben had some of its minions growing beans in Romania,
Austria, and the Balkan states. Recipe books distributed to
German Army cooks contained two hundred soybean dishes.
One contemporary historian went so far as to write that
"some commentators have ascribed almost as much significance to the German supply of soybeans as to her supply of
airplanes."

Hitler introduced Mussolini to soy. The Japanese, of course, had long been into it. Soviet troops were fed a porridge made of soybean meal, oatmeal, and salt. Soymeal was pressed into service as a Canadian Navy lifeboat ration. (One pound of it was reputed to be as valuable, and as unpalatable, as ten pounds of ordinary hardtack.) While few Americans deemed soybeans to be a high-priority part of any diet, they found a place, too, in the United States war effort. The magazine *Soybean Digest* crowed that PT boats in the North African landings were held together—as, presumably, was Lieutenant John F. Kennedy's in the Pacific until it came apart—with soybean-derived glue. And although not much found at military messes, soybeans were an ingredient of— along with helmets, uniform buttons, and rifles—GI mess kits.

From 1938 to 1945, Honeymead, of which Dwayne had quickly become executive officer, was on the food edge of the war effort, processing some fifty thousand bushels of beans daily, largely for animal feed, in its new oil-extraction plant. It was rapidly evolving, primarily, into one of the nation's largest livestock-nourishing enterprises. By 1945, Reuben Andreas was getting along in years, and with two of his sons engaged in other business pursuits, Dwayne was pretty much in charge of the company. That June, his draft classification was changed to 1-A. Having no reason to believe the war would soon end, and in anticipation of being called up, he sold 60 percent of the family's Honeymead holdings to Cargill, which was then, as it remains, the nation's premier exporter of grains. (Worldwide, in the 1980s, Cargill had forty-three thousand employees and 340 grain elevators, with a total capacity of 390 million bushels.)

Dwayne's personal share of the proceeds from the Honeymead sale came to about $1.5 million. He was twenty-seven. Ultimately, he wasn't drafted after all, and the war did end, and Cargill invited him to enlist in its well-remunerated ranks, offering him—"a Midwesterner of proverbial provinciality," according to one contemporary observer—a job as general manager of one of its Cedar Rapids plants at $25,000 a year. Reuben Andreas didn't much relish the notion of his son working outside the family, but Dwayne already had a mind of his own; he went to Cargill and stayed there for seven years, ending up as vice president in charge of soybean and linseed-oil operations at $35,000. In 1948, he hired as one of his assistants a twenty-year-old chemical engineer, James R. Randall, who in due course would become the president of Archer Daniels Midland.

Another of Andreas's deputies at Cargill was a man a dozen years his elder, Willard C. Lighter, who had returned to the company in January 1946 after being discharged from the army. Andreas handled the disparity in age and experience with, Lighter would recall, considerable skill and tact. At war's end, Cargill had built a new plant on the Minnesota River, south of Minneapolis, to crush flax for the extraction of linseed oil. That summer there was a shortage of flax, and its price had accordingly risen to a robust $7 a bushel. But any flax, to keep the plant running, was better than none. Andreas and Lighter and their associates learned that Dwayne's brother Albert happened to have some excess flax at a linseed-oil plant of his own, at Minneapolis, and Dr. Julius Hendel—another Midwestern Jew whose business acumen Dwayne was happy to partake of—was delegated to phone Albert and inquire whether he had, say, a few thousand bushels he could spare at $7.50 each.

As the day wore on, there was some confusion about just who had ordered how much of what, and by the time that got straightened out, the Cargill men learned that Albert had the impression that his brother et al. wanted all the flax they could get their hands on, and something like seven hundred thousand bushels were en route. It was far more than Cargill had the facilities to process. But within an hour Dwayne had found an idle plant that could be geared up to do the job, and Lighter found a customer for the incipient linseed oil. Lighter, who ended his career as a vice president at Central Soya, said afterward that they were "feeling mighty lucky that we had turned a very bad situation into a pretty profitable situation in half a day." Reflecting on his association with

Andreas, he would add, "I guess you could say he was unusual. During all his active years there probably has been no one that was or is his equal."

Of Cargill, Andreas said, nearly thirty years after bidding it farewell, "I don't believe there's a better private company in the world." He could afford to say so because his ADM is publicly owned and is also principally a processing company in the trading business, whereas Cargill is a trading company engaged in processing. When he moved on, he had to sell back to it a small stock interest he'd been granted on joining up; that added $400,000 to his till. His $1,500 capital investment was beginning to pay dividends.

Cargill was based in Minneapolis, and while there Andreas, by now separated from his wife, became an increasingly well-known bachelor about town—one of the few such indeed who, Mennonite upbringing notwithstanding, drove around in a Cadillac boasting a telephone. He got a kick out of parking outside a friend's house and phoning in to announce his arrival. After a bit, his most frequent stop and communications post was right outside the residence of Inez Snyder, a diminutive (5'2") blonde from Earlham, Iowa. The daughter of an Oregon-born farmer turned commodities trader, in 1947 Inez was a philosophy student at the University of Minnesota. By her first husband, the leader of an itinerant jazz band (the band broke up, as did the marriage, when he went into the wartime navy), she had a five-year-old daughter named Terry. Before the year was out, Dwayne was divorced and Inez and he were married.

With Dwayne at Cargill, brother Lowell, out of the army, was tending full-time to the family's remaining interest in Honeymead Products. Its principal activity was a soybean-crushing operation at Mankato, Minnesota, then a town of nineteen thousand. Lowell settled down there, and for much of his life since then Mankato has been his principal home. Before long, that plant was processing a thousand tons a day—more than was coming out of any other single site. Bankers—even some of those at the National City in Minneapolis, in which the Andreases had acquired a stake—thought the brothers were loony. How could they hope to sell so much emanating from so offbeat a source? What the bankers didn't know, and the Andreases saw no reason to enlighten them all about, was that the proprietors had made a deal with the Chicago & Northwestern Railroad to cart off their freight, for eventual sale abroad, at a special low trainload rate. Today that seemingly formidable output looks puny; a Rotterdam plant under the ADM umbrella is up to six thousand tons a day, and even good old Mankato is approaching three thousand.

One reason for Andreas's leaving Cargill in 1952—another being that he believed his commitment to the company was to make it the world's largest trader in oilseeds, and he had done that—was that his high-ranking colleagues there tended to have feelings about international relations considerably less flexible and more isolationist than his own. They had approved his Soviet expedition that year, but grudgingly. Andreas had a different view of the trip. "It was the best thing I ever did," he says. (In 1988, looking down on Moscow from Lenin Hills not long after a nine-hour flight from New York, he would recall that thirty-six years earlier it had taken him twenty-eight hours.) In Moscow that first time, one Russian official had told him that everybody over there believed that the US State Department had canceled the passports of more than a hundred Americans who'd evinced an interest in visiting the USSR. As Andreas was about to head home, already determined to fight for a right to return if need be, one of his hosts told him, "From now on, any United States businessman with a good reputation"—he did not spell out what that entailed—"can get a visa to the USSR. Let's see what your State Department has to say about that!"

Andreas, and all other American businessmen, and most of their customers, would shortly be dealing with an Eisenhower-Dulles, Cold War, scared-of-Joe-McCarthy State Department. Eisenhower's first term had barely begun when on April 16, 1953, the president, in a talk Andreas could have written himself and which in later years he would indeed commendingly repeat, told the American Society of Newspaper Editors:

> Every gun that is made, every warship launched, every rocket fired, signifies, in the final sense, a theft from those who hunger and are not fed, from those who are cold and are not clothed. This world in arms is not spending money alone. It is spending the sweat of its laborers, the genius of its scientists, the hopes of its children.... The nations are spending almost a trillion dollars a year on destructive weapons—more than one million eight hundred thousand every minute, day and night; the cost of one Trident submarine would pay for immunization and basic health care for all the needy children of the world.

In Moscow, twelve months before that ringing speech, Minister of Trade Anastas Mikoyan had mentioned to Andreas that the Soviet Union was unhappily short of fats and cooking oils and might be interested in buying some American linseed or cottonseed or soybean oil. That got Andreas to thinking, in due course, about butter. "We had so much butter on our hands—about two hundred and fifty million pounds of it—that it was a scandal," he says. He knew that Eisenhower, also soon after assuming office, had publicly declared that it would be better for his countrymen to sell butter cheap than to let it spoil. The president had told Andreas privately, "I think someday we'll start selling food, on a commercial basis, to all the Communist countries."

Andreas proceeded cautiously. He broached the matter with Richard Nixon, and the vice president said butter was indeed the ticket. Why? "McCarthy won't oppose you," Nixon said. "He's from Wisconsin." And Senator Joe did promise Dwayne that he wouldn't attack any trafficking with Communists as long as dairy products were involved. "I can't support you, but I won't say a word against you," McCarthy told him. Andreas says that the president, for his part, further told him, "I'm for selling them anything they can't shoot back."

A deal was eventually put together involving 150 million pounds of butter and an equal amount of cottonseed oil. The cost to the Russians would have been $185 million, or just about a hundred times the value of all United States exports to the Soviet Union for the entire year ending September 30, 1953. (A contemporaneous Gallup poll disclosed that 42 percent of Americans were in favor of trade with Russia, 44 percent were opposed, and 14 percent had no opinion.) Andreas thought it might make sense for the Russians to pay in some of *their* voluminous assets—gold, say, or manganese. The only hitch was that he and his associates would need an export license, which had to be granted by the Department of Commerce, whose incumbent secretary, Sinclair Weeks, had a mind of his own. (There were times when Eisenhower seemed to have surprisingly little influence on his own cabinet, but then did he not keep mum when McCarthy called his mentor George Marshall a traitor?) Weeks let it be known that if the plan was consummated, Russians would be paying less for American butter than American housewives were. There was predictable opposition. "No US butter for Boris," cried the Elko, Nevada, *Daily Free Press.* The *Wall Street Journal* also got into the act, complaining that it wasn't fair for Mrs. Smith to be paying eighty cents a pound for butter while Mrs. Ivanova was getting it for fifty.

Nobody bothered to note that it was costing all Americans sixty-seven cents a pound to hold the stuff in storage. "Of course, the housewife buying her butter at the corner grocery for eighty cents was paying about a third more than the world wholesale market price," Andreas said afterward. "But the Russians weren't expecting to buy their butter in quarter-pound packages." (The Mrs. Ivanova of that era was paying thirteen rubles a pound—the equivalent of $3.25.) Harold Stassen was then in charge of foreign aid—one of the few times when he managed to be in charge of anything outside Minnesota—and he was all in favor of the swap. But the Cold War was flourishing, and when Weeks balked at a license, with but a few other exceptions there was no demurrer from anyone of consequence in the administration, above or below him.*

Andreas shrugged, and puffing on the pipe he then smoked (he was thirty-five and trying to look more mature), he instructed his traders in Rotterdam to sell the Russians cottonseed and linseed oil from wherever they could obtain it. Dwayne and Inez also had to shrug off some five hundred threatening letters, conceivably from *Wall Street Journal* subscribers, consigning them more or less to the same category in which McCarthy had placed Marshall. For a while, Andreas carried around with him, to flourish if asked for identification, an envelope addressed simply "To the son of a bitch who wants to sell butter to the Russians." Much of the excess butter turned rancid and ended up being used to make soap.

---

* A *Washington Post* editorial said that "in denying to issue a license for exports at the lower world price, Commerce Secretary Weeks and the Administration are merely pandering to prejudice grounded on the false premise that this is the way to hurt Russia."

I'm just a farmer turned processor.

—DOA

D URING the Eisenhower years, the president at one point in 1954 wanted to send several million dollars in food aid to left-wing Poland, but he was once again worried about the possible reaction of right-wing Republicans. He didn't want them to nag him about the contemplated donation, and he thought he could avoid that if he could get it endorsed by the Democratic party and also by the Catholic church. More than that, he wanted Democratic senator Hubert Humphrey, as a bipartisan gesture, to support it and to go in person to Poland and to the Vatican to lay some useful groundwork. Humphrey asked his friend Dwayne Andreas to go along.* One thing Dwayne learned, to the

---

*Andreas liked to jot down notes about things or places or people he especially associated with prominent individuals. For Reagan one time it was "Decatur," for Eisenhower another time, "Butter & Pope."

distress of a man whose Mennonite forebears had eschewed tractors for horses, was that the Poles had butchered 20 million horses suitable for farm work in order to sell horse meat to France for money to buy tractors.

Walter F. Mondale, who like Humphrey hailed from Minnesota, and who was in a position to know what he was talking about, once said, "Hubert had a million friends. Dwayne was his best friend." Tip O'Neill, for his part, would say of Andreas, with perhaps a twinge of envy, "Hubert was his first love." The *Daily Worker*, for *its* part, once headlined an anti-Humphrey diatribe, "Meet Sir Hubert, Vassal of Soybean King."

The two men had similar backgrounds, Humphrey having been raised on a South Dakota farm. They first met, casually, in 1945, when Andreas was just starting in at Cargill and Humphrey was mayor of Minneapolis. Three years later, Humphrey was running for the Senate, and was more formally introduced to Andreas by Ray Ewald, a prominent Minneapolis dairyman and, as it happened, a Republican. Not long afterward, Humphrey's public relations man, a journalist named Dan Brennan, was surprised when Andreas strolled into a campaign office and handed over a thousand dollars in cash. "In those days, anybody who gave fifty bucks to a senatorial candidate felt he had a right to sit in his lap," Brennan said years afterward. "A thousand bucks was one hell of a big contribution, and Dwayne didn't even ask to shake hands. When I gave the money to Hubert, he was aghast. 'Who is this guy?' he asked. Dwayne was kind of a mystery man in those days."

Nearly twenty years after thus flacking for Hubert Horatio Humphrey, Brennan delivered himself of a roman à clef, *The President's Right Hand*, featuring a senator named Malcolm Milton Molander and a soybean magnate named Gaskin St. Claire, who was short and slim and dark. Because Brennan somehow had the impression that Andreas's immediate progenitors hailed from Lebanon, St. Claire was also of Lebanese descent. In the novel, a high-priced call girl, in bed with a rival commodities trader, asks him what line of work he is in anyway, and when the client says, "Soybeans," she says, "I can't stand any kind of beans. Ugh."

Andreas and Humphrey became intimate friends. So did their wives. So did their children. Humphrey was the godfather of the Andreases' son Michael. Michael and his contemporary Douglas Humphrey were Senate pages concurrently as teenagers. At times, their fathers seemed inseparable; by Dwayne's reckoning, they took eighty-five trips together over a twenty-year span. They used each other as sounding boards, sometimes the one casting himself as the other's devil's advocate. One aspect of Humphrey's philosophy that Andreas found especially appealing was: You can disagree without being disagreeable. Challenged one time to disclose some philosophy of his own, Andreas said that all he ever aspired to was to benefit from the experience of the legendary golfer who, on driving into a clump of trees and begging his caddie for counsel on how best to extricate himself, was told, "Get out the way you got in."

Andreas liked to describe his role on their joint excursions as Humphrey's "extra pair of eyes and ears." Ann Landers, who met Andreas through Humphrey, told a friend, "Dwayne was Hubert's conscience." She went on, "They were a wonderful team. Hubert was always vocal and ebullient. Dwayne, back when they met, was very quiet, just pleased to be part of the scene. That characteristic has carried throughout his career. I've known many CEOs, and Dwayne is the most understated of the lot. He never talks about himself. Most of them never ask a question. He wants to know about *you*, and that makes him unique."

Somebody was once impudent enough to ask her if Dwayne had ever sought her advice, or when it came to that, had she ever sought his.

"Of course not," she said. "We're *friends.*"

Andreas, understated though he seemed, had advice that Humphrey, not yet of large international stature, found helpful. Andreas says:

When Hubert was new to the Senate, I would take him to places like Switzerland and Germany, and London, and educate him about things like foreign exchange and the interlocking relationships of currencies. But then he became a *senior* senator, and afterward *he* took *me.* Oh, God, we saw a lot of people! There were Adenauer and Erhard, Harold Wilson, de Gaulle, Tito, Sukarno, Suharto, Mobutu, Haile Selassie, and all the rest.* And it was because of Hubert that Harry Truman once sent me to Argentina to look into the postwar bilateral trade in certain strategic materials. Nothing much came of that particular mission, but I did get to dine with the Peróns. That Evita was a beautiful woman. As a boy, I'd had to go to revival meetings, and you know who it was she reminded me of? Aimee Semple McPherson! There was this new oilseed plant dedicated, and Evita made a speech, and I said to myself while listening, "Wow! If she were an American politician!"

The 1954 Humphrey reelection campaign was being managed by Herbert J. Waters, a onetime West Coast newspaper editor who had moved to Minnesota and was later an assistant to Truman's secretary of agriculture, Charles Brannan. When Humphrey was elected vice president in 1964, Waters—who died, at seventy-seven, in January 1990—became assistant administrator for material resources in the State Department's Administration for International Development. He had already been instrumental in the inauguration of the country's food-stamp program. So had Humphrey and his fellow senator George McGovern. They thought it would be appropriate for food of any kind to be distributed through government warehouses operated much like post offices. Andreas told them that was ridiculous. Anything having to do with food, he argued, should be handled through food stores. But how, they wondered, could they ever get the leaders in that field, most of whom did not normally cotton to the views of liberal

*In the emperor's Addis Ababa dining room, Andreas saw and admired a painting by an Ethiopian artist of an African drought. His host only had it on loan, but at the guest's urging arranged for the American to buy it, and it is now on display at an Andreas residence in Florida.

Democrats, to go along with that idea? Andreas knew how; he had his, and Humphrey's, Republican chum Senator Bob Dole, along with Humphrey, talk to the Grocery Manufacturers of America.

Later in 1953, warming up for the Humphrey campaign, Herbert Waters—who thirty years later would often be visible in Washington, D.C., as an emissary from Andreas to any capital movers and shakers who seemed in need of on-the-spot stroking—was sent by Humphrey as an emissary to Andreas. The senator had excellent ties to labor, but was not yet especially close to agriculture. In a farm bill that was up for consideration, there was an amendment relating to price supports for soybeans, and what, Humphrey wanted to know, did Andreas think about it? When Waters asked him, Dwayne said the answer was very simple. If Humphrey voted one way, he'd be serving soybean growers, and if the other way, soybean processors—"like me." He added that if Humphrey was sensible, he'd vote the first way, because a lot more farmers were voters than were processors. ("I'm just a farmer turned processor," Andreas sometimes says of himself.) Humphrey was impressed. He knew enough about agriculture to be aware that relatively few processors put farmers' interests ahead of—or even equal to—their own. And here was a processor trying to give farmers a break!

Andreas has always insisted, whenever the subject was brought up—and considering his close relationship to eminent government personages, it often was—that ADM, unlike many corporations of its size and clout, has never had a resident lobbyist in Washington. In a technical sense, that was correct. The company has never paid anyone stationed there to seek to influence any legislator on any specific piece of legislation.

But as Herb Waters, through his formidable connections, proved a useful link between Andreas and Democratic powers-that-be, so on the other side of the political fence did Andreas have working on his behalf—as a consultant, that was, not a lobbyist—Martin Sorkin, who moved along smoothly in Republican circles: economic adviser to the secretary of agriculture, for instance, during seven Eisenhower-administration years, and more than thirty years later Senator Dole's adviser on agricultural matters during his 1988 try for his party's presidential nomination. When it came to seeking or receiving Washington favors, Sorkin once declared, "I never heard Dwayne ask anybody for anything."

Did that include Sorkin himself?

"Me? Oh, that was different," Sorkin said. "He was paying me."

During 1954—the year in which Andreas accompanied Humphrey to Poland and the Vatican—Dwayne's father, Reuben, died, at eighty-two. The son, who was becoming better and better known abroad, spoke then on "The Fats and Oils Situation in the United States" at the annual meeting, in Rome, of the International Association of Seed Crushers. There was a lot of talk at home not merely about leftover butter but of other agricultural surpluses. Andreas persuaded Humphrey—this time the Soviet Union and the Cold War did not much come into account—that it would make sense, and not cost much more than storage, to let foreign countries buy these foods with their own money. These currencies were generally worthless outside the jurisdictions of the treasuries issuing them, but the United States could find plenty of use for them in situ—supporting embassies and air bases, for instance. Thus evolved Public Law 480, formally the Agricultural Trade Development and Assistance Act of 1954, and more popularly the Food for Peace Program. It was at a 1954 meeting in Washington of the National Soybean Processors Association, where Martin Sorkin was explaining the then fairly new concept of Food for Peace, that he and Andreas had first met. Sorkin was surprised afterward when only two members of the audience seemed seriously enough interested in the subject to come up for further enlightenment. One of them was Andreas.

Early on, Humphrey would grouse to Andreas that most businessmen seemed to regard him as dangerously radical, a person to be avoided at all costs. "Why do they always make me catch every fly in left field?" he would lament. Waters had arranged a tight campaign schedule for him, with his time booked solid from ten A.M. to ten P.M.; Andreas began arranging breakfast dates with businessmen before the rest of the day got under way, and at least a few of them, willing to risk a get-together provided Dwayne also showed up, seemed pleasantly surprised to find their senator something short of ogreish. Reciprocally, Humphrey took pains to introduce Andreas to influential labor leaders, not least among them Lane Kirkland, the future head of the AFL-CIO. When President Reagan wanted to lift Jimmy Carter's embargo against grain shipments to the Soviet Union but the White House was afraid that the conservative longshoremen's union would balk, it was through Andreas that the American Farm Bureau, whose members wanted very much to resume that trade, got together with Kirkland and his deputies to negotiate a rapprochement.

In the spring of 1957, Humphrey took Andreas—Herb Waters, too—along on a three-week jaunt to Rome, Cairo, Beirut, Tel Aviv, Athens, Madrid, and Lisbon. In Humphrey's report on the trip to Senator Theodore Green, chairman of the Foreign Relations Committee, Andreas—who paid his own way—was described as "an advisor to the [Department of Agriculture] and a specialist in the problems of P. L. 480." The seventy-four-page report, which Waters and Andreas naturally had a hand in preparing, said, inter alia:

> The foreign policy of the U.S. has failed to keep pace with our obligations and responsibilities in the Middle East. In an area of the utmost strategic importance to ourselves and our allies, we have for too long pursued a policy of drift and improvisation.... The U.S. has an abundance of one resource unequalled as yet by any other world power. That resource is our food and fiber—and our ability to produce it in abundance.... Food is the common denominator of international life. Lack of adequate food is the underlying factor in many of the economic and political problems of the Middle East. The stocks of food and other agricultural commodities which the U.S. is fortunate to possess, over

and above its immediate domestic requirements, are a grossly underrated national asset. American food and fiber are vital to the very existence of millions of undernourished people. Utilizing this asset could provide a ray of hope for building stronger economies and greater stability in most of the countries I visited. But the full extent of this asset cannot be realized so long as it is regarded, not as an asset, but as a liability. We have cheapened the spirit behind our humanitarian food contributions abroad, and weakened our own bargaining power in negotiating trade agreements for food and fiber, by continuously proclaiming that our food reserves are something for which we have no use, and want to get rid of at any cost. If American foreign policy, not only in the Middle East and Southern Europe, but elsewhere, is to be of maximum effectiveness, a drastic revision is required in the prevailing official concept regarding disposal of our food and fiber in the world.

That time, Humphrey thought Andreas's eyes and ears needed amplification. The Egyptian authorities were temporarily miffed with the United States, which had cut back on food aid to their country because there was a Soviet adviser in Cairo. (The Russians didn't have much in the way of food aid to dispense, but Andreas was told that to demonstrate their supposed concern they shifted a load of it from one Cairo location to another overnight.)

In Greece, the two men were invited to attend a high-school graduation ceremony. Male honor students were awarded tool kits. At a time when a lot of their contemporaries were living out of, and sometimes all but in, garbage cans, this gave the recipients a chance to become carpenters, say, or brickmakers, and a leg up on their classmates. Andreas thought this was admirable but inadequate. When he returned home, he arranged—the Indiana Farm Bureau Cooperative was a principal conduit—for tool kits to be given that year to all male Athenian high-school graduates.

By 1959, his sphere of influence widening commensurate
with Humphrey's, Andreas was on the executive committee
of the National Soybean Processors Association and chairman of the Trade Development Committee of the Soybean
Council of America; was secretary of the Fats and Oils
Advisory Committee of the U.S. Department of Agriculture;* was a member both of the Chicago Board of Trade
and the Minneapolis Grain Exchange; and was the newly
elected president of the Chemurgic Council, an association
of ten companies—Ford, Du Pont, and Sun Oil prominent
among them—committed to pooling some of their know-
how toward the development of enhanced applications for
agricultural commodities. (*Chemurgy*, a word coined by a
nonprofit agency, the Chemical Council, was derived from
the Egyptian *chemi*, meaning "the origin of chemistry," and
the Greek *ergon*—work.)† In announcing his ascendancy at
the Council, the *Chemurgic Digest* noted that Andreas, then
forty-one, "has a wide acquaintance among industrial and
governmental people in this country and many overseas
contacts" and that "Honeymead operates the world's largest
deodorizer, designed to deodorize ten-tank carloads of soybean oil per day."

(One development fostered by the Council that proved to
be of particular interest, and profit, to its chief executive was
a method of refining soybean oil to keep it from reverting—

---

*The secretary of agriculture was Ezra Taft Benson, a hard-line, no-nonsense
Mormon. When Andreas was in his office one day, Benson asked, "Dwayne, do you
drink wine?" Andreas replied, guardedly, that he took a sip every now and then.
Benson was delighted. "Khrushchev gave me six bottles of red not long ago," he said.
"You take 'em." Andreas, who had met the Soviet leader but was not close enough
to be on his gift list, took the wine and opened it, bottle by bottle, on special
occasions, but by the time he'd uncorked the last of the lot, it had turned to vinegar.

†Andreas would explain later to the National Alcohol Fuels Commission that
"chemurgy means the utilization of agricultural surpluses to provide many of the
raw materials which are essential to industry. Moreover, it implies achieving this in
a way that does not jeopardize local and exportable food supplies, but indeed,
converts raw material from agriculture into more valuable forms of food and
chemicals. Chemurgy also involves the use of one of the inadequately recognized
energy sources plentifully available in Africa and elsewhere—sunshine—and repre-
sents the utilization of biomass as a means of exploiting solar energy."

i.e., turning rancid—and thus becoming unacceptable as an ingredient of, most importantly, margarine. For soybean processors—Honeymead was up to forty-five thousand bushels a day—this step forward could raise the value of their output by, the *Digest* estimated, a significant fifteen cents a bushel. There was only one hitch. In Spain and Mexico, people grumbled that the new technology made cooking oils too bland; they *liked* the taste of a bit of familiar old rancidity.)

Humphrey, by now an increasingly consequential solon, had a third-term campaign about to get under way, and it was no surprise to anyone even on the fringe of his orbit that Andreas was not only a diligent fund-raiser—Humphrey's letters of thanks to such supporters as executives of General Mills and Pillsbury all mentioned Dwayne's role in their solicitation—but the largest individual contributor.

When the two friends were together, they found time to relax as well as engage in high-minded, potentially world-saving endeavors. During that 1957 excursion for instance, they were happy to be able to spend a free weekend at St.-Jean-Cap-Ferrat, staying in the lavish villa of Marc Najar, a somewhat mysterious Paris-based Egyptian merchant. Before his death in a private-plane crash in the Alps in 1960, Najar, who was fluent in six languages, traded in, among other commodities, Vietnamese rubber and Argentine wheat, once reputedly expediting his dealings in the latter by means of a $20,000 platinum cigarette case that fitted neatly into the palm of Juan Perón.

By then, Humphrey was also a familiar visitor to a seaside place Andreas had himself acquired. Dwayne had first gone to Florida in 1933 as a boy of fifteen with his oldest brother, Osborn. While down south, they treated themselves to a brief fling in pre-Castro Cuba. In 1948, after his marriage to Inez, he began going to Miami Beach every year. (He gave up winter sports after a couple of nasty skiing spills.) In 1956, he bought one of two penthouses—and later an additional apartment for the use of his guests—at the Sea View Hotel, an elegant enclave at Bal Harbour, in Miami

Beach. Bal Harbour was relatively unsettled when Andreas first arrived. While his children were growing up, they and the Humphrey offspring could chase jackrabbits in the sagebrush abutting the hotel grounds, and when Dwayne's father came down to fish in the years just before his death, there were yellowtail, grouper, and red snapper, all but begging to be hooked fifty feet out, and the waters that were to turn murky in later years were so clear that one could wade out knee high, reach down, and grab a lobster.

Since 1965, diagonally across Collins Avenue from Sea View, Bal Harbour has boasted a mammoth shopping mall with such beckoning units as Gucci, Neiman-Marcus, Vuitton, and their gilded ilk. On the whole, though, the community has changed less than most of Florida. Between 1980 and 1986, Bal Harbour's round-the-clock population, now steady at around three thousand, even shrank a mite while that of the whole state was up by 20 percent—a tribute perhaps to the efficiency of exclusivity.

Despite the state's increasing growth and resultingly, importance, Andreas has taken little part in its political affairs. He is usually on hand when a president ventures into any portion of his territory. Surprised that while in residence at Sea View Andreas hadn't put in an appearance early in 1990 when George Bush graced a $1,500-a-plate fund-raising dinner at Miami Beach for Florida's governor Bob Martinez, a friend asked Dwayne how come he'd missed it. Andreas said he hadn't known about it until he read about it in the *Miami Herald* the next day. He was not fibbing; Inez, who believes there is a limit to any one person's participation in the rituals of democracy, had opened their invitation and thrown it away.

Andreas began to spend more and more time at his Florida place. That was especially manageable after he got his fourth and fastest airplane, a Falcon jet, in 1979. It took him just two hours to fly between Miami and Decatur, and inasmuch as there was a one-hour time difference, he could leave his Florida home at six o'clock on a Monday morning and be at his Illinois office by seven-thirty—before many of his employees turned up. Wherever he is, he can make do without much obvious sleep. Also, he has cultivated the knack, in the course of the innumerable banquets he *does* feel obliged to attend, of closing his eyes and napping without snoring, or even letting his chin drop.

Traveling in either direction, Andreas generally devotes much of his air time to phone calls, which are easier to make in the sky than to receive. (Since mid-1989, his airborne phone has had a fax machine appended.) "To get a couple of hours like that in a cubicle is a godsend," he said, adding, "Most of my work is done on the telephone, so it doesn't much matter where I am." The majority of the cabanas that go along with Sea View apartments have telephones. Andreas's has two. He has long felt uneasy whenever there was none within reach. Unless in a terrible hurry, when on a golf course he disdains to ride on a cart, but until he heard about a phone that would fit into his hip pocket, he always used a vehicle to transport one of his portable means of communication. By 1990, he had so many private telephone numbers in so many ports of call that his chief administrative assistant, Claudia Madding, was planning, if she ever found the time, to compile a directory of numbers belonging to no names other than her boss's.

10

The only goodwill you ever get in this
business is from feeding the hungry.

—DOA

FEW amateur golfers can ever have striven more reso-
lutely than Andreas toward self-improvement. Back in
Minnesota, the Andreases lived for a while beside
Lake Minnetonka. Dwayne had a putting green installed on a
spit of land that jutted into the water (there was a phone on a
nearby tree and another on the family speedboat), and with a
9-iron he would chip hundreds of balls toward it and would
then conscientiously hole out. When his son Michael was
ten, the father paid him a nickel a ball to dive in and retrieve
wayward shots. Michael says that his father sometimes chipped
a thousand balls at a clip—though at one every thirty seconds that would come to more than eight straight hours of
chipping, and the putting-out be damned. His father puts the
figure, more believably, at a mere five hundred.

Bal Harbour became even more convenient for Andreas

to stay at, work from, and play golf around after the airlines initiated transatlantic service to Miami from London, Frankfurt, and Paris, and it became just as easy for European business connections to touch base with him at Sea View as anywhere else. His ADM board of directors voiced no objections when their midwinter meetings began to be scheduled for sunny Florida instead of snowy Illinois. Bal Harbour residents got used to the sight also not only of Hubert Humphrey but other high-placed Andreas cronies, several of whom became fixtures of the Sea View scene. Tip O'Neill bought a unit there. So did Robert Strauss. So did David Brinkley. So did Howard Baker. So, in 1982, did the Bob Doles—actually, Mrs. Dole and a brother of hers. After that so did the wealthy Ambassador Emil Mossbacher, who paid less than the Doles. Some spoilsports—among them the *New York Times*—couldn't resist wondering whether it might conceivably affect Andreas's and ADM's relations with Congress that while he was the Sea View's dominant force the three-room Dole acquisition went for $150,000 at a time when, somebody had told the critics, a fairer market price would have been $190,000. Andreas found it hard to comprehend how a $50,000-per-room price tag could be a bargain extended to a politically powerful friend when in fact the average price for twenty-three Sea View rooms sold between 1981 and 1984 was $48,326. But then he had long since become resigned to being criticized for just about anything he does that involves any politician of any stripe. At one meeting of the ADM board, he told his directors, "The only goodwill you ever get in this business is from feeding the hungry."

All these Very Important People naturally imported Very Important Guests. Strauss, the Texan-turned-Washington lawyer, former chairman of the Democratic National Committee, and since 1981, ADM board member, has probably known just about everyone who matters. He once unreservedly described Andreas to the *Washington Post* as "the ablest man in America."

A Sea View proprietor since the mid-1970s, Strauss likes to muse on how much of a kick even he can get out of looking down from his balcony and seeing "Dwayne giving

Andy Young some advice, or conducting a political huddle of Bob Dole, Howard Baker, George McGovern, and Tip O'Neill." Strauss, not celebrated for humility, went on, "If anybody saw us all together, they'd bomb this place."

Senator Dole, unafraid, let it be known in 1988 that if elected president he might make Sea View his winter White House. If that had come to pass, the Secret Service would have been prepared, having taken as many as nineteen rooms when Humphrey and George Bush were guests while vice president. "They more or less have the place staked out," Andreas says.

Hubert Humphrey, who often visited Andreas in Florida, knew how to play golf, but did so rarely and then chiefly as an accommodation to his host. "Hubert felt guilty spending so much time chasing a little ball," Herbert Waters said. To circumvent any such compunctions Andreas might entertain, wherever he may be—unless the sun is inconveniently unrisen—he likes to tee off, in keeping with his early-rising legacy from the farm days, at seven in the morning. By starting then and playing fast—he walks at a brisk pace—he can finish eighteen holes in time to put in a decent day's work. "I like to play early, before my brain has to go to work," Andreas says. "Golf is a brainless game."

At Decatur one Friday afternoon, Andreas phoned James W. Stowell, one of his ADM vice presidents, and suggested a round the following morning. Stowell, knowing what that entailed, suppressed a groan and said by all means. He was relieved to learn later that evening that plans had presumably changed. Andreas had had a sudden invitation to dine in Washington with Bob Strauss. Surely, Stowell reasoned, he could now skip the dawn's early light. He reasoned wrong. Andreas flew to the capital, dined, flew back to Decatur, arriving at one in the morning, and was on the first tee taking practice whacks, as usual, at six fifty-nine.

Andreas is by no means rigid, however; in deference to Tip O'Neill's being five years older, Dwayne would consent to tee off at eight. "At the green once," the Speaker observed after one round, "I started to put down a six for his score, and

Dwayne said, 'No, I whiffed one back there while you weren't looking. Make it a seven.' What an honorable son of a gun!"

During an interview once with the *St. Paul Dispatch*, Andreas was asked whether golf was his hobby. "Business is my hobby," he replied. When he joined the Blind Brook Country Club, in Westchester County, in 1971, he wanted it understood that this was for business and that he be billed (initiation fee and dues: $9,064) at the office, though ADM ultimately charged his account. "As a mother relates things to her children," Michael Andreas says, "so does Dad relate everything to business and trade. He likes golf because he thinks of it as a means of negotiating his way into the hole." It was at Blind Brook that Andreas shot an 84, his best conventional round. He did once break 80, but only after taking a tranquilizer to steady his swing. That made him feel guilty, though, and he never took one again. He never again broke 80, either.

(In the view of Walter Klein, the nongolfing head of the Bunge Corporation and Andreas's longtime friendly competitor in trade, "life for Dwayne is all business, and business is his life. He is one of the few people who can successfully run our kind of business, with its excessive volatility. He's the only businessman I really respect. Zigging in the commodities markets one single day instead of zagging can make the difference between a good and a mediocre year. You have to be able to judge what effect world events will have on the current or future price of soybeans or grain, you have to be able to get to a phone wherever you are and tell your people to do this or beware of that. That's what I've had to do. But for me it's always been hard work, and for Dwayne it's second nature.")

In Florida, Dwayne belongs to the Indian Creek Country Club, a citadel with such tight security that one of the greatest playing hazards is an errant shot's hitting a patrol car. For times when they wish to escape the hurly-burly of Sea View, since 1988 the Andreases have had a second Miami Beach home on the country club grounds, accessible only by a guarded bridge. One of their neighbors is a rock singer. Driving past his spacious pad one day, Andreas revealed what in his opinion comprised genuine wealth. "That guy is really rich," he said. "He earns one hundred million a year and has three Rollses." More often than not Andreas goes around that course, as at Blind Brook and other well-combed pastures, with high corporate executives, among them, for instance, F. Ross Johnson, who was the CEO of RJR Nabisco until dethroned in a notorious multibillion-dollar Kohlberg-Kravis-Roberts takeover. Before he drifted off on a golden parachute, Johnson signed a $50 million sponsor's agreement—later abrogated—between RJR Nabisco and the Professional Golfers Association. After he was retired, Andreas kindly gave him a seat on the ADM board, and Johnson gave Andreas some Nabisco golf shirts. Another board on which Andreas has sat was that, for a year starting in 1980, of Columbia Pictures. He knew nothing about the motion-picture industry but joined anyway at the urging of Herbert Allen, the Wall Street eminence with whom Dwayne would occasionally go fishing in Canada. On becoming a director, Andreas felt constrained to buy some Columbia stock (he put it in his children's trusts), and it increased in value astronomically, especially when Coca-Cola came along and bought Columbia. "I contributed absolutely nothing to board meetings," Andreas said later. "I voted against every movie anybody proposed producing except *Annie.* Having endorsed that one, I felt obligated to go to auditions when it was being cast, which was interesting but not noticeably constructive. Herb Allen's getting me involved in all this kept stuffing my pockets with money, but I don't believe *Annie* ever made a dime."

Andreas has never been a heavy bettor—except, of course, on the future rises and falls of commodity prices, where he must in his line of work be willing to risk millions every day.* On the golf links, he is far more circumspect. He was

*Back at Cedar Rapids, after a round with Jimmy Hey, Dwayne and his cousin had some nineteenth hole fun with a gullible bystander. Jimmy pretended that Dwayne had lost $550 to him. "Double or nothing?" asked Dwayne. "Sure." Jimmy flipped a coin and asked Dwayne to call it. "Odd." Without showing Dwayne the coin, Jimmy said, "Even." Dwayne shrugged and wrote out a check for $1,100 on the Merchants National Bank. Their dupe drew Andreas aside and whispered, "How do you know that was an honest answer?"

once amused, during a round with Nelson and Laurance Rockefeller, when the brothers—in a somewhat exaggerated version of the penchant of their paternal grandfather—turned out to have silver dollars tucked into their pants pockets, which they would disburse to one another on the greens, hole by hole, whenever a bet between them produced a winner.

The resident professional at Indian Creek is Raymond Floyd, the nonplaying captain also of the 1989 United States Ryder Cup team. That links course can be challenged from either of two tees, and Floyd, not surprisingly, holds the record from both—62 and 61. Andreas's best score from the easier one is an 89. (His handicap at last report was 26, which his companions on the links say fits in nicely with a Midwestern joke: Your golf handicap is the average number of full working days you put in every month.) The pro and the amateur are not too often on the scene simultaneously— Floyd on the tour, Andreas on the go—but they manage to fit in eighteen holes together a dozen or so times a year.

During the ADM board meeting at Sea View in January 1990, some of the directors had their own little joke: that Ray Floyd had deliberately missed the cut at the Bob Hope tournament at Palm Springs so he could catch the red-eye out of L.A. and make it back to Florida in time to tee off with Andreas. When the two of them do, that competition is tough for the pro, too. His handicap is *minus* 2, so that if Andreas shoots a middling 95, Floyd, obliged to give him twenty-eight strokes, must score a 67 just to break even. Floyd uses adjectives like "intense" and "fierce" to describe his friend in action. "Dwayne is one of the most highly competitive people I've ever seen," says Floyd, who has seen his share, "with a wonderful touch around the greens." Floyd is not a teaching pro, but he did once proffer a tip on improving his friend's backswing; Dwayne needed to widen it, he was picking up the club too fast.

For a while, a very visible presence in the Indian Creek clubhouse was a masseur, George Burns, who by 1989, at ninety-one, was giving his namesake a run for his age. Frustrated because of poor eyesight in his ambition to become an architect, during the Depression the younger Burns studied physiotherapy, and he ended up, after the Second World War, at the country club. It was hard for him to work the way he liked to there, because whenever he had someone such as Hubert Humphrey on his table, there would be constant interruptions by members or their guests, who, whatever their political leanings, wanted to shake the eminent Minnesotan's hand. So Andreas and the Alabama businessman Poncet Davis, who was Sea View's president and bestrode its other penthouse, set Burns up in a hotel room of his own, where he could minister to Humphrey and others (sometimes with the Secret Service on guard in the hall) without being bothered by the hoi polloi.

During thirty years at Bal Harbour, Burns got to be on companionable terms with many of his clients. He would be invited to the annual Thanksgiving and Christmas dinners given by Poncet Davis and Jim Stewart, the then Lone Star Cement titan, who lived in a concrete castle on the Indian Creek Country Club grounds. (Andreas now and then borrowed Stewart's private helicopter if, say, he had to hop up to Palm Beach for a charity ball.) With the exception of some institutional investors, ADM was the largest corporate owner—more than $30 million worth—of Lone Star stock, and Andreas sat on his Florida neighbor's board for more than a decade. That connection was not inappropriate: Soybeans are one of the ingredients of some types of present-day concrete, and also of, to cite a tiny few other repositories, nitroglycerin and face cream. After the Chernobyl disaster, moreover, the soybean extract lecithin proved crucial as a purifying agent in bone-marrow transplants. Andreas once said of Stewart before his downfall—there may have been autobiographical overtones—"Jim doesn't look upon himself as a capitalist; he looks upon himself as a poor boy with money."

The year the Bal Harbour Burns turned ninety, he was seated alongside Andreas at one of Stewart's holiday feasts. Andreas told Burns, who was living in a retirement home, that he'd shortly be receiving some items that would keep him going for at least another decade. To be a beneficiary of Andreas's largesse is, as Mother Teresa and others have come to realize, rewarding. "At first he sent me four huge cartons containing protein powder, lecithin, and several other great things," Burns wrote an acquaintance, "also a Panasonic Bread Bakery and fifty packets of flour [it's called Multigrain Mix] that make the finest bread ever tasted. Since then, I have been receiving replacements of all things over and over. It is hard to understand how a man with so many important things on his mind could find time to think of a guy like me."

Andreas has never begrudged all the time he spends thinking about bread. One suspects that he dreams even more about baking loaves than breaking par. Awake, he often casts his mind to that perhaps not-too-far-off day when bread might somehow truly supplant rice as mankind's staff of life. (Bread consumption has been rising, at the rate of about 2 percent a year, to the point where average annual worldwide per capita consumption has finally reached the fifty-pound mark, but more than half the globe's inhabitants continue to be, as they long have been, largely dependent for their sustenance on rice.) Andreas's optimism is, of course, not entirely detached. Forever hoping to insinuate more and more soybeans into human stomachs, he has concluded that the most realistic and most practical way, instead of first passing them as meal through cows or pigs or hens, is by means of bread.

In his view, though, the big bakeries lack proper incentive. "They need to make bread cheaper, not better," he says. In 1988, he heard about the Panasonic Bread Bakery, a portable oven made in Japan. While not all the breads it turned out contained soy flour and were costlier than most, they struck him as manifestly tastier. Also, it was beguilingly novel. A housewife poured a bag of ingredients into it, and four hours later—presto!—in a kitchen filled with the aroma of fresh bread, her loaves were ready. Andreas ordered fifty of the devices, and after having the instructions translated into English and keeping one for each of his kitchens at his homes, distributed the rest to relatives and friends. One group of donees, Mother Teresa's nuns, seemed reluctant to lighten their self-imposed burdens by letting a machine do their routine labor. So his daughter Sandra McMurtrie arranged for their oven to go to a lay woman who put it to work and delivered its output to the sisters. George Burns would take his oven to the apartments of shut-ins at his retirement home and bake while they watched and sniffed. To Claudia Madding, Andreas's chief of staff at ADM, the nonagenarian wrote, "I have become so addicted I can't even look at store bread anymore."

Another frequent guest at Sea View, from 1955 on, was Thomas E. Dewey, who would die there, in 1971, an hour or so after finishing a round of golf with his host Andreas at Indian Creek. The twice-defeated Republican candidate for the presidency, sixteen years the senior of the two, was by then in private practice. They were introduced by another Bal Harbour sojourner, Frank Clarke, a Canadian shipowner who during the Second World War was reputedly a conduit for messages between Winston Churchill and Franklin D. Roosevelt—communications so very top secret, the story went, that it would be too risky to put them on paper, and accordingly they had to be entrusted solely to Clarke's head. Churchill and Dewey were both staying at Clarke's place in Florida, and it was at a party for his guests in 1953 that Andreas was introduced to the two-time Republican party standard-bearer. *

---

*A memorandum Andreas dictated after one of his trips abroad with Vice President Humphrey included the following: "Another interesting little event that took place at Chequers with Prime Minister [Harold] Wilson: Some years ago Winston Churchill was a guest in Miami of a very close friend of mine, Mr. and Mrs. Frank Clarke. On that occasion he told a story about a huge painting which is hung on the wall of the dining room in Chequers. It is a painting of a savage wild beast that has been tied with a network of ropes so that it will clearly be impossible for him to ever free himself. Churchill said that this totally helpless posture of this magnificent wild animal annoyed him so much that he corrected it by simply taking his brush and adding to the surface of the canvas a tiny little mouse gnawing away at a strategic knot that held all the ropes together, thus giving a signal that sooner or later the wild beast might have its freedom. At least it had hope as long as the mouse was gnawing. I asked Mary Wilson about the painting and she and the prime minister took me to the corner of the dining room and pointed out the mouse in the lower left-hand corner of the painting."

The two men hit it off from the outset. Dewey quickly endeared himself to his new friend by revealing, once apprised of Andreas's occupation and preoccupation, that while governor of New York he had once locked up soybeans in all bread baked for consumption in state prisons. "He seemed to be fascinated with the soybean," Andreas said later.

Not long after their meeting, Andreas arranged for Dewey to be suitably rewarded for such pro-soy efforts: he became special counsel to the National Soybean Processors Association. (Some say that its acquisition of Dewey as a spokesman had to be rated almost on a par with its espousal of getting the beany flavor out of soy milk.) Dewey also began to handle some of Andreas's personal legal affairs and to supervise a few trusts Dwayne had set up for his children when his ADM shareholdings became so massive that he was loath to have to keep worrying about them all the time himself. Counsel between them was not all one-way. Andreas was convinced that Dewey had missed out on the White House for two principal reasons, and although it was too late to make any difference, he would keep trying to explain to his friend what they were: Dewey hadn't understood how important it was to have an in with power blocs within the Congress, and he hadn't understood farmers.

Andreas and Dewey traveled around the world together a couple of times, mixing business with pleasure. They fished together in Newfoundland, and they played golf together, by Andreas's generous reckoning, five thousand times. (That would have come to a round every day, rain or shine, for more than thirteen years.) Dewey had a home in Pawling, New York, and sometimes they would play there, at a country club on top of a hill. Andreas particularly relished being on that course when the fog rolled in. "You could hit the ball out of sight," he says, "and that made you feel good."

Some observers of the American political scene found it bizarre that Andreas should have become so close to two men so seemingly antithetical as were Thomas Dewey and Hubert Humphrey. Andreas did not at all see it that way. He would often get the two of them together. "They loved each other," he says. "They had a lot in common. They would once in a while compare notes on things, national or international affairs, and it was amazing how often they were in agreement." Even Andreas had to concede, though, that they had *some* differences. Humphrey was not hooked on golf. Every so often, Dwayne managed to get both his buddies out on a course, and Dewey, seeking to make these outings more agreeable, once bought Humphrey a pair of golf shoes; but by and large Humphrey would beg off with some such excuse as that he was simply too busy with the demands of public life to squander the time eighteen holes would consume.

When Humphrey had his eye on the White House one time, he hoped to arrange a big fund-raising dinner in New York City. Andreas suggested that the guest list be made up mainly of the heads of big banks, big Wall Street houses, and big law firms. But, Humphrey expostulated, weren't they principally rock-ribbed Republicans? How could they ever be persuaded to attend? No problem, Andreas assured him; Tom Dewey could and would do it. (The event never materialized, but largely because an ocean liner on which it was to have been held switched scheduled days in port.) Andreas seemed to derive special pleasure out of throwing opposites together. He was happy to have been the middleman—in a New York theater lobby one evening—who introduced to one another Dewey and his 1948 unhorser, Harry Truman.

Andreas believes that one of his main nonmonetary contributions to the often acerbic 1968 presidential contest between Nixon and Humphrey was to prevail on the staffs of both principals to eschew derogatory personal attacks and counterattacks. "There were a few occasions when sparks began to fly, and I helped a little bit to pour a little water on the fire," he says.

You know, Tom Dewey once said of that election, while he and I were looking up at the sky from a Sea View cabana, that America was very fortunate, in that Nixon and Humphrey were probably the two best-qualified candidates to oppose each other in the history of our nation. Both had been vice president, both had served on the Senate Foreign Relations Committee, both were students of history, both had traveled the world and knew everybody of consequence in it, and both were masters of the art of compromise. Tom would hold two fingers up, parallel, slightly ajar, and then say that whichever man got to the Oval Office, when it came to foreign policy, he would move in the direction of the other until there was practically no space left between them.

Andreas had been Dewey's dinner guest the night the Republican convention designated Nixon its standard-bearer. As soon as the nomination became official, Dewey phoned to congratulate him, and mentioned whom he was with. Then Dewey put his hand over the mouthpiece and turned and said to Andreas, "You willing to go in the cabinet?"

Dwayne shook his head. "Well as I get along with farmers, can you imagine what some of those on the left would have said if a guy like me turned up in a Republican administration?" he said afterward.*

On the morning of March 16, 1971, Dewey, sixty-eight, had a checkup at the Miami Heart Institute and agreed to cut his cigarette consumption by half. That afternoon, on the seventeenth tee at Indian Creek, Dwayne thought his companion's face was too red and urged him to put on a hat. In the locker room not long afterward, they started planning their next overseas joint golf jaunt, and there was hushed, worshipful talk about Muirfield and St. Andrew's and Gleneagles. They agreed that they were both foolish to work as hard as they did rather than to concentrate on golf. Then they returned to Sea View, Dewey to rest up and change

---

*Does history repeat itself? On election night in 1972, not long after it became clear that Richard Nixon had trounced George McGovern, Andreas's phone rang. John Connally, renegade Democrat-turned-Republican, was on the line. Would Dwayne be interested in a cabinet job? He was free to join the winners now that he was no longer tied up with Humphrey and that lot of losers, wasn't he? Andreas asked the caller to hold on for a moment until he could turn the phone over to the man sitting alongside him—Hubert Humphrey.

before boarding Andreas's plane to fly up to Washington for a St. Patrick's Day dinner at the Nixon White House.

The next thing Andreas knew, his chauffeur, who was supposed to drive Dewey to the airport, phoned and said, "Tom's three minutes late." That worried both of them, knowing Dewey to be a bear for promptness, and they went to his room and found him dead. The plane took his body to New York instead. President Nixon flew up for the funeral. There were twenty-five honorary pallbearers, among them such familiar names as Lucius Clay, Lowell Thomas, Herbert Brownell, Frank Hogan, Roger Blough, and George Gallup, and one name that was probably unknown to most readers of the *New York Times*'s front-page obituary—Dwayne Andreas. "I miss him very much," Dwayne told a friend afterward.

In 1975, Nelson Rockefeller was raising money to embellish the Capitol Hill Club, a Republican watering place in Washington, D.C., which Andreas had joined years before at the behest of Dewey. Andreas responded with 3,500 shares of ADM stock—its market value then was $101,500—but on condition that the gift be in honor of Tom Dewey and that it be anonymous.

One of the traits that endeared Tom Dewey to the clients who courted his services was, not unreasonably, that he had ready access to most doors, however usually shut. Thus, while retained by the Soybean Processors, he could be a factor in 1966 in smoothing the way for Andreas and himself to be received by Generalissimo Francisco Franco. Andreas had for some time been trying to convince anyone of authority in Spain who would listen to him that it would make sense for that country to ease off from its traditional dependence on its indigenous olive oil. While it had not exactly been a crime there to cook with other sorts of oil, only in emergencies were substitutes—like soybean oil—even condoned.

But the Spanish were beginning to find justifications for altering, if not abandoning, their longstanding habits. They needed dollars, for one thing, and exporting olive oil diverted from their kitchens was one way of obtaining them. And in any event, as Spain's population caught up with and outstripped its olive production, there wasn't enough olive oil to meet domestic requirements. Some Spanish cooks, no doubt distastefully, had already been stretching their olive-oil resources by mixing them with soybean oil.

Still, Spain was a dictatorship, and no changes of consequence could be expected to take place without autocratic imprimatur. Franco, not long after receiving Dewey and Andreas, bestowed it. In due course Spain, where a generation earlier alien oil had been close to anathema, would become one of the largest importers of soybeans on earth and had ten plants busily processing them into thoroughly acceptable oil.

Andreas had no use for Franco's politics, but he came away from that trip to Spain with thorough acceptance of one of the generalissimo's innovations. Andreas says:

> I observed that Franco had done one extraordinarily intelligent thing. Whatever else he was, he saw that Spanish schools were deteriorating. So he had instituted vocational classes from the fifth grade on—for future carpenters, electricians, plumbers, auto-repair men, decorators, and others. As a result, Spain was becoming economically strong. Maybe something like that is what *our* schools should be doing now. They're little more than prisons as it is, and our teachers little more than wardens. If we had more vocational schools—Spain still has them—we could have a whole generation of skilled workers.

Andreas did not need Dewey, of course, to conduct him into oil-trading circles. In 1957, when he visited Spain with Humphrey, Dwayne had met a key figure in the olive-oil community, José Luis de Ybarra. They became friends and business associates. Late in 1962, Andreas reported to colleagues back home:

> It is extremely significant that Mr. José Ybarra came from Seville and met with me in Madrid. I consider his opinion on the olive crop in Spain to be the most reliable, as it has been during the past many years. He told me, in confidence, that he now believed the olive crop would be approx-

imately 265,000 tons. This is approximately 90,000 tons less than the official estimates shown up to now. He believes that the government officials are not aware of the drastic reduction in the crop.... Among the many other persons I talked with in Madrid, no one seemed to have exactly this picture of the oil situation.

I consider Mr. Ybarra's judgment, based on many years of experience, to be dependable. If this is the case, it will be a matter of four to five weeks before the situation begins to become public knowledge. This means to me that we might do well this year to hedge our oil, fill our tanks, collect the carrying charges, and be prepared to refine and ship on short notice in large volume after the opening of navigation next spring. This way we will collect the carrying charges in the meantime and still be able to do the refining and get good refining premiums when the time comes.

Ybarra, like other high-placed Spanish businessmen, belonged to the Opus Dei, the fraternity founded in 1928 of mostly celibate, mostly conservative, Catholic laymen. Sometimes known simply by the ominous-sounding abbreviation "The Work," the organization, whose seventy-odd-thousand members worldwide are supposed to devote a considerable part of their time, effort, and money to public service, was invested by Pope John Paul II with the status of a prelature, making it a quasi-religious order.

Spanish members of Opus Dei have by and large been staunch monarchists. One of those who helped persuade Franco to put a king, however ceremonial his powers, back on the throne was J. M. Barturen—"Manolo" to his fraternity brothers and other friends. A scion of a venerable Basque family with a four-hundred-year-old farmhouse outside Bilbao, Barturen's principal residence has been in New Jersey, where he runs an import-export business—Spanish truck and tractor parts, among other commodities—with headquarters at South Orange. Manolo and Dwayne have been friends and mutual admirers since they met in Spain in 1962. (Emulating Andreas, Barturen took to starting each day with a teaspoonful of Metamucil, and like him, too, began carrying around packets of bran flakes to sprinkle onto helpless soups.)

Barturen became much involved in Andreas's trafficking with Spain in soybeans. Barturen said:

> We never had a written agreement, and there never had to be one. If I told Dwayne, for instance, that I thought I deserved a better commission on a deal, he would say, "You've got it," and that would be that. I've always admired the way he operates. While I was at Bal Harbour once, I was in the process of buying a shipload of corn from ADM, and there was a lot of red tape involving some letters of credit or whatever without which the boat couldn't sail. I happened to mention the holdup to Dwayne, and he picked up a phone and talked to somebody somewhere and ended up with, "Tell 'em to sail," and that took care of that. You know, I've often wondered whether he's more interested in how business can help him in politics or how politics can help him in business. In any event, I regard Dwayne as the best-informed person I know when it comes to what's going on in both areas. And whatever else he may be doing, there's one thing about him that's constant: his mind doesn't relax.

When Barturen helped cajole Franco into giving Spain back a king, the generalissimo balked at reenthroning Don Juan, who since he'd been deposed was living, as the Count of Barcelona, in Portugal. Instead, the old king's son, Don Carlos, who still reigns, was installed. (Through Barturen, Don Carlos and his bride, the Greek princess Sophia, had spent part of their honeymoon at an Andreas apartment in New York.) When the son was crowned, the bypassed father was depressed. His supporters thought a change of scenery might be tonic for him and his wife, and they chose the Caribbean. Barturen suggested that they stop off en route as the Andreases' guests at Sea View, and presently they were comfortably holed up there for a couple of weeks.

Barturen joined the house party, and it was he whom Andreas was asked to summon to the phone at six A.M. one morning. (It was no problem for Dwayne to take the call; he'd already been up for a spell.) The Spanish ambassador to the United Nations was on the line. Would Manolo be good enough to rouse His Majesty?

At this hour? Manolo wondered. Whatever could be important enough to warrant that?

For a nation that honored the Salic law of succession, it was vital. Queen Sophia had given birth, and the baby was a boy, and so Spain had an authentic heir to its throne.

Barturen has an international reputation as an accomplished middleman. At Andreas's behest, he set off at once to procure two cases of (it seemed to be the consensus that the occasion was too grand to be celebrated in mere Spanish wine) Miami's very best French champagne.

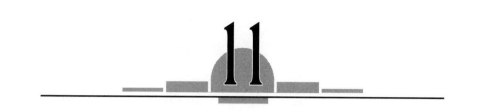

Food knows no boundaries. We are in
the international age of agriculture.

—DOA

I N the late 1950s, the soybean growers of Minnesota and
the Dakotas who sold their yields to Honeymead and
belonged to the Saint Paul–based Farmers Union Grain
Terminal Association, which they had organized in 1938,
decided that they could earn more money from their crops if
they processed them themselves. They were a substantial
group, with around one hundred thousand members. They
processed and marketed 138 million bushels a year. Their
semimonthly *Farmers Union Herald* reached 250,000 families. It had been at a meeting of the Association in 1952 that
Humphrey first publicly broached the idea of a Food for Peace
program.

In 1960, nearly a decade after Dwayne had left Cargill
and returned to the family business, the Association began
negotiating with Honeymead. The upshot was that in August

it bought out the Andreases for $10 million and hired Lowell and Dwayne as, respectively, vice president and executive vice president. Humphrey, aware that many of his and Andreas's contemporaries regarded all cooperatives as suspiciously radical, subsequently observed that installing Dwayne there constituted as bizarre a piece of casting as if the head of the United Automobile Workers had assumed the executive vice presidency of General Motors.

The man who mainly engineered the deal was Myron W. ("Bill") Thatcher, a friend of and adviser to Humphrey, who was secretary general of the Grain Terminal Association. A longtime Democrat and friend also of Franklin D. Roosevelt, Thatcher called Dwight Eisenhower "a man determined to force farmers back into a complete laissez-faire economy," and he described that president's two terms as "those terrible years." When Humphrey—who once told the columnist Jack Anderson, "Were it not for the Farmers Union Grain Terminal Association, the Democratic Farmer-Labor party of Minnesota would be a minority party, weak and without many officeholders"—introduced Thatcher to Andreas in Florida during the winter of 1960, Dwayne, who likes to reduce complicated matters, whenever possible, to elementals, told him, "I buy beans and make two things out of them—meal and oil. If I can do both and make money, farmers can, too."

The farmers of the GTA liked that kind of talk. In the spring of 1986, addressing the National Cooperative Business Association, Andreas would say:

> My own roots are in farm cooperatives.... Today, I am still deeply involved with cooperatives because my company, ADM, is a major customer and partner of cooperatives. Almost seventy percent of the agricultural commodities we buy come from farmer cooperatives. And most of the feed products we sell in Europe and elsewhere go through cooperatives.... Gone are the days when cooperatives were stigmatized by labels like "socialist." Today cooperatives are universally recognized as part of the strong foundations of our free enterprise system.... Together, we can help our

government to create the climate in which the free enterprise system of private corporations and cooperatives can survive in a hostile, state-dominated world market. Together, we must stand united in our cause. And as we do so, let us recall Ben Franklin's advice to his fellow patriots in the American Revolution: "Either we hang together or most assuredly we will hang separately."

During the 1960 presidential-election campaign, John F. Kennedy's advisers deemed the Grain Terminal Association to have sufficient clout to warrant his stopping by and paying his respects during a Midwest campaign swing. Andreas, who was becoming increasingly concerned with the problems of the Third World and the seemingly never ending hunger that afflicted it, would soon be writing Kennedy: "I think the next President of the United States and the next administrator [of foreign aid] should inaugurate a program of buying soybean oil and cottonseed oil and lard for relief feeding abroad, and I would do this before harvest time when the farmers have soybeans to sell." ("The secret of Andreas's success," the *St. Paul Dispatch* would say the following year, "is that he knows how and where to sell soybean oil.") Kennedy took him up on that, and he also appointed him to a low-level but high-sounding something called the American Food for Peace Council. *

Andreas was grateful, but not overly impressed. At times, he seems to have a reserved opinion of many elected officials. Among his known public utterances are "Washington is not made up of the smartest people" and "Dealing with governments is like trying to put a hundred volts through a ten-volt fuse." And no matter what friendships he has cultivated and relished, Andreas has tried—not entirely successfully—

---

*Andreas the do-gooding altruist occasionally seemed to be in conflict with Andreas the profit-oriented practical man. In April 1962, for instance, he sent Humphrey a telegram (it was back in the days when people still used telegrams) urging that the president persuade the Atomic Energy Commission to use water instead of milk as a measure of the strontium-90 level in foodstuffs, because if the AEC continued to put out announcements mentioning milk that could "lead to economic disaster for the dairy industry."

to shy away from being taken for a politician himself. He says:

> I've never been uncomfortable with either Republicans or Democrats because I've never attempted to do anything political. In any event, in the farm economy right-wingers and left-wingers and middle-of-the-roaders are all sort of mixed up, in a populist sense. Oh, there's a common enemy—two common enemies, actually. But they're not Democrats or Republicans. They're interest rates and depressed prices. Weather is not an enemy. Weather is something you can't do anything about. With the two real enemies, you think there *ought* to be something you could do, and when you're riding on your tractor, you don't get mad at politicians—you think about *them* and get mad.

In one of Andreas's first pronouncements as a Food for Peace councilman, he said, "Food knows no boundaries. We are in the international age of agriculture." In May 1961, a few months into the Kennedy administration, Humphrey and Thatcher and Andreas visited the Oval Office, and according to a memorandum the senator prepared for the compiler of his newsletter to his constituents, they "outlined the possibility of improving our foreign aid efforts in Latin America in particular by working through cooperatives and some of the private organizations rather than just the government."

Not long afterward, Latin America temporarily on the shelf, Humphrey and Andreas, accompanied by their wives, embarked on a month-long whirlwind excursion to Paris, Rome, London, Berlin, Brussels, Warsaw, Cairo, Damascus, Jerusalem, Athens, Tunis, Madrid, and Lisbon. In Belgium, Andreas was delighted to have his skepticism about men in public life confirmed when Paul-Henri Spaak told the visitors that when he retired he had it in mind to write a book titled *The Necessary Incompetence of a Politician*. Among the other dignitaries the two Americans called on that time were Harold Macmillan, Lucius Clay, Willy Brandt, Konrad Adenauer, Gamal Abdel Nasser, and the pope. To Humphrey, on returning home and catching his breath, Andreas wrote: "This was a tremendous educational experience for me....I wouldn't trade the experience for a million dollars or a college education."

Andreas could travel without Humphrey, too, of course. Representing the Grain Terminal Association, and in the company of Soybean Council of America executives, in 1962 he attended gatherings in Rome, Paris, Brussels, and Madrid, having to do in part with import duties on soybean oil in the Common Market area. On coming home, he submitted to his GTA associates a nearly four-thousand-word assessment of the trip, two of the concluding paragraphs of which hinted at the mathematical cast—who needed a college education if he had the right researchers?—of his thinking:

[A statistician] worked out the following simple little summary for me:

"The United States has a mixed feed business of 55,000,000 tons, serving 180,000,000 people. The Common Market area, including the anticipated associated countries, has a mixed feed business of 12,000,000 tons serving 320,000,000 people. If the meat consumption capacity per capita in the entire Common Market area were to rise to the level of the United States and if at the same time feeding practices were improved to approximately the same level as in the United States, the feed business in the Common Market area would have to increase from 12,000,000 tons to 100,000,000 tons—almost tenfold."

This would indicate a demand at some future date for the meal from more than 700,000,000 bushels of soybeans. It is only a question of when. He estimated that this could all take place within a period of 10 to 25 years, depending largely upon how rapidly wage rates, and hence meat consumption, continue to increase in the Common Market area. I am making a note of this not because I accepted the thesis 100 per cent, but because I want to continue to remind us that unless the soybean crop continues to expand at the rate of at least 8 per cent per year, we will run into serious shortages of meal again from time to time, and that we can safely plan for a crop of 1,200,000,000 bushels by about 1970.

12

Everything of consequence that I know
about business I learned between the
ages of eight and twelve.

—DOA

Bʏ 1962, Andreas's three children were grown. Michael,
the youngest, was approaching fifteen. Daughter Sandra
had lived as a youngster mostly with her mother,
who'd remarried, in Florida. The mother was Catholic, and
the girl attended parochial schools and then graduated, in
1962, from Marymount College. Before she got married, to a
lawyer, William McMurtrie, and had children, she worked in
New York City. She was a kindergarten teacher, department-
store model, and art-gallery assistant. Later, in Washington,
she served on Hubert Humphrey's vice-presidential staff.

In 1981, newly divorced and, thanks to her father, finan-
cially independent, Mrs. McMurtrie felt restless. Her children no longer needed her full-time. Dwayne, when consulted
about what she might do, proposed a trip to Haiti, where a
program was under way that involved feeding soy-fortified

formulas to infants. But Sandra wanted something with a strong Catholic orientation. (She is the first woman ever to become a director of her regional branch of the Knights of Malta, who have chivalrously escorted her to Lourdes.) She had recently seen a film about Mother Teresa's work in India, and that sounded more appealing. Besides, she had a friend who would accompany her to Calcutta.

Dwayne thought that sounded awfully far away, but she went anyway, and soon after three weeks at the Mother's sobering establishment there—an experience the neophyte would subsequently appraise as "a great joy"—she stationed herself behind a serving table at her patroness's Missionaries of Charity soup kitchen in Washington, D.C. Much of what Sandra served—and told her father her guests relished—was made of textured vegetable protein, ADM's meat substitute of many guises. After Mother Teresa opened a home in the capital for AIDS sufferers, called Gift of Peace, Sandra spent the better part of a year and a half there attending to the residents.

Most recently, Mrs. McMurtrie was involved in setting up a Missionaries of Charity soup kitchen in Tijuana, Mexico, where the menu features TVP-based tacos and tortillas. She had a hand, further, in teaching hundreds of barrio inhabitants, using TVP dispensed free by the kitchen, to make their staple dishes at home. The raw materials were easy enough to come by; Mother Teresa asked Andreas for them. On her own, Sandra did her bit toward making life more comfortable for at least one barrio dweller. With Mother Teresa's blessing, she adopted a six-year-old Down's-syndrome victim and welcomed the girl, Maria Guadalupe, into her Bethesda home.

In 1980, Inez's daughter Terry—who after two dissolved marriages adopted the name Terry Andreas—founded the School for Field Studies, a Cambridge, Massachusetts, institution of which she was and is chairman of the board. It would ultimately support the studies around the globe of more than two hundred men and women a year. Much of the School's own support came from the Andreas Foundation, the Archer Daniels Midland Foundation, and the Andreases themselves. Under Terry Andreas's far-flung wing there were affiliated centers in Australia (for rain-forest research), the Virgin Islands (marine resource research), Kenya (wildlife management), and Mexico (marine mammals). Had not the government of Zimbabwe put too many obstacles in her path, she'd have had an outpost there specializing in sustainable development. Her students, who get academic credit for their work through an arrangement with Massachusetts's Northeastern University, have dealt with posteruption elk return to Mount Saint Helens, the ecology of Alaskan bald eagles, the ecology of North Atlantic humpback whales, the collapse of the pronghorn-antelope population of Wyoming, the endangerment of monkeys in Mexico, and ecological-management conflicts in the northern Himalayas.

Inez Andreas's father had urged her to follow him into commodities trading, and as a temporary expedient, when she was on her own, she was willing enough to try. But she was frustratingly rebuffed when the head of the firm at which she wanted to open an account turned her down, on the ground that women cry too much. Ever since, she has emphatically demonstrated dry-eyed fiscal shrewdness. Some years ago, Inez and Dwayne bought a farm outside Decatur, with twenty acres in experimental soybean plots. They got bored with that, and Inez consulted the Forestry Department of the University of Illinois about what fruitful use could be made of the land. "Black-walnut trees" was the recommendation; their ranks had sorely been depleted, partly because the wood was used for rifle stocks in the First World War. In 1972, she had ten thousand of them planted. About half have survived. When the Andreases sold the house that went with the farm, they kept the twenty acres of black walnuts. Inez likes to tell her friends that the trees are a long-term investment for their grandchildren, of whom, by 1990, there were nine.

In Florida, Inez Andreas became well-known as the chairman of the board of trustees of Barry University, in Miami

Shores, where in 1975 she earned a master's degree in guidance and counseling. Barry, a Catholic institution, was founded in 1940. Its first student body comprised forty-seven young women. It turned coeducational in 1976, and by 1990 its enrollment had passed the five-thousand mark, and it boasted students from 162 geographical places. Among the courses it offers are podiatric medicine, nursing, computer science, Jewish studies, and most recently, aviation science. Many of the Andreases' friends became its friends. Hubert Humphrey was the principal speaker at its president's dinner in 1971, and Bob Dole did the honors the following year. James Stewart, the cement man, gave its scholarship fund a hundred thousand dollars. David Brinkley, whose name adorns a new television studio there, is also on the faculty as an adjunct professor, and one prize students compete for is the David Brinkley Award for Excellence in Communication. Tip O'Neill and Bob Strauss have been commencement speakers. Ray Floyd lets duffers play with him, for a stiff greens' fee, and gives Barry the proceeds. The administrator who welcomes them all to her domain, Sister Jeanne O'Laughlin, is an off-campus celebrity herself—the first female member ever of Miami's Orange Bowl Committee.

President O'Laughlin became another of the Andreases' close Florida friends. "If you see Inez Andreas coming toward you with dollar signs in her eyes and Sister Jeanne O'Laughlin on her arm, hang on to your wallet," the *Miami Herald* said in 1985. When Sister Jeanne took over, in 1981, Barry had a $500,000 deficit. She has since raised more than $35 million and is operating in the black.

Sister Jeanne, a high-spirited and unconventional nun (Adrian Dominican), has a PhD in educational administration from the University of Arizona. Extracurricularly, she likes to sing. She once received a standing ovation, during a performance of a local musical comedy called *Nunsense,* for her rendition of a parody song titled "You Can't Get a Man if You're a Nun." Not long after that, Sister Jeanne received a sporting proposition from Dwayne Andreas. He had just given Barry $1 million, and she wondered what she could do in return. First explaining that she reminded him of Evita Perón, he asked her if she'd sing "Don't Cry for Me, Argentina" in a white silk habit.

Nobody has ever pretended that fund-raising is easy. Sister Jeanne spent four agonizing months in prayer and meditation. Meanwhile, another wealthy admirer offered half a million more if when she performed it, she'd do so aboard his yacht. She prayed harder than ever. "I finally decided that if I was going to carry out this mission for God, maybe he would send me a sign," she says. On the evening of her scheduled performance, she switched on a radio, and the very first sounds she heard were the strains of "Don't Cry for Me." The money was soon all hers.

Inez Andreas is not without her share of nomenclatural honors. Her husband once christened a helicopter the *Inez*. Her full name graces one of ADM's fleet of Mississippi vessels called towboats, even though their function is not to pull but push—sometimes as many as thirty heavily laden barges at a clip. At Barry, one campus ornament, made possible largely because of a further $3.5 million gift from her husband, is the Inez Andreas School for Business Building. Friend Henry Kissinger spoke at its dedication. Dwayne, who already had an honorary LLD from Barry, was the new school's Executive MBA Distinguished Lecturer in February 1989, and Sister Jeanne seized the occasion to dub him— some scholars wait for years and even finish college first—a full professor. He told his auditors, echoing a favorite theme, "Everything of consequence that I know about business I learned between the ages of eight and twelve." And what, he went on, had he learned since? Principally that 90 percent of the paper that crossed his desk was irrelevant.*

---

*Until Andreas turned sixty or thereabouts, he repeatedly warned his children to shy away from the press, as had been his wont, and not to make speeches. At lunch one day, his son Michael happened to mention having just declined an offer to give a talk, during that area's most enticing weather, in Switzerland. But why? his father wondered. "Because you told me once, 'Never give your first speech, or you'll never give your last,'" was the answer. Dwayne, who by then had repeatedly disregarded his own advice, mulled that over for a moment. "I wish you'd reminded me of that ten years ago," he said.

Andreas himself, over the years, has probably generated far less paper than almost any other high-placed corporation executive. At a meeting of soybean-industry chieftains one time, it was suggested that somebody ought to write a letter to somebody about something, and that Dwayne, considering his exalted reputation, would be just the person to do it. He declined. "I've known the fellow for ten years, but I've never written a letter in my life," he said. "If you write a letter, you need a secretary, and if you have a secretary, you need a file, and if you have a file , the government wants to look at it." He was, of course, exaggerating, as his hardworking underlings well know; why, he once even wrote a long thoughtful letter to a woman who thought she had devised a new way to feed soybeans to pets.

Some of his six-figure senior executives share secretaries. His ADM president since 1975, James R. Randall, whose annual salary is more than $800,000 dollars, has said to an inquisitive outsider, "People around here make money instead of writing reports or going to meetings." At Cargill, where Andreas had hired him as a twenty-year-old production trainee in 1948, Randall had advanced to technical director by 1968. Then Andreas lured him away to ADM.* Randall leapt at the chance. When asked years later why he'd been so quick to cast in his lot with Andreas, he said, "He's the most brilliant man I've ever met."

In Decatur, Randall aims at hopping into his Ferrari or Mercedes and getting to his desk, at least six days a week and sometimes seven, by six-fifteen A.M. By nine, he will have conversed—not corresponded—with his ten division managers, all of whom are stationed within shouting distance. He does not consider his job onerous. As a small boy on a

---

*Andreas did not then practice what he has subsequently preached. In 1971, learning that the head of one of his subsidiaries had it in mind to recruit some of a rival company's employees, Andreas, belying his reputation for committing himself to paper as little as possible, wrote to him: "ADM has a long-standing firm policy of not raiding other people's organizations. We feel that it is simply poor business; and, in the long run, it is better to train our own people. Also, raiding is a two-way street, and we have to assume that we are as vulnerable as anyone in that regard." (Perhaps, considering how many people around him were namesakes, not quite as vulnerable.)

Wisconsin dairy farm, he had only one pair of overalls; his mother, fearing neighbors might otherwise catch on to the family's indigence, would lock him into his bedroom while she washed and dried them. While he was in high school, his father came down with leukemia, and Jim had to run the farm. While in college, he toiled nights in a box factory and weekends at a garage. "I've *never* worked at ADM," he says. "This is a *game*."

Administration and production are Randall's two primary playthings. He is a strong believer in higher education and likes to take on young PhDs. He had twenty-seven of them around at last count, but he is always careful to point out that they constitute a special breed, and that instead of being white-sneaker types, they have crap on their shoes. He can be tough. After reducing the employees at one new ADM acquisition from eighteen to eight, and at another from twelve hundred to four hundred, he himself acquired the sobriquet of "Neutron Jim." It has also been said of him that he's the only big businessman known to get seriously unhappy when he has to take a vacation.

13

You know, I'm not sure I'm the right
person to be lecturing somebody on how to
be a good loser.

—DOA

MICHAEL Andreas, born in 1948, is the only child of
Inez and Dwayne. There seemed to be little doubt
that *he* would follow paternal business footsteps.
He began catching on to the appropriate lingo at the age of
four, when Dwayne left Cargill and for a while worked out of
his home, conducting trades by telephone while the boy
crawled around under his feet. The story goes that in Sunday
school one day, someone asked "What's a prophet?" Mickey
piped up, "What's left after you've paid your expenses." It has
been suggested by at least one friend of his father's—an admir-
ing friend—that to him religion and money are both also often
intertwined. "I sometimes think of Dwayne as a person with
a Bible in his hand," the friend says, "and a dollar bill for a
bookmark."

Andreas *père* is sometimes accused by people he does

business with of being hard-shelled, but one has to wonder after hearing about an alleged incident from Mickey's later childhood. The son was playing Little League hockey and, when his team had been trounced one day, came home in a terrible sulk and misbehaved, as many a kid will in such circumstances. "You just wait till your father gets home," Inez adjured him, and when Dwayne duly materialized, he was instructed to give the boy his desserts. The mother heard no sounds of spanking, not even a raised voice, and indeed heard nothing more about the incident until, a couple of days afterward, Dwayne confessed to her, "You know, I'm not sure I'm the right person to be lecturing somebody on how to be a good loser."

Michael Andreas went to Northwestern, and he graduated in 1970. A fellow student there was a stepdaughter of David Susskind, and they got married that year. (That set the stage for Susskind's saying on television, while guest Dwayne Andreas beamed appreciatively, "The world doesn't understand the miracle of soybeans.") The union ended in divorce. Michael and his second wife, Sally, who runs a children's clothing store in Decatur, make no special effort to eat soybeans at home, although he has conceded that he has been used as a guinea pig when novel soybased foods are brought around ADM for testing and tasting. "I leave the office at the office," he says. "But Dad has always believed that the real future of human beings lies in his TVP food and the like. The truth is that the protein shortage hasn't come yet. When it comes, though, we'll be ready."

During a run-of-the-mill week retrieving golf balls for his father at Lake Minnetonka, young Mickey could count on ending up with at least five dollars. Unlike the generation ahead of him, he never had to cope with predawn farm chores. (His father, though, did eventually turn over to him the responsibility of dealing with three A.M. phone calls from customers in Europe.) There was a stint as a message carrier on the Chicago Board of Trade (on which Michael later bought a seat), and he did for a bit wield a shovel in a San

Francisco malting plant; but at ADM he made headway relatively fast. (Also at golf, getting to the point where he could give his father a stroke a hole.) By the time Michael was forty-one, he was executive vice president at ADM, a member of its board of directors, and the owner of $60 million worth of its stock, with an annual salary of over $500,000.

Michael Andreas had joined ADM in 1971, at twenty-three, and even before that the paterfamilias had planted the son very firmly in his footsteps, turning him over for tutelage to Julius Hendel, who when Dwayne first went to work at Cargill was in charge of commodities trading there and had initiated him into the arcana of hedging: in essence, letting somebody else—a speculator, say—take the risks in commodities trading, while you protect yourself through the futures market, always being in a position to sell if a price goes up or to buy when it comes down. Another preceptor of those early days—like Hendel, yet another Jew who strongly influenced Andreas's thoughts and actions—was a Fargo, North Dakota, grain dealer, Max Goldberg, the father of the Harvard Business School professor Ray Goldberg. The senior Goldberg, escorting a youthful and attentive Dwayne around the frenetic Minneapolis Grain Exchange one day, had had these long-remembered words to impart: "Put your hands in your pockets and keep your head down and say to yourself ten times, 'Don't believe the sons of bitches.' "

It was the junior Goldberg, by now enthroned as Cambridge's Moffett Professor of Agriculture and Business, who in the summer of 1990 would tap Andreas to become president-elect of a newly formed high-level entity called the International Agribusiness Association.

Cargill enforced compulsory retirement at sixty-five then. Hendel, willy-nilly on his own, took a room in a Minneapolis office building and launched the Julius Hendel School of Practical Hedging. Just how many students it attracted, or he desired, is moot. Michael Andreas knows of only one other. The academy's chief assigned reading was Hendel's own *Principles and Practices in Grain Trading and Hedging*. It was a pamphlet in two sections: "Relationship Between Cash and Future Prices of Grain" and "Theory and Practice of Hedging."*

Hendel had a home at Minnetonka, and it was there that he took on Michael as a pupil, to learn all about cross-hedging wheat and corn or flax and soybeans, and to familiarize himself with commodity spreads and carrying charges and the complex like. "The fundamentals that Julius Hendel instilled in both Dad and me still apply," Michael says.† "There may be only a handful of traders who comprehend the real fundamentals of hedging, and it's useful to know that we have that understanding. That's good for my future." (He has probably had less cause than most mortals to be concerned about *that.*) Michael clings to his timeworn copy of *Principles and Practices* much as a clergyman might to Scripture. "I've read it so many times," he says, "that I don't need it anymore."

According to Michael—who since January 1989 has been a director also of such ADM enterprises as Alfred C. Toepfer International, ADM/GROWMARK, Golden Peanut Company, and ADM-UCO Grainco:

> I am the only guy around who always knows where Dad is and what he's up to. While he's running around talking about hundreds of millions of dollars, we take care of the millions here. When he's in Decatur, we have lunch together every day. Wherever he is, we talk three to five times daily. We talk about everything. We have a good understanding of each other. We think alike, so it's easy to

*"One should never attempt to use hedges for the purpose of making additional profits," the pamphlet enjoins. "True hedges are protection, and should invariably be used as such. Trying to profit from hedging will lead to speculation, and if a trader is speculating, his mind will not be on business.... Maintain a policy of hedging at all times—experience has shown that hedgers tend to grow and prosper. Speculators may have spectacular success, but in the long run they tend to disappear."

†One of Hendel's "fundamental principles of trading in grain" (in his treatise, the words are, for emphasis, both capitalized and underlined) was "Under conditions of inverse carrying charges, carry very low inventories, and if possible maintain a net cash short position (forward sales) hedged by long deferred futures." And one of his no-less-stressed warnings went: "You never go broke taking profits.... A bull and a bear make money, but a hog gets slaughtered."

communicate. Also, we don't have any organization chart or chain of command. If a guy from General Motors ever came to work here, where you have to make decisions in a hurry—the wrong guess about the market can lose you millions of dollars in a day—he'd be shocked. If our corn man gets involved with beans, or our beans man with barges, that's fine with everybody. This is a company of Indian trails. Nobody not in the grain business can really have any idea how it works. I've been in it my whole adult life, and I'm beginning to learn it. It's a kind of fraternity. It's important to keep things secret, but I know of no case where anybody has actually spied on anybody. All our trading is done on the phone, and your word is your bond.* When people come here for the first time and ask for instructions, I simply tell them to sit back, keep their eyes and ears open, and learn the Indian trails.

By 1963, Hubert Humphrey was much more than just another farm-belt member of the upper house. As its majority whip, he had become a national figure, and being ever more widely recognized as the senator's best friend and trusted confidant was clearly to Andreas's advantage in both business and political circles. Social invitations accelerated, too. It was a mutually beneficial relationship for two men who, among other things, shared one very practical goal: to open up as many foreign markets as possible to the produce of Midwestern American farmers. Was it not Humphrey, that year, who had brought forth a joint resolution calling for the appointment of a bipartisan congressional committee to look into the nation's requirements of food and fiber and in connection therewith had urged that American companies be allowed to sell grain—preferably for gold—to the Soviet Union and its satellite countries?

---

*Sometimes it gets nice and chatty. "Because of our very special relationship to you," Michael Andreas will say to a Soviet soybean buyer negotiating for eight hundred thousand tons, "we would be pleased to accept your bid"; and the deal is consummated with "My father sends his best" and "Thanks and my personal regards to Mr. D. Andreas."

Through Humphrey, Andreas gained access to the inner workings of government on a high level; and through Andreas's farflung connections on a no-less-lofty business level, Humphrey was sometimes made privy to intelligence superior to anything he could obtain from the State Department or the CIA. Typically, when Dwayne learned of one economic meeting on Hubert's schedule, he sent his friend a memo that began:

> In preparation for next week's conference, I have communicated with people well-known to me in (1) The Dreyfus Company, Paris; (2) Rothschilds, London; (3) Bunge Corporation, Rotterdam; (4) Continental Grain Company; (5) The Andre Corporation, Lausanne; (6) Tradex (subsidiary of Cargill), Geneva; (7) Superintendence Company, Geneva; and (8) a large private investor in Paris.

Reflecting one time on Andreas's place in the general order of things, John H. Daniels, a retired CEO of ADM and a continuing member of its board of directors, said:

> [A] factor which sets Dwayne apart is his sophisticated understanding of the critical interrelationship between business and politics. This is no accident. Some of his critics have said that he has spent an inordinate amount of time—and money—in the political arena and have labelled it an ego trip. I believe that they have misread DOA's motives. My own feeling is that he is one of the few people who have a very clear appreciation of the frequently antagonistic, unfriendly, and almost always uninformed attitudes that bureaucrats—and especially most people in Congress and the Executive branch at the national level—have towards his particular agricultural-processing business. Agricultural policy is particularly prone to being misinterpreted, mangled, and mishandled. It is extremely complex, and most people never truly understand it. It tries to serve so many diverse masters—the consumer and the farmer; the exporter and importer; the State Department and the Department of Commerce; the northern farmer and the southern farmer; to give you a few examples. The food processor is often caught in the middle. DOA is a successful practitioner of

the art of imparting accurate and timely information about the position of agribusiness to people in government.

Humphrey's and Andreas's joint trips together in 1963 included one to Scandinavia, principally to attend a meeting, convened by Prime Minister Tage Erlander of Sweden, of some twenty labor-oriented leaders in order, according to Humphrey's notes, "simply to exchange ideas among these people [among them, Harold Wilson, Willy Brandt, and Walter Reuther] who represent the power in the liberal forces in the various countries." Reuther, who as head of the United Automobile Workers was a powerful labor leader in the United States, sought to forestall whatever thrusts right-wingers back home might be tempted to level at the Americans for thus consorting with a bunch of European lefties by saying, according to the senator's jotting, that "the most important item on the agenda of world politics today was for the leaders of the Democratic left to demonstrate clearly to the people of the world that there is an ALTERNATIVE [Humphrey's capitals] to Communism."

Humphrey, for his part, with Andreas's attentive and enthusiastic concurrence, spoke when it came his turn of "a massive technological revolution already manifested in the farm economy: in production of foodstuffs we stand on the eve of the possibility of eliminating hunger from the world, but our economists and fiscal people are so puzzled by this new development that efforts to make this miracle available to [the] world are endangered."

Another trip that year took the peripatetic pair to Caracas, for a session of the Inter American Development Bank, following which Andreas, once again belying his reputation for never putting anything on paper, wrote to Humphrey: "Thanks for giving me the opportunity to make the Venezuelan trip, which was extremely fruitful from my point of view. . . . It was a great opportunity for me to make several acquaintances of great interest to me in the pursuit of the [Grain Terminal Association's] business and objectives." And three weeks after that, Latin America still evidently much on Andreas's mind, he would be deploring in another letter to Humphrey an American government decision to stop buying sugar from Cuba. That, Andreas wrote, had been our chief means of having any economic impact at all down there. "We handed our best—perhaps only—weapon to Russia," he lamented. "Khrushchev and Castro must be having a good laugh. We did the whole job for them."

The year 1964 would be crucial for Hubert Humphrey. Lyndon Johnson, president by virtue of Kennedy's assassination, would be seeking reinstallment by election, and Humphrey would be his running mate. Andreas didn't know Johnson especially well, but at the president's request did once go to West Germany to warn Ludwig Erhard, then the chancellor, that a European Economic Community tariff on American chickens would be unwelcome. Johnson told Andreas to remind Erhard that United States foreign-aid appropriations had to clear the Senate Foreign Relations Committee, and that J. William Fulbright, its chairman, came from Arkansas, a big chicken state. "Erhard looked me right in the eye," Andreas recalls, "and he said, 'Dwayne, you go back and tell the president that my farmers vote, too.'" While Erhard remained adamant about chickens, Andreas's pilgrimage was not without results; the Germans relaxed their restrictions on chicken feed.

Johnson, who rarely used one syllable where two would do, always pronounced the name "Dee-wayne." The story goes that someone interrupted a cabinet meeting once to say there was an urgent phone call for Secretary of Agriculture Orville Freeman.* The president glowered. Who on earth would have the effrontery...? Dwayne Andreas was on the line, the courier said. Johnson beamed. "Oh, say hello to Dee-wayne for me," he told the departing Freeman.

---

*Humphrey, in a letter to Andreas about his middle name, wrote, "You Orvilles always work together. Orville Andreas, Orville Wright, Orville Freeman, and all other Orvilles are deserving of special commendation."

Andreas surmised years later that the call might have related to a pending decision on whether the administration was going to introduce legislation to pay farmers not to grow crops, and that he had phoned to try to make sure that the entire cabinet was aware that the Farmer-Labor people would not support any such move. (The legislation, when finally introduced nonetheless, failed to pass the House.) Andreas, who has persistently professed not to have any track with lobbying—how can people never understand, he wonders, that Herb Waters and Martin Sorkin have been just *consultants?* —has said of this episode, "I wasn't dealing in politics. I just happened to be a guy who dealt with Farmer-Labor groups and wanted to make sure their point of view got passed along."

Humphrey and Andreas kept in close touch during the 1964 campaign. The vice-presidential nominee would send along drafts of speeches he contemplated giving, for any comments Andreas might have. Andreas appears to have refrained from reacting one way or another when given a glimpse of a Humphrey oration, less than a month before Election Day, in which the Minnesotan planned to tell a Sioux Falls, South Dakota, crowd gathered for a National Corn-Picking Contest, "Whatever I am, I owe to you."

During the campaign, also, the editors of the Grain Terminal Association's *Farmers Union Herald* sent for Andreas's advance approval a cartoon showing hungry children on one side of a fence while on the other dry milk of United States origin was being fed to European cattle. Andreas complimented the paper's editor, saying that the drawing "made a very good and valid point." At the same time he ordered him not to publish it because "it raises an issue which might work against us during the election campaign."

At Atlantic City, at five forty-five A.M. on August 27, President Johnson, who'd been renominated only a few hours earlier, phoned Dee-wayne at his convention hotel and asked him to be at the airport there in half an hour and fly to the LBJ ranch in Texas, along with vice-presidential nominee Humphrey, for a strategy huddle. During one three-hour session down there, Johnson had some blunt things to recall about when, four years earlier, *he* had been a vice-presidential nominee and the Kennedy people had all but ignored him, and how in order to procure a plane to barnstorm in, Lady Bird and he had had to go to a bank and borrow a million dollars on their own. Johnson said he was, by contrast, prepared to work closely with Humphrey and Humphrey's people. While he was at it, he also apprised them of his suspicion that the Republicans, before they were through, would accuse him personally of having had a hand in Kennedy's assassination.

As for Andreas, Johnson had one specific request: it seemed that he anticipated some opposition from organized farm groups, and he wanted Humphrey's friend, starting right away, to neutralize them. Andreas remembers his instructions from the president as simple and succinct: "Tell them to stop squealing and shut up, and to let us win. Eight weeks of silence—that's all I ask for." To the best of Andreas's ability, Johnson got his wish.

During the Johnson years, Andreas, on a couple of sorties to Brazil, ended up disappointed. Brazil is an estimable place for the tillage of soybeans. For several years, the Agency for International Development had run an experimental program in northeastern Brazil to learn what effect an infusion of soybeans into children's diets might have on juvenile development. The results had been heartening: a 23 percent improvement in growth, a 25 percent improvement in the ability to pass tests.

Andreas went to Rio de Janeiro soon afterward for a meeting with Brazilian officials. Brazil hadn't yet embarked on large-scale cultivation, but Andreas was told that if he would build a soybean-processing plant there, they would mandate the inclusion of a minimum of 5 percent of the legume in all indigenous bread. Andreas began to put up a processing plant, but when it was just about finished, the mandate was canceled—after complaints, he heard later, from local wheat-flour mills and a few other parties who felt themselves threatened. "I'm kind of a trusting fellow, and I took the officials at their word," he said later. "I'm usually considered not a bad salesman, what's more, but maybe that one time I oversold them." He was further hoping—also in vain—to have his pet Nutri-Bev produced there commercially. "I've been frustrated every time I've tried to make it," he says. "We always lose money on it. Only a little, fortunately, so it doesn't hurt too much."

14

Just as war is too important to be left
to the generals, food production is too
important to be left to the economists.

—DOA

For some time, presidents had been appointing Andreas
to various posts, some more honorary than productive. With Truman, it had been a consultant
on price controls, with Eisenhower an adviser on foreign aid,
with Kennedy his American Food for Peace Council. Johnson—
who had a cold at his inaugural ball and passed it along,
while dancing with her, to Inez Andreas—saw fit to name
Dwayne to a General Advisory Commission on Foreign Assistance Programs. After three years on it, Andreas expressed
doubt that whatever advice the group had given the president
had materially affected any distribution of foreign aid.

It was to the vice president, though, that Andreas, naturally enough in view of their intimacy, paid the most attention. They continued to travel together, but in far grander
style, accompanied now by an entourage of Secret Service

operatives and other image enhancers.* On the manifests that preceded or accompanied these excursions, for the convenience of hosts and hostesses having to arrange banquet-table placements and the like, Humphrey would have Andreas designated as "personal friend," thus ensuring that, by some arcane protocolary fiat, he would be accorded status superior to that of much of the rest of the official party. Now Humphrey would carry along, and dispense, vice-presidential keepsakes: specially marked tie clasps, cuff links, bracelets, photographs, et al. Andreas, whose support of his friend included putting a Humphrey son through school and administering a blind trust under the legal counsel of Tom Dewey—some of it invested, to Hubert's good fortune, in ADM stock—footed the bill for most of the giveaways. (The financial relationship was not exclusively one-sided; Humphrey once had a jeweler fashion just three brooches in the form of his vice-presidential seal—one for Inez and one for each Andreas daughter.)

One journey took them and their wives to seven European countries and the Vatican. There were discussions all the way—on the highest governmental (Charles de Gaulle) and diplomatic (David Bruce) levels—about nonproliferation of weapons, monetary reform, foreign aid, and other such topics. This time Andreas, unequivocally turning to paper, composed a summary memorandum approximately six thousand words long. Along with a revelation of some of his views on important issues, it was illustrative of some of the enormous admiration he had for Humphrey and of the almost innocent pleasure—a near-boyish enthusiasm—at being admitted to the courts of the great. A few excerpts:

Meeting with Prime Minister Harold Wilson at Chequers.
[An] interesting feature was Wilson's quotation from Jonathan

*Andreas and his staff were obliged to spend a good deal of time, in connection with these trips, filling out security-clearance forms. When *Barron's* ran an article observing testily that "some Americans see nothing wrong in trafficking with Communists," Humphrey, who knew that his favorite fellow traveler was an irreproachable capitalist despite his efforts to promote trade with the USSR, clipped it and passed it along to Andreas with the comment, "Now do you realize what a real rascal you are, even to the point of being a threat to national security?"

Swift to the effect that "a man who can make two blades of grass grow where one grew before is more important to mankind than all the politicians in the history of the world." Later I heard the vice president use this same quotation in an address concerning the worldwide food problem. But I could not help thinking that some of the things that went on at Chequers proved this quotation may not always be the truth. For example, we here in the United States have in fact made two blades of grass grow where one grew before, but we have encountered difficulties. The economists of the thirties and forties have not been able to keep up with the sixties and develop ways and means of making this vast technological improvement in American agriculture available for the benefit of mankind. Just as war is too important to be left to the generals, food production is too important to be left to the economists....

I had an excellent opportunity for an interesting little exchange of ideas with the prime minister of England about the Kennedy Round and the significance of multilateral food aid in the total picture. That was an opportunity for give and take that was well worth the entire trip to me because of the sense of participation and sense of achievement that I experienced in the process of doing one bit of service for the policy of my government at the request of our vice president.

Preparation for meeting with de Gaulle. This is a little event but it is significant. We were on the plane en route to Paris. As was usual, the vice president was being briefed with a good deal of very current information supplied by his intelligence officers so that he would be absolutely up to the minute on the various events of importance around the globe. Then he was discussing with the State Department experts the intricacies of the subjects that might come up in the conversation to be held with de Gaulle. At this moment, though, there were just four of us in the center lounge of the presidential plane, Air Force I, which is a large private compartment with six large chairs, two cots, a working desk, and a table. The vice president handed me a paper which said, "Proposed toast for the de Gaulle lunch." He said, "Dwayne, read this and see how it sounds to you." Long before I had a chance to read it and answer he had called in an aide. He said, "I want to change the format of the toast for the de Gaulle luncheon. This toast is a long recitation of all the things we have done for France. I haven't the slightest intention of entering a man's home and lecturing him on all the things we have done for him. In the two and one half hours we have between now and the time I arrive at the lunch, get me a well-prepared list of all of the things that France has done for the United States of America since the time of Lafayette, and from that I will make my own toast." ... At the luncheon the vice president delivered an eloquent dissertation on the long history of friendship between France and the United States. Ambassador Chip Bohlen remarked later that when the vice president delivered his toast, de Gaulle had tears in his eyes and running down his cheeks and was very emotional as he leaned to the ambassador and said, "Your vice president is a great scholar and has a magnificent understanding of history." That is professional diplomacy at its best, but more importantly, it was the result of the kind of instinctive reaction that is the hallmark of a great political leader and a talent that is very rare, even among people in public life.

I have been asked why Mrs. Andreas and I accompanied the vice president on this trip. I do not know the answer. They will have to ask the vice president. However, I will be glad to tell you how it came about.... Late in March at two in the morning my phone rang. It was the vice president. He said, "Dwayne, I have spent considerable time today with the president and I am now sitting here with Muriel. I want you to know that we are planning a two-week trip to Europe for vital and important purposes. We would like it very much if you and Inez would accompany us, but I want to warn you that it is going to be a rugged trip. The schedule is a very difficult one. There is a lot of work and briefing involved. We believe that you and Inez could be helpful. Do you want to think it over and let us know?" By this time Inez was wide-awake and nodding her head, and I simply said, "We have thought it over and the answer is yes." He did not tell me what he wanted us to do and I didn't ask.... [I]t could very well be that Mrs. Humphrey, who on her own had a very rugged schedule making trips nearly every day to hospitals, mental institutions, and other things, wanted to have Mrs. Andreas along for the reasons that most women would have for needing help on a trip like that. In that case, perhaps I was invited only because I am Mrs. Andreas's husband! And still another possibility is that a person in public life does not always want to be surrounded only by staff, other government people, and subordinates. In that case, I suppose it is only natural to think of a friend on whom you have "tried out" an idea or two before and whose idiosyncrasies and prejudices you are already wise to. But whatever the reasons, I considered it a unique opportunity to serve my country.

We are at the crossroads with our great technological improvements and our ability to actually "make two blades of grass grow where one grew before," which can provide mass quantities of food to the hungry parts of the world. There are strong forces at work here to limit the amount of food production in order to avoid price-threatening results of excess production. That is an unfortunate situation.

Of course, no one wants to deprive humanity of the benefits of this great technological revolution. On the other hand, it is not likely that Congress will appropriate huge sums of money to ship food abroad if indeed we are the only ones in the world willing to help out. If the other richer countries of the world are willing to participate in the same program on a matching basis, it is far more likely that our representatives will be willing to continue to devote substantial portions of our resources for the prevention of starvation abroad. Therefore, with the multilateral food aid program, we can look forward to far more abundant production and good prices for farmers, which will maintain the farm income and help many other segments of our economy. On the other hand, without multilateral food aid, it is likely that we can look forward to artificial limitations on production.

Here again, launching a multilateral food aid program has vast implications for our political posture in the world.

This factor, as much as anything else, could tip the scales in this century toward the way of life of the free nations as opposed to the regimented existence of the communist countries.

There was another long memo after another trip with Humphrey to Africa, where Andreas was dismayed to find that several national leaders, educated in Europe and influenced by the liberal-leaning London School of Economics, were more interested in office buildings and airlines and steel mills than in increasing their much-needed production of food. And he was saddened at more than one stop by "the occupational disease, megalomania," which he deemed to be even more debilitating than malaria. He observed, for instance, that of $500 million poured into Tunisia by the United States, Habib Bourguiba, who at an earlier encounter had struck him as "a Spartan middle-road socialist of great and unshakable convictions," had taken an estimated $200 million... and spent it on four of the most extravagant palaces of world history—money that, by Andreas's reckoning, could otherwise and much better have been allocated to a badly needed harbor, two cement plants, two thousand miles of highway, and four hundred schools. Rural Africans were becoming urbanized, he noted further, just as rural black Americans were moving to northern cities, and he mused, "unless we substantially improve their standard of living, we will be lucky if they do not become the guerrilla fighters of the USA."

And then, in the fall of 1967, there was Vietnam. "After the usual high-level meeting with, in this instance, Nguyen Van Thieu, Hubert took off in one helicopter," Andreas remarked, "and I was told to board another one, with a Vietnamese pilot, who, it developed, didn't know a word of English. We were all supposed to rendezvous on an aircraft carrier. I ended up—only temporarily, thank heaven—at an American jungle base so secret it didn't show on any map. Meanwhile, I heard later, Hubert was storming around the carrier deck yelling, 'Where the hell is Dwayne?'"

Dwayne was inspecting rice paddies. While others in

Vietnam were preoccupied with ideology and territoriality and death and destruction, he was mainly concerned, as always, with food, and as would happen more than once, his concern led to dismay and disappointment. "One of my principal objectives, that trip, was to talk to indigenous rice merchants," he said. "They quickly disillusioned me about our presence in Vietnam. We'd been sending in rice to be sold to South Vietnamese farmers at a so-called controlled price. Well, it seemed that the North Vietnamese and the Vietcong would come along and pay them much more for native rice, and would then sell it for even more than *that* to Indonesians and use the proceeds to buy arms, and then we'd have to send more rice to fill the gap."

By 1967, Andreas—and no doubt the vice president, too—was contemplating the day not far off when the two of them might be greeted by the ruffles and flourishes and multigun salutes attendant to *presidential* travels. Indeed, a good two years earlier, thinking well ahead, Dwayne had reminded Hubert that a big Republican corporation executive in Missouri "tells me that among the top people around Saint Louis he hears many highly skeptical comments about Humphrey. There is no use repeating them. You are familiar with that problem." A solution Andreas proposed then was for him to arrange a closed session—"an engraved-invitation affair"—for Humphrey to sit down with "the presidents of the four large banks and the presidents or board chairmen of twelve or fifteen of the largest institutions in that area." Andreas added that "I would estimate we would have as guests persons who control approximately seven billion dollars of assets." It was a low-key, getting-to-know-you-better sort of evening, which Andreas hoped might end up with some of the guests believing that his friend was, after all, not hostile to big business and had a middle-of-the-road approach to high finance.

And again anticipating 1968, Andreas jotted down some notes on a conversation with Humphrey, in the course of which Dwayne stressed two matters: first—this was on the level of routine partisan politics—how to try to go about

taking the farm vote away from the Republicans; second—
now Andreas was warming up, talking about something
closer to his heart than mere ballot boxes—why and how the
Democratic standard-bearer should come out with a bold,
forthright plan for alleviating world hunger.

I stated that the president has great and ample justification
to make a dramatic change in the direction of the farm
programs. An ideal time to do so would be at the time he
signs the executive order which was proposed to him by the
Advisory Committee on Aid. Our committee proposed the
creation of a cabinet-level committee chaired by the secretary of state which would gear food-production policy to
foreign policy. The committee would include the secretary
of the treasury since food production is vital to his balance-
of-payments problems. The president could change the scheme
of things by stating that the food situation is so important
that *he himself* has elected to chair that committee with
the vice president as vice chairman.

He could say that ... what is needed now for the world
economy is rapidly stepped up production of food. The
farmers need to have more income, which can be achieved
in two ways—more volume and better prices. In order to
achieve the better prices, he could freeze all government
stocks and permit them to be sold only at prices which
would show a better return to our farmers than they are
now getting. In lieu of better prices on many commodities
he could offer direct production payments which could be
made from the savings which accrue to the government
from suspending the payments for crop reduction.

He could say that he and the vice president are now leading
the worldwide War on Hunger, and considering the extra
trucks, railroad cars, ships, barges, and all kinds of business
and processing activity that this program will create, it will
generate a lot more tax income for the treasury and the net
cost to the government will be very small indeed in relation to the benefits.

He can say that America has developed the greatest agricultural technology in the world, but we are interested not only in selling to or providing food for other nations but we are equally interested in assisting in any way the developing nations in the world to improve their own productivity. To this end he could ask Congress for an additional $1 billion in capital to be turned over to the World Bank in the form of long-term debentures with the request that the World Bank institute an immediate program to make this capital available to nations for facilities and capital requirements of all kinds for the purpose of increasing food production.

I see this as a magnificent opportunity and a timely one for the Johnson-Humphrey team to identify themselves with the War on Hunger. The newspaper stories that have been appearing in recent months ... can be a tremendous asset to an administration that adopts the posture of leadership in a massive effort to overcome hunger. This program could be the background not only for great economic advances during 1968 but great improvements in political prestige of the participants and the advocates.

When the Andreases sold their Honeymead holdings to the Grain Terminal Association in 1960, they put the $10 million they received into an investment entity rather grandly called the First Interoceanic Corporation, which got them into foreign trade banking, and, far more consequentially for Dwayne, it bought a modest soybean-crushing installation at Decatur, where the Minnesota firm of Archer Daniels Midland had long had an outpost of its own. Dwayne had been to Decatur, of course, when he had had his memorable lunch with August Eugene Staley. And he had met ADM functionaries at various gatherings of feed-and-grain men. But he had had hardly any business dealings with their company.

Now in 1965, Archer Daniels Midland was up against uncertain conditions in the processing industry. For three years running, its earnings had gone down and hadn't covered its dividend. Shreve Archer, Jr., and John L. Daniels, third-generation pillars of the founding families, invited the Andreases to come to the rescue—specifically, to buy one hundred thousand shares of ADM stock from an Archer family trust, at thirty-three dollars a share, which, considering that the stock's book value was nearly double that figure, was a tempting proposition. It was swiftly taken up. That $3.3 million accounted for 6 percent of all ADM stock outstanding. Had the Andreases hung on to all of it, that 6 percent would, as 1990 rolled around, have been worth close to a billion dollars. As it was, even after diverting a good deal of stock for other investments and to philanthropies, they still retained, among them, more than $300 million worth.

How different was the Andreases' takeover of ADM from the snarling, grasping ones that came to characterize American corporate shuffling a generation later! (Different, for example, from the rude exodus from RJR Nabisco of ADM director Ross Johnson.) The Archers and the Danielses were not at all distressed about being nudged aside. Nudged aside? Anything but. There has been at least one Archer and one Daniels on the ADM board ever since. Once, Shreve Archer, Jr., John Daniels, and Robert Strauss happened to approach an ADM security gate *à trois*. After Archer gave the guard on duty his name, and Daniels followed suit, the temptation for the often roguish Strauss to say "I'm Mr. Midland" was awfully strong, but he refrained lest the three of them be peremptorily hauled away as patent mischief-makers or worse.

Archer, observing his forty-first anniversary as an ADM director in 1989, told *Fortune*, "Having been actively involved with Dwayne Andreas has been the most stimulating experience of my life." (And could there be a much better example of mutual trust than that when Dwayne asked Hubert Humphrey to get Inez and himself on a roster of future civilian space-shuttle passengers, he suggested that Shreve Archer *et ux.* would make admirable traveling companions?) And asked another time to characterize Andreas, Archer said, "How do you describe one of the most brilliant business minds in the world?" Most cost-conscious, too, Archer was quick to add; why, when once through a computer malfunction he received sixty-five copies of the same

ADM report and asked Andreas what in the world he was supposed to do with them, had not Dwayne instantly replied, "Distribute 'em"? (Andreas, for all his enjoyment of creature comforts, has long been aggrieved by waste. "I'm a natural-born Midwestern conservative," he often says.) Now long since retired to Arizona, this Archer has no part in the company's day-to-day affairs, but a son of his is its assistant treasurer—a fourth generation of the Archers to share in its destiny.

Archer Daniels Midland was, as soybean-related enter-prises went, a venerable one. It was a direct successor to the turn-of-the-century Archer Daniels Linseed Company, formed by two old friends, George A. Archer and John W. Daniels, who grew up together in the Miami Valley district of Ohio, where the cultivation of flax for linseed oil was concentrated in the midnineteenth century, before that crop, like others and their growers, migrated westward. On the eve of the Civil War, there were twenty-six flax-crushing mills in the Miami Valley. Minneapolis, where the two former Ohioans started their joint venture, became one of the nation's principal flax markets. By the time they opened up in Minneapolis, Archer, fifty-five, and Daniels, forty-seven, had had more than fifty years' experience between them in various linseed-oil ven-tures. Like other early-twentieth-century business partners, they were happy to share an office. Theirs, with two facing rolltop desks, was tucked into a corner of a crushing mill. They were frugal and formal: they saved incoming envelopes to use as scratch paper, and they addressed one another, at least within a third party's hearing, as "Mister." Archer tended to be the in-house member of the team, Daniels the man of the world who fraternized hither and yon, to the point where he seemed a natural choice for the presidency of the National Paint, Oil, and Varnish Association.

In 1923, the firm became Archer Daniels Midland when the partners absorbed the Midland Linseed Products Compa-ny, a few of whose crushing plants abutted theirs. Forthwith, ADM, with 344 presses in nine mills, became the largest linseed-oil processor extant, offering eighteen different grades of it to manufacturers of paint, varnish, printing ink, oilcloth, and soap. By then, both founders had welcomed sons into the business. Thomas Daniels was its treasurer, and Shreve Archer vice president. (The following year, though only thirty-six, he'd be president.) Before their deaths—John Daniels, at seventy-four, in 1931, George Archer, at eighty-two, in 1932—the fathers turned over ever-increasing responsibility to the sons.

ADM soon began to diversify. It started processing grain in 1927, and in 1929 it converted two linseed plants into soybean crushing. When the owners decided, in 1939, to build a plant specifically to handle soybeans, they picked Decatur as a site.

Shreve Archer was willing enough to commit himself and his firm's capital to faith in the potential of the soybean, but by and large his associates remembered, and respected, him for his caution. When they were engaged in trading grain and other commodities, he never stopped preaching to them the virtues of hedging. He would say over and over, "If I wanted to speculate, I wouldn't need any flour mills or processing plants. All I would need would be a desk and a telephone." Julius Hendel, the Andreases' hedging schoolmaster, would ringingly have concurred.

After Shreve Archer's death, at only forty-seven, in 1959, Thomas Daniels was in charge. He was an uncommon Midwesterner. He had gone to Yale, taking a string of polo ponies along, and had embarked on a career in the Foreign Service until he was persuaded to come into the family fold. He did a considerable amount of traveling abroad—his Foreign Service training clearly was an asset—and one thing that worried him was how standoffish Europeans seemed to be when it came to using soybean oil in the preparation of food for human consumption.

In Germany, Daniels was distressed to learn, a big margarine maker wouldn't touch the stuff. Italy had declared such blending illegal. In Spain, of course, it was olive oil or *nada*.

Daniels, whose sentiments would be reprised by Dwayne Andreas a generation later, said in the 1950s:

> The Americans are a value-conscious people. The protein hunger of the American people is a potential multibillion-dollar market. The soybean is our finest source of vegetable protein. It is best qualified to satisfy that hunger. The industry needs all the research and merchandising it can muster. And both at home and abroad we need to do some good old-fashioned American selling.

The company kept growing. By 1962, it was selling in good American fashion in Europe and Latin America, and it was into new products, among them Airy Fairy coffee-cake mix, castor oil—much in demand as an aircraft-engine lubricant—and whale oil. With some Peruvian partners, ADM ran a whaling station near Lima, a berth for three ships that went out and killed two thousand whales a year. The seven thousand metric tons of sperm oil these hunts garnered—ideal for cosmetics and for automatic motor-car transmissions because temperature changes didn't affect its viscosity—made ADM the largest United States marketer of the product. The company's participation in that questionable sideline lasted until 1967, when it was abandoned as unmanageable and unprofitable.

15

I didn't make the company grow. It just grew
under me. I feel like a june bug sitting on
top of a heap of ever-increasing manure,
wondering how he ever got to be king of
so big a mountain.

—DOA

O F the five Andreas brothers—their sister, Lenore,
who died in 1969, was married to Marvin Steele, a
Miami Airport Administration employee—Dwayne
was next to the youngest. All but the oldest, Osborn, born in
1903, were business partners for much of their lives. Osborn
was the maverick. He was at one time or another a concert
pianist, an English teacher, the author of books on Henry
James and Joseph Conrad, and in the end a suicide, in 1967,
while awaiting trial on a stock-rigging indictment. He left
trusts to take care of his widow and two sons, but Lowell and
Dwayne didn't want any of that money to be touched, so they
undertook thenceforth to assume responsibility for their kinfolk.

Albert, the second-oldest brother, and overall probably
the one closest to Dwayne, was born in 1907. An active
trader on the Minneapolis Grain Exchange, he was on the

ADM board of directors, starting in 1972, for fourteen years. In 1985, at seventy-eight, he was named director emeritus. He was credited by his brethren for thinking up the melliflu-ent name "Honeymead" for *that* venture. More significantly, in 1970 he established, and then ran, one of the new family company's most flourishing subsidiaries, ADM Corn Sweet-eners. Albert was also the main investor in the North Ameri-can Cement Company, a non-ADM-affiliated organization located in New York City, or "out East," in the idiom of his son Martin, who succeeded him as the head of Corn Sweet-eners and as a full-fledged ADM board member. Meanwhile, Albert had handsomely profited from a sale of North Ameri-can Cement and was spending most of his time in Florida. He liked the South. Once, in younger and more larksome days, he had gone to the Minneapolis airport to catch a plane for a business meeting in Chicago. But it was cold, and when he noticed that a plane was about to take off for Miami from a nearby gate, he hopped aboard.

Lowell, the youngest of the brothers, joined Dwayne at Honeymead in 1947 on getting out of the army, and they worked together ever afterward. Dwayne's closest ally when First Interoceanic bought into ADM in 1965, Lowell soon joined him on its board, and in the ensuing years he filled a number of high-level slots there—president and chairman of the executive committee among them. At last report, he owned $60-odd million worth of ADM stock. Sometimes he liked to jest about the family's rise to affluence. One time when he was playing gin rummy on an ADM plane with Dwayne's son, Michael, they were about to land. Michael, who was a few dollars ahead, wanted to quit. "If you don't give me one more chance to get even," his uncle said, "I'm going to tell your father's old-est brother how much Dwayne spent on this here airplane."

Browsers through the proxy statements issued by ADM on the eve of its annual meetings have become accustomed to such explanatory paragraphs as the 1989 one:

D. O. Andreas [elsewhere in statement: common stock owned: 8,891,568; cash compensation: $1,337,500] and L. W.

Andreas are brothers. G. Allen Andreas, Jr., Vice-President of the Company, President of ADM Leasco, Inc., a subsidiary of the Company, and Chief Financial Officer for European operations, is a nephew of these two Directors. M. D. Andreas [that's Executive Vice President Michael, with 2,186,526 shares of his own and cash compensation of $512,500] is the son of D. O. Andreas and a nephew of L. W. Andreas. M. L. Andreas is a nephew of D. O. Andreas and L. W. Andreas [and son also, of course, of A. M. Andreas, but *emeriti* don't rate being listed]. G. Allen Andreas, Jr. [no shareholder asked how come he got a name spelled out], M. D. Andreas and M. L. Andreas are cousins.

Glenn Allen Andreas, Sr., brother, father, and uncle, was an ADM shareholder himself when the family first moved in on the company, but he sold out to Dwayne and Lowell and concentrated on banking—Iowa's Pella National Bank becoming his base of operations. At Pella, Glenn handled the bookkeeping for much of his brothers' scattered interests. His son G. Allen has since mid-1989 been stationed in Brussels, from which outpost his kith and kin hope he can keep a watchful eye on continental developments foreshadowing the fateful European economic year of 1992. "We trust him," his cousin Michael says, "and besides, he's an Andreas, and that helps with connections." Dwayne's son also said, not long after his uncle Albert bowed out as one of thirteen active ADM directors, "We don't want to have too many Andreases on the board. We don't want the rest of 'em to think they're surrounded, even if they are."

At Dwayne A.'s insistence, ADM's annual reports, markedly unlike those of comparable corporations, never carry photographs of high-level company executives. If they did, there would have to be identifying captions, and some shareholders might get apprehensive at the proliferation of the same surname.

Michael's first cousin Martin, reflecting on family-cum-company, has said, "We all love the business and are working toward a kind of common goal—making things change and making things grow." Dwayne Andreas is not much given to hyperbole, but his relatives do not consider themselves bound by his reticence. "I always say that Uncle Dwayne is our number one salesman," Martin Andreas says, "and by 'one' I mean in the whole United States of America. He has his fingers on the pulse of the trade world." Martin A., incidentally, makes his wife irritable when they go grocery shopping together because he has an unbreakable and irresistible and time-consuming penchant for scrutinizing the small type on labels of food products to ascertain whether all the products that contain soybeans—and they are legion—clearly say they do.

By 1967, when the Andreases, still operating out of Minneapolis, had moved into ADM—its annual sales stood at $370 million—Dwayne's name was familiar throughout the farm belt, but he was less well-known beyond it. A *New York Times* dispatch from Rome, reporting that the Hubert Humphreys had called on Pope Paul VI, mentioned that the vice president and his wife were accompanied by "Mr. and Mrs. Duane Andrews."*

BusinessWeek knew better. "Already Minneapolis grainmen see the Andreas influence at work in a tightening of ADM management," it said. "In the future they expect the Andreas name to play a more active role in company affairs." The magazine also said, without citing any specific sources, "Many find him exceedingly charming and affable; some feel he is icy and ambitious." Icy charm, ambitious affability; the man seemed to have everything, including an unlimited potential. Andreas himself kept expressing surprise that he had got as far as he had. "I didn't make the company grow," he said. "It just grew under me. I feel like a june bug sitting on top of a heap of ever-increasing manure, wondering how he ever got to be king of so big a mountain."

*On October 17, 1989, Mikhail Gorbachev dropped in at the opening of USA '89, a trade show in Moscow. A photograph transmitted by the Associated Press identified the man at the Soviet president's right as Prime Minister Nikolai Ryzhkov. But it wasn't; it was anonymity's long-suffering favorite Dwayne Andreas.

For Andreas, as 1968 came around, having a big company to run was one thing. Having Hubert Humphrey running for president was another, and more than once it seemed to take precedence. Aside from contributing $100,000 of his own to his friend's campaign, Andreas was an assiduous raider of others' funds. There were many large-scale potential donors who might have refused another solicitor but who for business reasons found it prudent to respect his requests. (Big businessmen are resignedly aware that they inhabit a quid-pro-quo world. Many soft-drink manufacturers have dropped sugar as their sweetener in favor of fructose, which ADM coaxes from corn. "If the president of Coca-Cola calls me and says, 'I'm raising money for so and so for the senator from Georgia,'" Andreas says, "what am I going to do? Say no to our biggest customer?")

For Humphrey, Andreas was also a doubly valuable sounding board. He could, with proven expertise, predict reactions to proposed statements or policies of both the Grange and the boardroom. He could also be entrusted with confidential missions: to phone David Rockefeller at his summer home in Maine, for instance, soon after Humphrey became the Democratic nominee, to inquire whether the banker would, depending on how the vote went in November, care to be secretary of the treasury. Rockefeller said he'd think about it. When the presidency went to Nixon—who would no doubt have been equally happy to have him on board—there was no need to respond. Robert Strauss has since said he is positive that if Humphrey had won, his first choice for Treasury would have been Dwayne Andreas.

Once again, Humphrey and Andreas spent election night together, dining at Andreas's Lake Minnetonka home (no wine, said the inquisitive *Minneapolis Tribune*) on—their appetites apparently unaffected by early returns—boned pheasant with cream sauce, wild rice with fresh mushrooms, squash, green beans, water chestnuts, salad with cherry tomatoes, caramel rolls with Minnesota butter, and homemade apple pie with both ice cream and cheddar cheese.

For all his loyalty to and love for Humphrey, Andreas was never one to put all his political eggs in one basket. As he had been Tom Dewey's guest at the Republican convention that nominated Nixon, so now did he accept another Dewey invitation, to attend the new president's January inaugural. Soon afterward, Nixon would appoint Andreas—Dewey had a hand in that, too—to something called an Advisory Council on Management Improvement.

Andreas, as usual, did not feel the least bit uncomfortable about hobnobbing with the chieftains of rival political tribes. Years after that election, the *Washington Post*, curious about his capacity for hedging in government as well as hedging in business, asked him about substantial contributions he had made, in 1972, to both Humphrey, vainly seeking renomination, and Nixon, successfully seeking reelection. The answer:

> I talked to Hubert before I gave to Nixon, and he said, "Dwayne, you'd be a fool not to give money to Nixon," said Mr. Andreas. "They were good friends, Nixon and Hubert. My God, I carried messages back and forth between them for 10 years."

Another time, mulling over some of the important personages who had crossed his path over the many years, Andreas said that among them all there were three he would characterize as heroic—Winston Churchill, Hubert Humphrey, and Richard Nixon.

In 1969, Andreas shifted ADM's headquarters from Minneapolis to Decatur. By then, feeling that it did not mesh properly with food processing and commodity trading, and also because it was unprofitable, he had got rid of a chemical division that made resins, plastics, alcohols, and various additives to fabric softeners, waterproofers, and the like. By 1989, though, Andreas would be far more receptive to chemistry, and ADM was building two new plants at Decatur so it could branch out into biochemicals. The ones he had in mind were incontestably complementary to the company's traditional lines of business, for corn was the raw material from which the output of both facilities would be fabricated: from the one, liquid sorbitol, bacitracin, penicillin, and vitamin C, destined for the pharmaceutical and cosmetics industries; and from the other, amino acids—tryptophan, threonine, and lysine—for the feed industry. Lysine enhances growth in chickens and hogs and also makes meat leaner. Andreas, who never thinks small (and who carries scraps of paper in his pockets to remind himself of all these additions to his cornucopia of products), has expressed the hope that by 1995 one hundred and seventy thousand tons of this additive will be used world-wide every year, and that ADM will be churning out half of that.

An inveterate global traveler such as Hubert Humphrey would not change his ways merely because he'd failed to become chief of state. In the summer of 1969, he embarked on a grand tour of half a dozen European nations and the Soviet Union. Andreas, to nobody's surprise, went along. (It was earlier that year, after a stay at Sea View, that Humphrey wrote to Inez and Dwayne: "Both of you have done so much for the Humphreys that there is no possible way that we can ever repay you except through sincere affection and appreciation.") Humphrey was by now chairman of the board of a Washington think tank, the Woodrow Wilson Center for International Affairs. (In 1986, President Reagan named Andreas to be vice chairman.) Its full-time director, Benjamin H. Read, who'd rated high in Dean Rusk's State Department, also went along. The *Apollo II* had just landed on the moon, and during a Yugoslavian stop Marshal Tito remarked, when the trio dropped in at his summer residence at Brioni, that he wished America and Russia would thenceforth worry less about celestial objectives and worry more about resolving problems on earth.

Andreas had dropped in, alone, at the White House not long before, and the president had told him that he wanted to end the war in Vietnam, and that he was prepared to extend a considerable sum in new credits to the Soviet Union if it would help. Humphrey et al. had a two-hour session at the Kremlin with chairman of the Council of Ministers, Aleksey Kosygin. When the subject of Vietnam came up, Andreas slipped Humphrey a note: "I...have talked with President Nixon. [He] is eager to throw open all possible avenues of trade. But public opinion won't permit congressmen to agree until Vietnam is over. *Then* he will pursue trade questions urgently....Would it be fitting for me (or you) to say this?"

Humphrey scribbled back: "If it can be brought in, I should do so, since the discussion seems to be entirely between Kosygin and myself."

But he didn't, and a while later, when he excused himself for a moment, Andreas delivered the message himself. Kosygin listened with, near as Andreas could determine, impassivity.

In April 1988, at another Kremlin get-together with another Soviet leader, Andreas rose and said, "Mr. Gorbachev, the day I was leaving New York, Mr. Nixon, a friend of yours, with whom you do not always agree but who you know is a friend of détente, gave me a message to be passed on to you secretly. So I am going to give you his message here in privacy with you and eight hundred of your closest friends. Mr. Gorbachev, President Nixon sends his congratulations that you were on the cover of *Time* magazine as Man of the Year, and he believes devoutly that, when the world sees that you are achieving the goals of glasnost and perestroika you, for certain sure, Mr. Gorbachev, will be the Man of the Century. I propose a toast to that."*

Whoever transcribed the proceedings set down: "(APPLAUSE, STANDING TOAST)."

During the Kosygin meeting, the chairman told his guests he'd heard of a boar hunt they'd just been on with Minister of Defense Alexei Grechko. Did the Americans know, Kosygin

---

*In 1990, *Time* did at least designate Gorbachev its Man of the Decade.

added, that the purchase agreement signed when the United States acquired Alaska gave the Russians the right to hunt big game there for something like ninety-nine years? They hoped he was only kidding.

The boar hunt had begun as a sort of joke itself. After his loss to Nixon, Humphrey had made courtesy calls, in a bid-you-farewell gesture, to several foreign ambassadors. One was Jakob Malik, the Soviet envoy to the United Nations, not widely celebrated for a sense of humor. During their exchange of banalities, Malik had said something about hoping he would see Humphrey one day soon in Russia. Humphrey had joshingly replied that a half dozen years or so ago, when as a senator he'd been in Moscow witnessing the formalization of some sort of bilateral pact, the subject of hunting had come up in a chat Humphrey had had in 1963 when Grechko had been head of the Soviet Missile Force. "That defense minister of yours is a deadbeat," Humphrey now said jocularly to Malik. "He invited me to go boar-hunting in the Urals and then never followed up."

Malik had evidently dashed off a cable to Moscow about how the former vice president of the United States had been grievously insulted. And in due course, Ambassador Dobrynin passed along an invitation from the minister of defense.

Humphrey took Andreas and Read along. They were never told in advance what the next step would be. They were in the middle of a meal in Moscow when somebody said, "Your cars are waiting." They were whisked off to an elaborate hunting reserve a couple of hours north of the capital. Catherine the Great, they judged, would have found it acceptable. A hunt master appeared and announced they'd be boar-stalking that evening. They were issued Red Army fatigue uniforms—what the Republican Party wouldn't have given for a snapshot of Humphrey so accoutred!—and Red Army rifles and tendered a bit of instruction in handling them. The recoil of Read's rifle gave him a bloody nose.

Then they were packed off to four separate blinds—or tree houses, each a commodious perch reached by a spiral staircase and shrouded in yards of mosquito netting. Inside each was a table with yards of alcohol. Soon, some animals that looked like pigs arrived, lured by a trail of bread crumbs, and the visitors politely fired a few can't-miss volleys. Although Andreas liked to make light of his marksmanship, he brought down an eighty-pound boar, and one of his hosts later sent him, as a memento of the outing, a ten-pound iron elk. Then it was back to Catherine's lodge, and an interminable sequence of toasts to boars' ears and tails and snouts, and practically every other part of their anatomy that could be isolated.

It was at midnight only that their titular host materialized, and that called for a banquet, with seven or eight glasses at each table setting. Andreas and Read, for what they maintained was the first and only time in their experience, found themselves almost as talkative as the notoriously voluble Humphrey.

The following day, the last words Andreas and Read could recall their hosts' having uttered at bedtime was an announcement that the vehicles to take them elk-hunting would be departing at five A.M., and the last word heard from Humphrey, to the astonishment of his companions, who had never heard Hubert turn down anything, was a ringing, if a trifle slurred, *"Nyet!"*

"Hubert Humphrey was an unusual man in many ways," Andreas says of his departed friend. "He could read a book and digest it in one short plane flight. He had an extraordinary respect for brains. One of his strengths [one that Dwayne shared] was that he knew how to deal with both Republicans and Southern Democrats. When the history of his period is written, Hubert will emerge like Henry Clay. He knew how to compromise, and to do it without confrontation. He was always looking for things that two sides could agree on."

When the Hubert H. Humphrey Institute of Public Affairs was established, in 1977, at the University of Minnesota, one of the first checks received to sustain it was for a thousand dollars, delivered by Dwayne Andreas, from Richard Nixon. Henry Clay would surely have approved.

(Andreas himself has been one of the Institute's most faithful benefactors. In 1976, after Spain finally got rid of Franco, Dwayne's plenipotentiary friend Manolo Barturen sent a delegation of technocrats from Madrid to seek his advice on restructuring the liberated nation's economy. One upshot of that visit was the underwriting each year by Andreas of the cost of exporting two economists from the Humphrey Institute to the Spanish government. In Madrid they are known as "the Minnesotans.")

Later in 1977, with Humphrey gravely ill, Senator Robert Dole, who, of course, is a Republican, succeeded in getting a new Health and Human Services headquarters building in Washington named after his longtime colleague across the Capitol aisle. A Humphrey portrait by Charles Levitan, on loan from the artist, was duly hung inside. In 1981, Levitan asked the administration—by now a Reagan one—either to return the portrait or to buy it, for a reasonable $3000. Someone in the department balked, so Andreas got together with an old friend, John G. McMillan, of the Northwest Pipeline Corporation, and they paid for it and donated it to the nation. Humphrey died on January 13, 1978, shortly after he and Muriel spent a long weekend at Andreas's country home in Moweaqua, Illinois. Andreas persuaded his widow to invite Nixon to the funeral. The only time an Andreas daughter ever saw her father cry was at that ceremony.

Are you aware that a pound of catfish
requires a mere one point one pounds
of feed? Think of it!

—DOA

I n 1971, a year in which Andreas was called "a little-
known but powerful businessman" by the *New York
Times* and by the *Minneapolis Tribune* "a prominent
supporter of the Democratic party nationally and locally," he
was accepted for membership in the largely Republican Blind
Brook Country Club in New York State's largely Republican
Westchester County—initiation fee and dues: $9,064, but, he
wanted it known, a strictly-for-business outlay, and accordingly his office address was to be used on its membership
roster. Concurrently, his status at the office became more
lofty; he assumed the titles, never to be relinquished, of
chairman and chief executive officer. ADM's sales had ascended
to what then seemed an almost giddy $660 million a year,
and it was making itself heard well beyond food processing; it

set up one dominion, called Independent Bancorporation, to furnish various services to Midwest banks.

That was a big year, too, when it came to Andreas's persistent proselytizing for the soybean. The Food and Nutrition Service of the Department of Agriculture gave its imprimatur to the use of soybeans as an alternate food for part of the meat requirements in child-nutrition programs. That translated into the channeling of 50 million pounds of soy protein into school lunches every year. A rather exclusive promotional outfit called the Food Protein Council, later the more boldly named Soy Protein Council—it had only three members: ADM, Cargill, and their rival, Central Soya—let it be known that 17 pounds of unadorned meat would yield one hundred lunch portions, but if you added to it 5.1 pounds of hydrated soy protein, you'd end up—presto!—with one hundred and *forty-three* nourishing servings. Those were the kinds of statistics that Andreas always relished. He liked to point out, for example, that whereas a single acre of farmland could yield (through grazing) 58 pounds of edible meat protein, that same plot given to tillage could account for 180 pounds of wheat protein, 313 of corn, and—here came the clincher—584 of soybean.

Andreas likes to think ahead, and globally. As early as 1966 he was contemplating doing business with China— specifically, becoming a large-scale purchaser of that then-isolated country's surplus soybeans. He was a member of a President's General Advisory Committee on Foreign Assistance Programs, and in that capacity wrote to the State Department requesting that the prohibition against travel to China be deleted from his passport. He wanted to go there, he explained, "to get some feel, at first hand, of economic conditions, especially in agriculture." The State Department said all right, but if he got into any trouble not to expect Washington to bail him out. That was all irrelevant, because Peking wouldn't let him in. In June 1971, even before President Nixon's memorable gulf-bridging trip to the People's Republic, Andreas made another move. He wrote to Huang

Hua, then Chinese ambassador to Canada, proposing that Andreas and—who else?—Hubert Humphrey be allowed to visit China. A similar request was cabled to Peking for the attention of Chou En-lai, who Andreas hoped was in fact his acquaintance from Moscow back in 1952. Andreas was too far ahead of the game; his overtures went unacknowledged.

That same year of 1971 got him involved in other far-flung connections. Back in his Cargill days, traveling on a plane between Nice and Paris, he had fallen in with Ismail Habib, a member of the leading banking family in Pakistan, the chairman of a construction company and a director of a dozen corporations in, among other areas, sugar, cotton, insurance, and investments. Habib, whose wife had taken ill while they were in Europe, had used up most of his available foreign currency for medical expenses. Andreas, though they had barely met, offered to lend him any amount of money he needed, interest free, and didn't even bother about a receipt. Habib was understandably impressed. Over the next twenty years, the two men became close friends and also business allies, sharing an interest in a Karachi-based venture mainly to convert Pakistani rice into fructose.

Habib was traveling in Europe in December 1971 when Pakistan and India went to war. He was told that it would be inadvisable for him to go home. He'd sent Andreas postcards from various stops in Germany, Holland, and Switzerland, but without any return addresses. Andreas, hearing that he was stateless and near penniless, had him traced to Zurich, phoned him there, and said right off, Habib recalls, "Ismail, how much money shall I send you?"

Over the next few years, Andreas footed the tuition bills for Habib's two sons at a Swiss boarding school, put their father on the ADM payroll as a two-thousand-dollar-a-month consultant, with the vaguest of responsibilities, and finally arranged for him to immigrate to Canada. After all that, it is hardly surprising that in 1989 a Habib appraisal of Andreas— "In the name of God the Beneficent the Merciful"—would go: "He is one of those rare people who is a real friend in good times and bad. If I phoned him and he was not in his office, he returned my call within a couple of hours from whatever part of the world he was in. He is God's good man and the world is so much nicer because of him."

Just a few months before Tom Dewey died in 1971, he had introduced Andreas to an international figure who emphatically didn't need monetary aid—the multimillion-aire shipping magnate Daniel K. Ludwig, mentions of whom in the press were usually embellished with some such adjective as "legendary," "enigmatic," or "reclusive." Andreas and Ludwig began meeting for lunch whenever they happened to be in the same place at the same time. "People seem to think of DK as a kind of tough old man," Andreas says, "but he's really very pleasant."

They traveled together to Brazil for an inspection of a million or so acres in the Amazon jungle to which Ludwig had been granted exploitative rights. They were able to fly in readily enough; Ludwig had his own landing strip. He also had a paper mill in operation; he had had it built in Japan and floated up a river. DK thought Dwayne might be interested in jointly producing palm oil and rice out there. (Palm oil had not yet become ostracized in cholesterol-conscious circles.) Andreas was indeed, but their plans ran afoul of the relevant Brazilian authorities. "The problem," Andreas said afterward, "was that the government was all smiles while Ludwig was putting in money, but once it was in, they began to turn hostile."

Andreas and Ludwig still wanted to do something together besides eating lunch. For a while, they pinned their hopes on catfish. The study that they commissioned Martin Sorkin, Andreas's liaison with Washington Republicans, to make for them read promisingly enough, but on reflection they concluded that the field was less well suited for large corporations than for small farmers. They reverted to lunch. But Andreas had got hooked, as it were, on catfish. Fewer than 6 million pounds of *Tetalurus punctatus* had been marketed in the United States in 1970. Its ugly appearance and off-putting name in English were no help when it came to competing with swordfish or brook trout or filet of sole. Andreas thought the species had great promise notwithstanding. And there was method in what some looked on as his madness; catfish, like chickens, thrived on soy meal.

Catfish, fattening themselves contentedly on soy, began to crack the acceptance barrier. By 1989, they had become one of the ten most popular species of fish in America. Catfish farming—8 percent of it in man-made ponds that covered ninety thousand acres in the Mississippi delta—became the biggest aquacultural industry in the country, with a yearly output (hardly a "catch," since they were cultivated) of 300 million pounds. A World Catfish Festival became an annual lower-Mississippi-River event.

Andreas hasn't yet found time to put in an appearance, but he has been very much involved in the booming business. ADM has a plant north of the Delta, at Clarksdale, churning out high-protein soymeal. When in a statistics-citing mood, Andreas may interrupt a conversation on haute cuisine with an aside on feed-to-food conversion ratios—the weight of feed, that is, necessary for the generation of so-and-so-much food. "Are you aware," he will say, "that it's seven plus to one for cow, four to one for pig, and two point two to one for chicken, whereas"—here he may pause for dramatic effect—"a pound of catfish requires a mere one point one pounds of feed. Think of it!"

Decatur restaurants now feature Friday-night catfish specials. At Andreas's home there, broiled catfish is apt to be the pièce de résistance almost any night, and guests have noticed that his eagerness to have them share his fondness for it is as touching as a bride's hoping to have her fare approved by her mother-in-law. "Good as Dover sole, isn't it?" he will inquire with a trace of anxiety. More and more people across the nation are beginning to agree with him. The *Boston Globe,* with no prompting from Andreas or any other interested party, has declared: "The pampered darlings have a heavenly taste."

Pampered they are indeed. The proprietors of the Mississippi ponds treat their growing fish to a diet, along with soymeal, of fish meal, vitamins, minerals, and corn. This last appeals to Andreas, too, because corn is never—*can* never—be far from his thoughts. (For all the money he has made from other commodities on earth, he would be the last to dispute the assertion of the late Paul Christoph Mangelsdorf, perhaps America's preeminent corn breeder, that corn is "a cereal treasure of immensely greater value than the spices which Columbus traveled so far to seek in his search for a westward route to India.") In season, Inez and Dwayne serve corn on the cob, fresh picked, naturally, with their broiled catfish, but that kind of tasteful use of corn consumes a mere one-thousandth or less—sweet corn is grown on 174,000 acres, field corn on 72 *million*—of America's 8-billion-bushel annual crop.

The nerve center of ADM's headquarters building at Decatur—the war room, or situation room, some liken it to—is an open area, with the offices of President Jim Randall and his top brass around its flanks, in which one hundred commodity traders and their one hundred assistants sit at desks surrounded by and attached to computers and screens and telephones and other up-to-date miracles of technology that keep them in constant touch with commodities markets around the world. (Andreas, en route from his sixth-floor aerie to the executives' dining room, has to pass through their ranks. At lunch, he usually sits facing yet another monitor above the door, from which changing market quotations can be ingested with every mouthful. For all that he has risen above the nitty-gritty of trading, it is still in his blood. He can hardly pass a ringing telephone anywhere without picking it up.) Every so often, the second-floor traders, their reliance on ultramodern gadgetry be hanged, are graphically reminded what their feverish buying and selling is fundamentally all about. On a table alongside their battle stations, in times of market instability, there is laid out for their sober observation and reflection and perhaps even to instill in these mortals to whom six-figure deals are run-of-the-mill a modicum of humility, a couple of piteously shriveled and crippled ears of honest-to-goodness *Zea mays*.

*   *   *

For much of ADM's history, its processing of corn—currently about 2.5 billion of the 8 billion bushels of the annual crop pass through its many hands a year—consisted mainly of grinding out corn oil and syrup and starch and grits and meal. There were many uses, of course, for each of these prosaic categories. Cornstarch, for instance, could become a valued constituent of, to cite just a few of its destinations, paper, adhesives, charcoal briquettes, olives, vitamin pills, chewing gum, and instant soups designed specifically to be microwavable.

ADM Milling, one of, at last count, twenty-four subsidiaries and divisions in Andreas's ever-expanding realm—among others, by the end of 1989, were the Tabor Grain Company, the Fleischmann-Kurth Malting Company, the Southern Cotton Oil Company, the American River Transportation Company, the Agrinational Insurance Company, and Gooch Foods—sells 4 million pounds' worth daily of some one hundred ingredients for cereals, bread, muffins, and mixes. One ADM food-ingredients catalogue lists seventeen different varieties of corn syrup alone.

ADM Milling, né Commander Larabee, had joined the Andreas business family in 1943. A few years later, its proprietor, John Vanier, had casually mentioned to Andreas that he'd like to sell him another important milling company someday. Now, Vanier was on the phone. He had turned eighty, he said, and was putting his affairs in order and wanted to make good on his pledge.

Andreas, who sometimes seems to feel that the orderly progress of business is impeded by such roadblocks as lawyers and accountants, hustled to Salina, Kansas, in twenty-five-below-zero weather, and rendezvoused with Vanier in a hotel room. The older man said right off, "You have to know where we stand," and fished a scrap of paper out of a pocket with some figures scribbled on it. Then he quoted a price and held out his hand and Andreas shook it and that was that. There was one caveat: "I may be a couple of hundred thousand or so off on our twenty-million-bushel inventory," Vanier said, "but we can straighten that out."

No problem, Andreas said, and it wasn't.

The ADM stock that Vanier's children received for their mills as a result of that corporate merger was, seventeen years later, worth nearly $150 million. And just as the Archers and the Danielses had remained friendly after they were taken over, so was it with the Vaniers. John Vanier's son John, Jr., and his son-in-law H. D. "Joe" Hale joined the ADM board, and they have sat there contentedly ever since. Hale managed their six flour mills. Andreas was happy to have him continue to manage them, and while he was at it, also to run ADM's own mills, all of which were banded together as ADM Milling. Now Hale manages 30 flour mills.

Early in 1990, Andreas had a call from Joe Hale. Some Japanese wanted to buy ADM Milling, he felt obliged to report.

Andreas, his shareholders' interests necessarily to be considered—and Hale of course was a major one—asked, "How much?"

"Well, our book value is a hundred million and they're offering three hundred," Hale said.

"Gee, that's a lot of money," said Andreas, hoping he wouldn't be talked into accepting it.

"We have a lot of money," Hale said. "What we need is more mills."

Andreas was much relieved at this meeting of minds.

The traditional derivatives of corn were large-volume products, but also low-profit ones. What revolutionized and modernized and made potentially far more lucrative the manipulating of the dependable old crop was wet corn milling. In this process, cornstarch—itself the result of soaking kernels in a caustic solution—is treated with an enzyme, and various sweeteners are the result. The Western world became aware in 1969 of a new technology, perfected in Japan, for converting cornstarch's dextrose into more highly sweetened fructose. ADM didn't get into that until 1971, and its first enhanced sweeteners were all right as a substitute for sugar in baked and canned goods, but they weren't sweet enough for the finicky soft-drink industry. (Fructose, though usually less costly, is unlikely ever to displace sugar altogether; it's a liquid and doesn't sit well on a tea tray alongside a creamer.) What that industry's giants, the cola people, wanted and eventually got was HFCS—high-fructose corn syrup—extra-sweetened dextrose that was obtained through the further rearrangement of dextrose atoms, thanks to the catalytic influence of yet another enzyme.

Today, more than 7 billion pounds of HFCS—nearly 3.5 billion of them bearing the ADM stamp—end up each year as soft-drink sweeteners. The company began to take a serious interest in this alternative to sugar in 1973, largely at the instigation of Dwayne's nephew Martin, a fructose buff from way back. (His Decatur office is decorated with framed portraits of the preeminent objects of his affection: wife, children, grandchildren, and cornstalks.) In 1970, Martin and his father, Albert, had launched a modest fructose-making enterprise of their own, called Corn Sweeteners, which Albert's younger brother Dwayne bought into for ADM in 1972 and acquired whole hog the following year. (For a spell, the city of Decatur's championship women's softball team was called ADM Pride. The name was dropped because the ladies were too good; Dwayne didn't cotton to the idea of an outfit identified with his company beating up on its opposition right and left.)

Martin Andreas became ADM's chief HFCS salesman, and he spent long, patient hours as a missionary trying to persuade the soft-drink industry leaders of the merits of the new sweetener. More than 50 percent of all the sweeteners bottlers now use stem from corn. (The message imparted by one ADM Sunday-morning television commercial was that it would take 18 billion honeybees a year to produce the equivalent of the company's single-day output of fructose.) But before this could come to pass, ADM had to build a $50 million plant to turn dextrose into the higher-quality fructose that Martin had learned in his pilgrimages to soft-drink shrines would be acceptable. And before Uncle Dwayne would persuade his board of directors to authorize that outlay, he asked his nephew one question that Martin didn't especially want to have to answer: "If we make it, how do you know you can sell it?"

Martin got a go-ahead mainly on faith. "It was a major gamble," he said afterward. "The only thing it changed in the soft-drink world was everything."

Welch's Sparkling Grape Soda and Mountain Dew were relatively easy converts. But it took longer and was harder to please the finicky taste buds of Coca-Cola and Pepsi-Cola flavor factotums. In due course, they saw the light. By 1977, HFCS accounted for 25 percent of Coke sweeteners; and by 1980, 50 percent. In 1983, when Coke got to 75 percent, Pepsi, which had held back, came in at the 50 percent level. By 1983, fructose was in all the way, and sugar was out.

By 1989, ADM had a $300 million plant at Decatur dedicated exclusively to the production of HFCS, and forty corn-sweetener storage terminals scattered across the country, from Clewiston, Florida, to Tacoma, Washington, and from Alameda, California, to East Cambridge, Massachusetts. (And at Clinton, Iowa, there was an enzyme-making facility of such magnitude that it inspired the company to boast once to its shareholders that "ADM has become the world's largest commercial practitioner of biotechnology.") Even in 1984, a hundred railroad tank cars brimming with fructose were pulling out of Decatur every day, many of them toward the Southeast, and ADM, which had become the nation's largest shipper of freight, asked the railroads involved for a more favorable rate. The railroads demurred. ADM shrugged and at a cost of $2.5 million, installed huge stainless-steel tanks on a couple of barges and headed them down the Mississippi. It took only one such competitive shipment to persuade the railroads to capitulate. "These are some of the things you have to do," Martin Andreas said afterward.

While the nephew was plugging along toward his goal, the uncle was exhibiting his own brand of missionary zeal.

For a while, Dwayne carried around pocketsful of high-fructose pills, which he would tell people would not only raise a body's "sugar level" for four hours—more than the duration, his auditors could reflect, of most sugar-depleting athletic contests—but were also a first-rate hangover preventive because they reduced one's craving for alcohol, as had been determined—he would assert without much risk of on-the-spot refutation—by experiments at the University of Arkansas on pigs. (As Andreas hedges his political connections, so has it been with sweeteners; while he was pushing a sugar substitute, he also took over as yet another ADM subsidiary a Louisiana outfit with the challenging name of Supreme Sugar Company.)

When soft-drink aficionados get together at their favorite soda fountain to swap legends, they sometimes regale each other with accounts of how Dwayne Andreas personally brought about the surrender of the two men who counted most, J. Paul Austin and Donald Kendall, the omnipotent CEOs of, respectively, Coca-Cola and Pepsi-Cola. First, the yarn goes—and Andreas has yet to dispute it publicly—he had lunch at the Links with Austin, who said right off, "Dwayne, don't put your fifteen million or whatever it is into that fructose stuff. The Coca-Cola Company will never go for it. We use pure sugar and we always will."

"Paul," was Dwayne's response, "I'm telling you you're going to do it."

"Why?"

"It will save your company two hundred million dollars, and your shareholders would never stand for your *not* doing it."

Austin, a practical man even though he went to Harvard, left the matter up to his successor, Robert Goizueta, who had already seen the light.

Next, Andreas got together at "21" with Don Kendall and said Pepsi-Cola ought to join Coke on the fructose bandwagon.

"Dwayne, I've heard the Paul Austin story," said Kendall,

"and I want you to know right off that Pepsi is never going to switch to fructose."

"Yes, you are going to."

"Why?"

"Don," Andreas persisted, "you know how your sugar gets over here?"

"Sure, in big ships."

"Kept in holds, isn't it?"

"Yep."

"Ever look down inside one?"

"What for?"

"To see the rats. Biggest goddamn rats in the world. They feed on sugar. And sooner or later, unfortunately, they have to urinate."

"Oh, come on now," said Kendall.

"Don," said Andreas, moving in for the kill, "what happens when you put sugar in water?"

"It melts."

"Yes, and it turns yellow, too, doesn't it?"

Andreas's own on-the-record recollection of his persuading of his friends and customers is less vivid. "There was never any question in my mind that they'd have to use fructose," he says. "How could anybody have continued to run either company and not use it?"

Reuben Andreas and his family at home in Lisbon, Iowa, circa 1924. Dwayne is sitting, with dog, at his mother's feet.

Dwayne and Inez on one of their many White House visits.

A high-level agricultural conference in 1960. Left to right: Hubert
Humphrey, Orville Freeman, Dwayne O. Andreas, John F. Kennedy, and
M. W. Thatcher of the Farmers Union Grain Terminal Association.

The Andreases and the Humphreys call on Pope Paul VI at the Vatican.
(Photo by Pontificia Fotografia.)

Mother Teresa and two of her principal American friends and supporters.

Settling the affairs of the world? They have certainly tried.
(Andreas with Gorbachev and translator.)

At a Kremlin dinner that Gorbachev gave for Andreas as Chairman of the US-USSR Trade & Economic Council.

Never a man to put all his eggs in one basket, Andreas numbers Boris Yeltsin among his Soviet friends.

"I was just saying to the president that there'd been no negative reaction when I told Gorbachev to tear down the Berlin wall," Andreas said, "when a photographer popped out of an antechamber and snapped us."

With Supreme Court Justice Warren Burger, when President Reagan asked Andreas to be Chairman of the Foundation for the Commemoration of the U.S. Constitution.

The ever-expanding Decatur, Illinois, skyline prepares to embrace yet another ADM edifice, this one a plant for the production of multiple biochemicals.

Just a few of the products dependent on Archer Daniels Midland for their ingredients.

The proprietor of a newly opened Moscow fast-food establishment poses outside with a prospective customer.

I consider politics to be just
like the church.

—DOA

LIKE many another person of substantial means, Andreas
has a family foundation—ADM has another of its
own—which currently doles out about $800,000 a year.
"You think of that sort of thing as a way to make friends,"
Andreas says, "but the way it works out what you get is
thousands of requests, and when you can't respond to all of
them, you end up making enemies." There was no danger old
friend Hubert Humphrey would be among these. One of the
Andreas Foundation's investments was the 1965 purchase of
a lakeside cottage in Minnesota where Humphrey could
relax. In 1977, the Foundation inaugurated an annual
Hubert H. Humphrey First Amendment Freedoms Prize in
the amount of $10,000. The first recipient was Humphrey
himself.

The *Wall Street Journal* once dubbed Andreas a "generous

maverick," and his bounteousness has by many criteria been uncommon. His foundation, for instance, underwrote the June 1990 visit to Washington of a six-member Soviet delegation—part of a US-USSR Exchange on Mobility Technology—who attended the annual meeting of the President's Committee on Employment of Persons with Disabilities. His contributions are by no means exclusively charitable. Many of his principal beneficiaries, to be sure, have been conventional enough: the Anti-Defamation League of B'nai B'irth, the Southern Christian Leadership Conference, Decatur Boys Baseball, assorted schools and colleges. (Sister Jeanne O'Laughlin, asked once how importantly the gifts of Dwayne and Inez figured in Barry University's welfare, said, "I'd be dead in the water if it weren't for the two of them.") Low as is his opinion of how a lot of people in Washington perform, he has consistently urged his associates and employees, even if they stop far short of his inherited commitment to tithing, to donate at least 1 percent of their earnings to political campaigns— channeled, if they choose, through an ADM political action committee. Politicians are one thing, in his view, politic another. At least one of his notions about fund-raising and -giving would doubtless have confounded his Mennonite antecedents: "I consider politics to be just like the church," he says.

However other people may feel about such PACs, in his view businesses should interact with government in every legitimate way possible. Reflecting on his dedication to corporate political involvement at one ADM shareholders' meeting, and using the kind of farm lingo to which he often turns by way of emphasis or illustration, he said, "Living with the government in a state of coexistence is like a turkey living with a farmer until Thanksgiving. And we don't want to be the turkey in that relationship."

(To divert the smaller Andreas grandchildren, Inez would occasionally buy baby fowl from a Decatur hatchery and raise them. One year her menagerie comprised a turkey, a goose, and a brace of ducks. The goose became the leader of the flock. It conveyed the others to the Andreases' swimming pool and jumped in. The turkey obediently followed—and sank. While the children looked on in horror, Inez fished it out, gave it mouth-to-mouth resuscitation, wrapped it in a towel, and then, because it still seemed chilled, popped it into an oven. She was merely attempting, as she sought to explain instructively, to succor yet another innocent who had succumbed to peer pressure, but she had to pull it out in a hurry because the children thought she was trying to cook it alive.)

It has more than once been suggested, not surprisingly, that there is a touch of insensitivity to Andreas's largesse, and that it should not surprise him when critics wonder if his and his company's generosity, especially when politicians are involved, might not be a bit self-serving. Andreas's defenders like to point out that this staunch upholder and defender of do-gooders and liberals and even Democrats has also stoked the coffers of, for one, Senator Jesse Helms.

There have been times, though—difficult times—when Andreas has been accused in a very literal sense of being generous to a fault. The year 1972—a year in which *Parade* listed him among the thirty most powerful individuals in American politics—turned out to be one of those times. It was Hubert Humphrey's dream, when the year began, of once again running against Richard Nixon and reversing the outcome. Andreas was by now on companionable enough terms with Nixon, who had told him in the Oval Office in 1969, perhaps even then anticipating his own historic trip, "Dwayne, you'll be selling wheat to China before this term of my office is ended."

Still, Humphrey was Humphrey, and Andreas was happy to pledge $75,000 toward his old friend's persistent aspiration. That bubble burst abruptly when he lost the Democratic primary in California to his political protégé George McGovern. Andreas was fond of McGovern as a person and was more than once pleased to have him as a Sea View guest, but one Democratic contender per campaign appeared to be his limit. Before the year was out, he had lavished $157,000 upon various Nixon treasuries. When somebody asked Andreas how it was that he'd been so nearly concurrently supportive of both parties, he said it had been "an act of good citizenship."

In a speech Andreas would have given at Kansas State University had not a higher priority taken him to Moscow instead, he'd have said, "In your political activity, as a good citizen, I urge you to be flexible. Almost all good legislation is bipartisan. Remember, Democrats in power need good ambassadors to the Republicans, and Republicans need ambassadors to the Democrats. Both parties are seeking converts from the other side. That's what it's all about." There was yet more to come that election year. A new law, the Federal Election Campaign Act, went into effect on April 7, 1972. After that date, all political gifts had to be disclosed. A good deal of last-minute scrambling ensued, to beat the deadline. Notable among the heavy-breathing solicitors was Maurice H. Stans, the former secretary of commerce who was heading up the Committee to Re-elect the President. (Some people could not resist calling it CREEP.) Andreas was in Florida, on April 5, when he got a phone call from Stans. Could he count on Dwayne for a quick, off-the-record twenty-five thousand? Andreas hesitated. After all, it was for the nomination of Nixon, not the election, and Humphrey was running against other Democrats for the nomination, not against Nixon. But it couldn't hurt to hedge, especially if anonymity still prevailed. No problem, Stans assured him; he would send an emissary pronto to pick up the money. (Even then, leaders of the free society seemed to harbor doubts about the efficacy of the U.S. Postal Service.)

The courier was to be Kenneth H. Dahlberg, a hearing-aid entrepreneur from Minneapolis, a longtime Andreas acquaintance, and at the moment the head of the Minnesota Committee to Re-elect. (Later that year, Dahlberg and Andreas would be co-organizers of a new bank in Minnetonka, Minnesota, the granting of a federal charter for which was challenged by McGovern's headquarters as "unusually quick." It perhaps said something about American government bureaucracies that that characterization was applied to a procedure that took eighty-six days.) Andreas talked by phone with Dahlberg, who said he was on his way south. Until he arrived, Andreas said, he'd get some cash and put it in a safe deposit box. The immediate sequence of events thereafter is uncertain, but no matter. What did matter was that Dahlberg's plane to Florida was late, and that a weekend intervened, and that it was Monday, April 10, before he collected the money and converted it into a cashier's check and delivered that to Stans in Washington.

The next time anybody knew or much cared about the episode was in June, after the arrest of seven Republican-hired "plumbers" who broke into the Democratic National Committee's headquarters at the Watergate office building. The $25,000 check was soon found, along with other funds, in a bank account of one of the seven, Bernard L. Barker. When the source of that item was traced through Barker to Stans and the reelection committee, it was the first inkling the nation had that there might be—patently was—a link between the plumbers and the president.

Hubert Humphrey, asked to comment this time on the first and least of the revelations, said, with restraint, and maybe also amusement, "Let's put it this way: Dwayne has friends in both parties." And Andreas seemed perfectly willing to concur with that sentiment. A *Minneapolis Star* colum-nist would be purporting to quote him that summer—during the Republican nominating convention at Miami, where Andreas had shelled out $10,000 for a $500-a-plate dinner at the Fontainebleau and had had at his own table such unarguably top-drawer guests as the president's wife and daughters and the Nelson Rockefellers—as saying, like a career speculator, "I don't care who's president, just as long as I've got ten minutes' advance word." Dwayne says he never said it.

That wayward $25,000 was not the only political gift that was to cause Andreas embarrassment. On October 19, 1973, Archibald Cox, the Department of Justice's special prosecutor to delve into Watergate shenanigans, filed some charges against Andreas at Federal Court in Minneapolis. It was alleged that several contributions Andreas had made to

Humphrey during the 1968 campaign—in this instance, four, of $25,000 apiece—were illegal because they'd come from a corporation (the First Interoceanic, the family's private investment company) rather than from the donor's personal funds. Such corporate gifts were forbidden. As far as Andreas was concerned, it was all a technicality. He had simply borrowed the $100,000 from a company that he and his kin owned outright and within a month had paid it back.*

That, however, was not the way it looked to Cox—whose own role in the proceedings expired on October 20, when the president summarily fired him. The precise nature of the complaint against Andreas was "a criminal information," an offense in the misdemeanor class, and it had had to be filed suddenly because a few days later a five-year statute of limitations covering such transgressions would have expired. Mere misdemeanor notwithstanding, the accusation was no joke; if Andreas had been found guilty by the judge weighing the evidence alone in the absence of a jury, he could have been fined $1,000 and sentenced to a year's imprisonment on each of the four counts. As it turned out, he never even once showed up in court. (Cox and his staff did not press for his appearance, having heard—erroneously—that he was in China selling soybeans.) Andreas, who happened to be in London, made sure, however, that he was ably represented. He retained the celebrated Washington lawyer Edward Bennett Williams, and all the charges were presently dismissed.

For a while, it almost seemed to have become fashionable, if indeed not outright fun, to go after Andreas for his broadside generosity. There was to be a brouhaha, for instance, in 1978, that had its genesis way back in 1963, when

---

*Asked yet again to comment, this time Humphrey had his office release a statement that sounded as if it had been dictated, or at least cleared, by a lawyer: "In 1968, as in all of my campaigns for public office, fund-raising was handled by my campaign finance committees. However, Dwayne Andreas is a longtime close personal friend and supporter. I know through many years of being associated with him that he would not knowingly violate any law. He is a highly respected member of our community and a man held in high esteem by his associates in business and civic life."

daughter Sandra McMurtrie, working in New York at the art gallery, came home to Minnesota for Christmas. The Humphreys were around for the holidays, too, and as usual the two families saw a lot of each other. Soon Sandra had a new job, working for the senator in Washington as secretary to his principal assistant, a twenty-eight-year-old lawyer from Iowa named David G. Gartner, who'd joined Humphrey's staff in 1961. When in 1965 Humphrey became vice president, Gartner moved along with him, and so did Sandra. She stayed on altogether for three and a half years.

As the Andreases and the Humphreys had become close, so did the McMurtries and the Gartners. As the wealthier Andreas had helped support the less-well-off Humphreys, so would Sandra, comfortably endowed by her father, lend a hand to her former boss's family. By 1975, Gartner had four children. Starting then, and for two successive years, she put $3,000 worth of ADM stock a year in trust for each of them. Her father knew Gartner well, too. The younger man had accompanied Humphrey and Andreas on several of their foreign excursions, and both of them had been attendants at his 1965 wedding. Accordingly, when Dwayne heard about Sandra's philanthropic gesture, he decided to match it. That added up to three annual installments of $24,00 apiece —$72,000 altogether, which were part of a larger family gifts program. Other similar gifts of several hundred thousand dollars went to close relatives.

All that remained fairly private knowledge until, early in 1978 and shortly after Humphrey's death, President Carter, who had never met Gartner, appointed him, on the recommendation of Vice President Mondale and other knowledgeable Capitol hands, to be one of five commissioners in charge of the Commodity Futures Trading Commission. It was a $50,000-a-year post that entailed Senate confirmation. The Senate Committee on Agriculture, Nutrition, and Forestry— Herman Talmadge was its chairman and among its seventeen members were Bob Dole, Jesse Helms, and George McGovern— would pass judgment first. Their staffs, along with those of the president and the vice president, had all been apprised in detail of the four trust funds. Gartner's nomination was approved by both the committee and the full Senate in a single smooth-sailing day.

But then the press latched onto what seemed to be a hot story. Curiously, the ringleaders were the *Des Moines Register* and the *Minneapolis Tribune,* the president of whose parent company was none other than Gartner's brother. Could a man function as a CFTC commissioner, it was wondered, if he was beholden to a big commodities trader? Was there a conflict of interest? And hadn't Gartner the year before, as a key aide to Humphrey, been instrumental in getting legislation passed that kept the wholesale price of sugar high enough to make fructose marketers happily competitive? Gartner conceded he had done that, but for an altogether unobjectionable purpose: to benefit those of Senator Humphrey's constituents who were sugar-beet growers. And as for the conflict of interest, Gartner's supporters argued, the CFTC dealt mainly with commodities markets, and not with individual companies involved in them, so a commissioner would be hard put to favor any company or company official even if he wanted to.

President Carter, when asked about Gartner's appointment at a press conference just after the story broke, professed not to know much about him. Two weeks later, Carter said that he thought Gartner should resign—the president didn't have the authority to fire him and impeachment was the only other means of departure—because of "an allegation of impropriety." Vice President Mondale agreed. But Gartner declined to accommodate them. "To me the issue is friendship, not one of stock," he said. "If I was inclined to do something for Andreas, I'd do it for him stock or no stock. But I'm not inclined to do it."

The Senate committee decided to reconvene. This time Gartner, though himself a lawyer, brought along an attorney. Right off the bat, the committee was handed a letter from the chairman of the CFTC, William T. Bagley, who wrote:

> I wish to relate the following facts re new CFTC Commissioner David G. Gartner. I do not presume to pass judgment upon any matter before your committee nor upon

any past circumstance but only to report these present factual observations to you.

Mr. Gartner has served with us for the five weeks since his confirmation by the United States Senate. Though we do not and in all likelihood will not agree on all issues, I have found Mr. Gartner to be a very hardworking and conscientious commissioner. He has become aware of the numerous issues facing the Commission and, with his history of public service, he is certainly awake to the complex public interest involved. He does his homework, contributes significantly to our discussions, and has been and is a constructive force on the Commission.

Further, one other factual observation is in order. I have read and heard that Mr. Gartner's close friendship with the chief executive of one large agribusiness company will somehow affect "all" or a "significant part" of his actions as a Commissioner. That conclusion is simply not true. A given company will have a particular or unique problem with the jurisdiction of the Commission only on rare occasions. On such occasions a Commissioner can—and some Commissioners do—simply abstain. All Commissioners have friends somewhere.

As differentiated from such particular circumstances— usually a case subject to quasi-judicial actions—the vast majority of actual Commission work, perhaps as high as 90 percent, deals with general rulemaking. This function is much akin to legislating, adopting for example customer protection rules, uniform financial standards and transactional reporting requirements of general industry-wide application. No one company is affected and no one company has any relevance in these matters.

Again, without passing any judgment on matters before you, these are facts which I believe should be brought to your attention.

Gartner himself was extensively questioned and said at one turn, "Archer Daniels Midland basically is a user of the futures markets. It is analogous to a large investor in the stock market. If and when its positions in the futures markets exceed specific limits, it is required to file reports with the CFTC, much in the same manner as people with large stock holdings in a company have to notify the SEC. This is the only direct regulatory impact the CFTC exercises over Archer Daniels Midland.... The CFTC has no more effect on the price of soybeans or soybean futures than the SEC does on the price of General Motors stock."

On sugar and fructose:

> Now, Senator, I read that story in the *Des Moines Register* and I resent the insinuation contained in it. I will bring it out. Mr. Andreas is a corn refiner. He makes a product called fructose, and when the price of sugar goes up, it is easier for him to supply the very large users, but I don't think any Senator sitting here at this table would refuse to respond to the requests of his constituency because coincidentally it might help a friend of his, and that is exactly what happened, and I have no apologies at all.

On what he and Dwayne and Sandra considered the crux of the matter:

> Now, Mr. Chairman, there is another matter that is not directly at issue here, but which I feel I should address myself to. That is the question of why I permitted the stock gifts in the first place.
> In this connection there are two considerations—the legal question and the moral question. There is agreement that acceptance of the gifts constituted no violation of the law or of the then-existing Senate Code of Standards and Conduct.
> The other question is whether I violated any moral principles when I did not object to the gifts being made in trust for my children. This leads to the nature of my friendship with Dwayne Andreas.
> Dwayne Andreas was one of Hubert Humphrey's closest friends. Their friendship goes back well before I ever met either one of them.
> It also is important to understand that Hubert Humphrey, in addition to being my employer, was one of my closest friends.
> Given these circumstances, it was quite natural that there would develop a very special relationship between Mr. Andreas and myself. Add to this the fact that his daughter

and her husband were, and continue to be, close friends of my wife and me.

So I thought it perfectly understandable that this friend of mine, who I had known for fourteen years and who had asked no favors of me, who, along with Vice President Humphrey, was a groomsman at my wedding in 1965, would want to share a portion of his wealth in order that my children might be assured an education. I felt that he was making the gifts in the spirit of a very close friendship—expecting nothing in return—and I can assure the members of this committee that at no time prior to the gifts or subsequent to them has he sought any special favors from me or have I extended any special favors to him.

The *New York Times* remarked editorially, "Although there is no evidence of wrongdoing, most people must wonder over the event. So generous a gift—for what? Whatever the details of the Andreas-Gartner relationship, it is too close for public comfort." Soon, more urgent affairs of state and nation inevitably occupied the attention of all concerned. Gartner stayed on, the trusts remained intact (though along the way the trustee, at Gartner's bidding, had swapped the shares of ADM for less controversial holdings), and the storm was over. Andreas, who has rarely been accused of naïveté, never did seem altogether to comprehend what the fuss had all been about. (Had Humphrey lived a few months and had his say in the matter, there might never have been a tempest at all in this particular teapot.) When he had helped his daughter help their friend, Andreas told the *Wall Street Journal*, "I never dreamed he'd have that kind of job."

Soon afterward, though there were others who strongly concurred with the *Times*'s editorial conclusion, one longtime acquaintance of Andreas's was moved to remark, "Did anyone seriously believe that Dwayne would expect any reward for a small gesture of friendship? Why, that would be as ridiculous as it would be to accuse him, merely because he's unloaded enormous sums of money on one daughter's School for Field Studies and on another's Mother Teresa, of hoping thereby to obtain a shortcut to heaven or avoid being gored by an elk."

18

I don't mind doing business in a goldfish
bowl. Our kind of business is all structured
by governments to begin with. There is no
longer any free market in agricultural
commodities.

—DOA

Of the big grain companies—Bunge, Cargill, Continental, Dreyfus, et al.—ADM is the only one whose stock is publicly traded. It consistently pays low cash dividends; Andreas is partial to stock dividends or better yet, reinvestment of profits. "Most of our stock is owned by pension funds," Andreas says, "and if we gave them dividends in the form of cash, they'd just have to reinvest it somewhere. We do that for them. When security analysts ask me about this, I tell them our cash dividends won't be increased while I'm alive, because they have to be taxed and I won't work for the government. 'Our shareholders' money is in our company—their company—working for them,' I say, 'and it isn't in Vietnam or Panama.'"

ADM's competitors have supposedly clung to their privacy, in part, out of conviction that if they went public, they'd have to reveal carefully guarded and nurtured trade secrets. Andreas contends, contrarily, that the agricultural economy worldwide has become so socialized that everybody in it is involved in pretty much the same operations. There have been differences. The other four companies are principally engaged in buying and selling grain. ADM concentrates on processing it—half its revenue deriving from that—and as a result Andreas is sometimes known in commodity circles, not at all to his displeasure, as Mr. Added Value.

He is seldom unaware, too, of an additional difference. "These other guys all come from third-generation families," he says of his rivals, "and they've long had it made. I went public because I'm a latecomer. If I wanted to become important, I had to leapfrog. I couldn't wait to build a fortune. Anyway, I don't mind doing business in a goldfish bowl. Our kind of business is all structured by governments to begin with. There is no longer any free market in agricultural commodities."

Andreas's leapfrogging has paid off. When in 1988 his ADM board declared a 5 percent stock dividend, that meant for him a further four hundred thousand shares, worth about $10 million. As the company's stock has gone up and down, albeit for the most part in a fairly narrow range, it has taken him on and off *Forbes*'s roster of the five hundred wealthiest Americans. (He has also been in and out of *Who's Who*, but largely for neglecting to comply with its requests for updated data.) "If you do your job well, money—ink on paper, that's all it really is—just seems to pile up under you," he says. He is unembarrassed about disbursing it. Frustrated in Florida because it took two hours to get from the Indian Creek golf course to a bonefishing rendezvous at the Anglers Club, he bought a thirty-two-foot power boat that could skim along at sixty miles an hour. It is deemed prudent for passengers aboard it—like those on parade in his stretch Rolls-Royce—to fasten their seat belts.

By the mid-1970s, though like his company Andreas was still relatively unknown to the general public, because of

ADM's increasing growth and his increasing clout he had become a bona fide member of what for better or worse is sometimes called the Establishment. Along with entrée to such further clubs as the Capitol Hill in Washington (for a 1975 gift to this Republican hangout of a hundred thousand dollars' worth of ADM stock, he was rewarded, not surprisingly, with a life membership), he began turning up at such annual affairs of the in crowd as the larksome banquets in the Capitol of the Gridiron and Alfalfa Clubs, not to mention at more formal dinners, invited by hosts both Democratic and Republican, in the White House. "I go to every White House thing I'm asked to, out of fear. I might miss out on something," Andreas says. "I wouldn't dare not go. Unless you have honest fear, you're not much of a businessman."

Then there were fall weekends at the two-hundred-acre game farm in Minnesota owned by the Cowles Communications people (he sat for a spell on its board), where he could rub shooting-jacket elbows with such other establishmentarians as the CEOs of General Electric and Goldman Sachs, as they took aim against flocks of ducks and quail bred there for the guests' handy stalking. (Searching for an apt analogy after he became more widely known and more often solicited for his views on this or that issue of the moment, Andreas told the *Wall Street Journal*, "It's just like being a duck. If you get two feet above the horizon, a lot people are ready to shoot at you.")

Then, too, were the celebrated—if not indeed notorious— gatherings of his ilk at the twenty-seven-hundred-acre California enclave seventy-five miles north of San Francisco called Bohemian Grove, where several hundred CEOs and their high-placed cronies would assemble, in a college-fraternity-initiation mood, for part or all of a couple of carefree weeks each year, bedding down in cabins with arch names such as Cave Man, Wild Oats, Dog House, and Woof. Andreas first joined those ranks as a guest in 1977, on receipt of an all-but-irresistible invitation from a pension-fund manager who wrote him, "It is the greatest experience of a businessman's lifetime." An undercover reporter for the magazine *Spy* who once managed to penetrate the Grove during the proceedings seemed to gather the impression after prowling around that the adult personages on hand spent most of their time urinating against trees.

There were other groups to participate in, or preside over, of loftier caliber. For a couple of years, Andreas served as president of the Economic Club of New York, an institution founded in 1907 that puts on a half dozen hotel-ballroom dinners a year and that Wendell Willkie called America's "foremost nonpartisan forum." That club's claim to that fame was fortified by the speakers it attracted over the years: Winston Churchill, Nikita Khrushchev, Dag Hammarskjöld, Dean Acheson, Louis Brandeis, Averell Harriman, Indira Gandhi, Corazon Aquino, U Thant, and Presidents Wilson, Eisenhower, Kennedy, Nixon, Ford, Carter, and Reagan. It was characteristic of Andreas's professed evaluation of his own celebrity that when somebody asked him how he happened to be tapped to join the list of those captains of industry who had presided over the club before him—among them Thomas J. Watson, Winthrop Aldrich, Frank Vanderlip, David Sarnoff, and Alfred P. Sloan, Jr.—he replied, "I haven't the remotest idea."

Andreas always likes to tie together various scattered threads that run through his life. Thus to one Economic Club dinner he invited Ellen Stoutenberg, a onetime television producer who in 1962 had founded an organization that became known as the Executive Council on Foreign Diplomats; he was chairman of its board of overseers. The Council, which has described itself as "the secretary of state's Private Sector Briefing Program for U.S. and Foreign Diplomats," started out, at the instigation of Adlai Stevenson when he was at the United Nations, to make diplomats from abroad, especially those from smaller and nonwhite countries, feel at home in the United States, and to help them cope with problems like finding apartments and parking spaces. It arranged for them to become acquainted with such American institutions as Old Faithful at Yellowstone Park and all-soy lunches at Decatur, Illinois. In later years, the Council also began trying to brief American diplomats heading overseas about some of the things they could expect to encounter. In the spring of 1990, after a dinner at the State Department in Andreas's honor, he turned over the Council's reins to Robert Strauss.

When Andreas invited Mrs. Stoutenberg—also her son James, who had succeeded her as full-time director of the Council, and his wife—to the Economic Club dinner, they somehow got the date wrong and were no-shows. As soon as Mrs. Stoutenberg realized their gaffe, she phoned Claudia Madding and said she hoped in the presence of what was surely a large crowd (the dinners usually drew more than a thousand) their absence hadn't been noticed. Mrs. Madding hesitated, then confessed that they had indeed been missed; they were supposed to have been sitting at Mr. Andreas's very own table. Mrs. Stoutenberg was still reeling when her phone rang. It was Andreas. "Ellen, not showing up was the smartest thing you ever did," he said. "The air-conditioning was on the blink and everybody was sweltering, and when it came my time to talk, I made a lousy speech." That convinced her, if she needed any reassurance, that in Andreas the Council has a chairman well versed in high-level diplomacy.*

All such activities and responsibilities are obviously easier for a busy man to juggle if he has his own airplane. Not having to hang around airports like ordinary mortals, one statistically minded observer of the contemporary corporate scene has calculated, can save the average CEO 213 hours a year, or the equivalent of more than a round of golf a week. Notwithstanding, Andreas is well aware of how burdensome the demands can be on someone of his status. "If

---

*Nobody's perfect. During one around-a-table meeting at the Kremlin between some Soviet government ministers and, representing the American Trade Consortium, Andreas and James Giffen, one of the Russians proposed something and said, "What do you think of it, Mr. Andreas?" Andreas replied, "That's the dumbest goddamn idea I ever heard in my life." Before he could go on, Giffen grabbed his knee under the table and muttered, "Remember where we are."

you went to all the things that as a CEO people want you to," he says, "it would be a terrible life."

When he took over ADM in 1965, it had only a single propeller-driven airplane. By 1989, it had a five-plane fleet, and eleven pilots on the company payroll to ferry them around. At the Decatur airport, which is spacious enough to accommodate Air Force One, ADM has its own terminal. The star of the fleet, which Andreas bought for $12.5 million in 1987, is the Falcon 900, a three-engine jet made in France that can comfortably seat nine and sleep four. (It has been cited as a measure of his business acumen that not long after he purchased that plane, which he has yet to name after anybody, its price shot up to $18 million.) For longish flights, such as the eight-and-a-half-hour one from Decatur to Copenhagen, en route to Moscow, Andreas keeps a jumpsuit aboard, though before landing he gets himself up as dapper as ever, pearl stickpin firmly in place. "I sleep better on a plane than at home," he says.

When Andreas is flying toward New York City, his plane usually touches down either at the Westchester County Airport or at Teterboro, New Jersey. The latter's terminal has good facilities for servicing Falcons. He eschews La Guardia because it doesn't always have last-minute berths available for people who fly about on short notice. "If I knew a day ahead where I was going to be," Andreas says, "I wouldn't need a private plane." For trips to many of his more distant destinations, there is always the Concorde.

Way back in 1961, while still with the Grain Terminal Association, Andreas had to spend enough time in New York to warrant having a permanent place to bed down there, and he had enough money to spend to rent a four-thousand-square-foot apartment on a floor of the Waldorf Towers otherwise occupied by the United States ambassador to the United Nations. His friend Adlai Stevenson, the incumbent plenipotentiary, heard that the space was available and didn't want some stranger poking about the corridors. When the ambassador, whoever he is, is physically present, Andreas and his overnight guests enjoy a perquisite shared by very few other New York apartment dwellers: State Department security vigilance.

In 1986, though, he concluded that there was too much traffic, however well policed, in and out of the area. By then he had additional New York digs, and so while he continued to use the Waldorf apartment for some business breakfasts and as a place to put up guests, and to keep its shelves well stocked with soy-based foodstuffs, he rarely slept there anymore himself.

When somebody who should have known better asked Andreas one time if he was acquainted with Nelson Rockefeller, he replied, "I would naturally know Nelson. How could I not know Nelson?" After Nelson married his second wife, Happy ("Everybody knows *her*, all over the world," Andreas has said), they bought an apartment on Fifth Avenue adjacent to one the husband already owned and broke through the dividing building walls to splice them. Nelson died in 1979. His widow, having no need for all that space, had the gap resealed and in 1982 sold one of the apartments to Andreas, thus affording him a comfortable alternative to the Waldorf.

The following year, Mrs. Rockefeller became a member of the ADM board. "I know an awful lot of people," she says, "and Dwayne is unique. Why, if it hadn't been for him, I'd probably never have met Mother Teresa or Gorbachev." For her directorial services, she receives $25,000 a year, and if assigned to enough ADM committees, she could extend that to $65,000, which she may not need. At last count, she owned 4,385 of its shares, worth just under $70,000. (Andreas himself, when it comes to that, can get by nicely without touching the income generated by *his* service on other people's boards: $15,000 a year, for instance, from Salomon, Inc., plus $500 for each directors' meeting he attends, and a $3000 pourboire for chairing the board's nominating committee.)

Mrs. Rockefeller has been conscientious about making the trip to rural Illinois for ADM board meetings. After Andreas took her along on one such occasion to a party at the home of Decatur's leading banker, the host, whose family has been around so long that when General Grant stopped by its post office the banker's grandmother sat on his lap, said afterward, "Getting a chance to talk to people you'd normally never get to meet in a million years—Bob Dole, Andy Young, Chinese and Indians, even Happy herself—these are the fun things that happen when you know Dwayne Andreas."

In October 1975, while Nelson Rockefeller was vice president, he came to Decatur to speak at the biennial fund-raising dinner of the Macon County Republican Central Committee. A number of the committee's officials hoped to have a private word with the distinguished visitor the following morning. They had to cool their heels for quite a while; Andreas had got to the veep's hotel room at seven-thirty for a breakfast à deux that lasted until ten.

Andreas has never proposed erecting a statue to the vice president there, but to this day the Rockefeller influence remains visible in Decatur—specifically, on the walls of the corridors that lead to Andreas's top-floor office at ADM's headquarters building.* Rockefeller was, of course, a noted art collector. Andreas was impressed during one of their get-togethers when the onetime president of the Museum of Modern Art observed that while anybody could buy a recording of a great orchestra's rendition of a symphony, wasn't it a shame that great paintings were by and large seen only by those fortunate few who could get to the homes or museums where they hung?

Andreas was quick to ingest such expert food for thought. Research disclosed a store that sold laser-produced, three-dimensional, exact-same-sized replicas of masterpieces for the bargain price of only about $1,500 apiece. Before long, the Decatur corridor walls boasted, among eye-catching others, Pissarro's *Boulevard Montmartre*, Monet's *The Artist's Garden at Giverny*, Manet's *Monet and His Floating Studio*, and Van Gogh's *Starry Night over the Rhône*. Escorting a visitor

*When he finds time to read, he can reach to a shelf behind his desk for *Soviet Agriculture, Managing Human Assets, KGB Today, The Staffs of Life,* or *Ending Hunger.*

along his gallery, Andreas remarked in front of that last work, "I'm getting some Van Goghs that are absolutely fantastic" (one, and a Renoir, would soon occupy prominent wall space at his Decatur home), and added, abreast of the Manet, "I'll bet this one would cost seven hundred thousand." Told that a seven- or eight-figure speculation would probably be more realistic, he gasped.

The only hitch is that probably three-quarters of ADM's nearly twelve hundred Decatur employees may never get to appreciate his collection, because they seldom have occasion to ascend to his aerie.

Back when it was Hubert Humphrey's turn to be vice president and Nelson Rockefeller was merely governor of New York, Andreas took Humphrey along on a weekend visit to the Rockefeller enclave at Pocantico Hills. Humphrey said at one point that in his view the Ford administration was ruining Midwestern farmers. Why, he went on, instead of paying them not to produce and letting their land lay idle, it should help them conserve it by paying for retaining walls and grading and windbreaks and trees. Andreas vigorously concurred. Nothing came of that out of Washington, but Peggy—Mrs. David—Rockefeller later asked Andreas to join the board of directors of the American Farmland Trust, an organization she sponsored that was dedicated to keeping farmland, as much as possible, for farmers instead of letting it disintegrate into shopping malls—sentiments that Andreas saw to it were thumpingly echoed in ADM television commercials.*

---

*The words—all carefully vetted by Andreas before being released—that accompanied twelve pictures went: "The dust bowl. Nature's devastating reply to man's neglect of the land. Some say it could never happen again. But the truth is, what you're seeing isn't something that took place fifty years ago. It's going on right now. Each year, some of the most important food-producing land in this country loses an average of ten tons of topsoil per acre. And with it goes the chance for future generations to expect what we've come to take for granted. Abundant, low-cost supplies of food. Considering the millions of jobs tied to American agriculture and the worldwide dependence on it for food, soil erosion is a problem that must be solved. And it can be if we all recognize its seriousness. At the Archer Daniels Midland Company, soil conservation is one of our primary concerns. We ask that you make it one of yours, too. Before [nothing to look at but dust] it's too late."

On a more personal level, when Secretary of Defense Caspar Weinberger invited a dozen CEOs of large corporations to dinner at the Pentagon one evening, to introduce them to a forthcoming military budget, Andreas startled the gathering by suggesting pleasantly that it might not be a bad idea to divert some of the billions of dollars under consideration to paying unemployed young men to leave city streets and go out into the countryside to terrace rapidly eroding farmland.

Through David Rockefeller, Andreas had been admitted to yet another inner Establishment circle, the Bilderbergs. They are sometimes thought to be mysterious, behind-the-scenes, manipulative movers and shakers of world events, but this is probably because their annual meetings are closed to the public and the press. In 1954, Dr. Joseph Retinger, a Polish economist living in London, thought it might be useful for leaders of the Atlantic community of nations to get together periodically and discuss—off the record—matters of mutual concern. Soon a meeting was convened at the Hotel de Bilderberg, at Oosterbeek, the Netherlands. Prince Bernhard presided, as he has continued to ever since, during sessions held in Austria, in Spain, and in the United States, at Williamsburg. Among the ten dozen or so participants from a dozen nations (Europe represented by such as Hugh Gaitskell, Jean Monnet, and Harold Wilson), some of the Americans involved over the years have been Dean Acheson, Dean Rusk, Christian Herter, Jacob Javits, William Fulbright, David Rockefeller, and Dwayne Andreas, who was happy to note that at the 1989 session there was for the first time, along with the usual conversations about reductions of armaments, a discussion about preserving the environment.

The Bilderbergs, says Rockefeller, who has attained the rank among them of an honorary adviser, never reach conclusions and have never tried as a group to influence any government. Notwithstanding, the feeling persists among those not privy to their deliberations that they constitute some kind of shadowy supergovernment, for all anybody knows a capitalistically seditious one to boot. There is reason to believe that at least one presidential appointment to a high office that required Senate confirmation was held up because of alleged guilt by association—a member of that august body contending that the designee deserved special scrutiny because he was rumored to have had close dealings with an American Bilderberg.

Andreas's consistent and generous support of Jewish causes has been reciprocated. In 1990, the Anti-Defamation League of B'nai B'rith dubbed him its Man of the Year. In 1981, the League had given him a Man of Achievement Award. Among the guests at a presentation dinner were a suitable cross section of the honoree's close associates and admirers: Happy Rockefeller, Bob Dole, Danny Kaye, Andrew Young, Bob Strauss, George McGovern, Tom Dewey, Jr., Ross Johnson, and Walter Mondale, who acclaimed the man of that hour as "the world's most successful businessman." To some of those present, however, it seemed especially significant, and illustrative of how Andreas never permitted himself to forget what had been his priorities ever since he left the farm, that the master of ceremonies was Morton I. Sosland, from Shawnee Mission, Kansas (though to be sure he also has a flat in London), the editor and publisher of *Milling & Baking News, World Grain, Agribusiness Worldwide, Baking Buyer,* and *Baking & Snack Systems.*

19

It is becoming a fact of life for
all American industry that we must
be prepared to work within a global
reference of supply and demand
and no longer hide our heads in the
soybean fields of Illinois.

—DOA

DURING Jimmy Carter's administration, Andreas had access to and affinity with the president not only because Robert Strauss had been his campaign manager but also because Carter was, or had been, a farmer. (Those circumstances helped make it easier to forgive and forget the flap over the Andreas beneficences to David Gartner of the Commodity Futures Trading Commission.) Toward the end of the Carter years, the United States, to Andreas's delight, signed a trade agreement according to which the Soviet Union was to buy four hundred thousand tons of soybeans. The first twenty-thousand-ton shipment was en route when the USSR invaded Afghanistan. The deal was off, and Carter proceeded to embargo all such commodity shipments.

One result of that was the loss to American farmers, according to Andreas's expert reckoning, of 17 million tons' worth of sales. (Another was the lamentable absence of an American team at the 1980 Olympic Games in Moscow.) "We shot ourselves in the foot," said Andreas, who believed that United States trading, or nontrading, with Communists had long been characterized by extraordinary shortsightedness. "It didn't hurt the Soviets, who just took their business to other countries and the Common Market."

Andreas had been sitting in New York with the Soviet Union's principal grain buyer when news of that embargo—"disaster" was one of the American's gentler descriptions of it—reached them. "He at once booked flights for Canada, Brazil, and Australia," Andreas recalls. "They increased their production and permanently took a lion's share of that business away from us. The Japanese soon invested more than a billion dollars in Brazilian soybeans, and the EEC tripled its production of oilseeds. Even worse, many former customers of ours seemed determined to exclude the US as an only supplier." As a result of this chain of events, 28 soybean plants have closed in the U.S.

When Ronald Reagan took over, he was reluctant to try to lift his predecessor's embargo, first wanting to be reassured that if he did, the emphatically anti-Russian longshoremen's union wouldn't refuse to load the ships taking the goods to their destination. The American Farm Bureau wondered if Andreas could help. Through Hubert Humphrey's old aide Herbert Waters, the Bureau set up a meeting between the ADM man and his friend Lane Kirkland of the AFL-CIO, who, happily for all concerned, had a maritime background himself; that helped to remove that particular roadblock.*

The very word *embargo* makes Andreas bristle, or at least sigh. Although he never finished college, he can, when the occasion demands, display as much erudition as any CEO.

---

*Unions sometimes don't like to deal with individual businesses, preferring trade associations. (Kirkland had a bone of his own to pick; his people didn't take to the idea of agricultural commodities, such as the ones ADM handled, being processed abroad rather than at home.) In due course, there evolved in Washington, D.C., to facilitate needed dialogue, an Export Processing Industry Coalition, with Waters as its coordinator.

One of his favorite quotations, which he attributes to Socrates, is "No man is qualified as a statesman unless he understands the problems of wheat." For embargoes, he is apt to turn to Santayana's "Those who cannot remember the past are condemned to repeat it."

It distressed him that few others in or out of government seemed in his view to have ended up any the wiser from President Nixon's 1973 ban on soybean exports. A poor harvest had seemed likely, and that would have raised the price of soybeans and thus of domestic livestock feed—and with it, inevitably, the cost of meat and milk and butter and eggs and much else. But what happened was that Japan, which had been importing $700 million worth of soybeans annually from the States, had to turn elsewhere. It turned—while Japanese newspapers were reporting that many of their countrymen were suffering from a novel ailment: Nixon Soybean Shock—to Brazil, which quickly and gratefully became a prodigious exporter of processed soybeans. That nation has ever since subsidized its growers and has paid in large part for the subsidies, as Andreas likes to point out whenever he contemplates the crazy universe he inhabits, with loans—sometimes a trifle late in redemption—from the United States.

Andreas, who regarded Carter's attitude toward international trade as parochial, if not outright isolationist, made his own contrary viewpoint clear midway through the ex-peanut farmer's reign in a September 1978 address to some New York security analysts:

At the start of the last fiscal year we were facing the prospects of a bountiful soybean harvest. Large crops are usually favorable for the processing industry, and the year did start out on that tone. However, early in calendar 1978 it became known that the Brazilian soybean crop would be substantially below both expected and usual levels. That created a situation where both European and Asiatic soybean crushers intensified their competition with the US crushers for the American supply of soybeans, and the processing margins deteriorated thereafter. The fact that the year turned out to be only an average one for soybean processing shows both the vicissitudes of world markets and the importance of what is going on outside the US to US industry itself. It is becoming a fact of life for all American industry that we must be prepared to work within a global reference of supply and demand and no longer hide our heads in the soybean fields of Illinois.

It is just as important for the US processors to know what the French processor thinks of the Brazilian soybean supply situation as it is for Detroit to know what Honda and Volkswagen have in mind and for the money managers of New York and Boston to know that the dollar is doing in relationship to the mark and the yen.

In 1981, not long after Carter was deposed by a nonfarmer, ADM bought the president emeritus's struggling peanut business, for $1.5 million. Soon ADM's scattered peanut holdings would far eclipse those at Plains, Georgia. By 1987, Andreas's legion of peanut minions, some of them joint ventures, had the capacity to shell five hundred thousand tons a year—25 percent of the country's total—at seven installations. A food-ingredients catalogue published by ADM listed four varieties of Spanish-shelled peanuts, and five of runner-shelled. (There were further discrete subcategories: in-shell Virginians for ballparks, large-kernel Virginians for cocktail snacks, small-kernel Virginians for peanut butter.) By 1984, ADM's own tough-shelled leader would be a robust enough personage in the field for the monthly *Peanut Journal* to offer its subscribers, as a headline over an article about American industry vis-à-vis European, "Andreas Urges Combative Stance." Among the fringe benefits enjoyed by ADM's employees at Decatur are free peanuts—also popcorn—in their cafeteria. Popcorn-eaters there have the option of dousing their kernels with an in-house product called Gold 'N Flavor, dispensed from one-gallon jugs—outside of ADM's research laboratories, perhaps its smallest-size containers. Most of the liquids the company deals with end up in fifty-five-gallon drums or tank cars.

Also in 1981, on the eve of a ten-day trip to China, the ex-president phoned Andreas in Decatur and said he'd like to become better acquainted with the soybean. (Like most people with a modicum of familiarity about agriculture, Carter probably did know that the Chinese have long worshipfully called it the miracle bean.) Andreas's hospitable instincts never flag. "'Hell, come on up here and you'll go away knowing more about it than anybody in the world,' I told him," he says.

Jimmy and Rosalynn and an entourage arrived, wandered around, asked, in Andreas's recollection, 450 questions, and were treated (Ronald Reagan hadn't had time when he stopped by) to ADM's all-soy lunch—from soy-based taco-dip appetizer to soy-based ice cream with all intermediate culinary stops. "We give the soybean lunch anytime we think we can get by with it," Andreas says.

Some years after the Carter visit, the special meal was sampled, with Andreas enlighteningly presiding over the soy-groaning board, by a delegation from the People's Republic of China to an Illinois State Fair. China, with more than a billion potential consumers of ADM products of one sort or another, has never strayed far from Andreas's thoughts. How could anyone in his line of work not feel warmly toward a nation whose children skip off to school carrying paper bags with cooked whole soybeans in them and when they hanker for a snack, rip open the pods and lick off the beans inside? And whose millions and millions of inhabitants, Andreas was fond of stressing when in one of his antimeat moods, got by quite nicely without abject dependence on the bloody stuff. "Chinese eat meat like we eat caviar—a speck at a time," he would say. "And they're not hungry."

Andreas had long had it in mind, indeed, to start a peanut-oil plant in China, or perhaps some other venture such as a wet-corn-milling enterprise turning out fructose as well as starch convertible into paper. "They print a lot of things over there," he says.

When Robert Strauss went to China, in 1979, as head of

a Carter trade mission of twenty or so American business-men, Andreas tagged along and took part in the negotiations, much as had been his wont in the Humphrey days. "I was able to sort of help Bob get to people who could be helpful to him" was Andreas's response to a question about precisely what role he'd played. On the plane going over, he was less reserved. Often when abroad he carries, like any other consci-entious traveling salesman, a sample kit of goods he hopes to peddle. This time, he was up and down the aisles passing out imitation bacon bits and other soy-based delicacies. Strauss recalled later that his compatriots, who seemed quite con-tent with the flight attendants' proferred treats, all but shoved Dwayne back into his seat.* But China was not yet much accustomed to foreigners' weird tastes, and, Strauss further remembered, within a few days the members of his flock were beseeching Dwayne for some of that TVP or whatever he called the stuff in his handbag, so they could sprinkle it on their bland breakfast eggs.

For Andreas, other men's breakfast times were in China, as at home, practically the middle of his day. In Shanghai, at five o'clock one morning, with no Jacuzzi or golf date to preoccupy him, he took a stroll and was impressed, coming upon a bakery, to find people lined up outside with pails and other receptacles, waiting to fill them with hot soy milk from big tubs on the sidewalk. (The potion is fashioned from dried beans that have been soaked, ground, and boiled.)

The Chinese had been familiar with soy milk for centu-ries, but it had mainly been served as a hot soup until a medical missionary from Ohio named Harry W. Miller turned

---

*It amuses and naturally pleases ADM operatives who fly Pan Am that that airline's packets of "coffee whitener" list more than a half dozen ingredients—none of them milk—and that the very first two are "corn syrup solids" and "partially hydrogenated soybean oil." (Andreas and his cohorts have long been cognizant that people on kosher diets can combine soy-meat substitutes with genuine cow's milk or combine soy milk with beef without violating any religious laws. In the United States today, there are such esoteric eating establishments as kosher macrobiotic vegetarian restaurants. Perhaps after patronizing one of these, an American versifier was inspired to pen: "Soybeans can be the cream in your coffee, the dog in your bun, the chow for your cat, and then some.")

up there early in the twentieth century. To enhance the nourishment of some of the infant orphans who arrived on the doorstep of one of his sanatoriums, he began to experiment with it. It had an odd flavor, which was generally described as "beany," and to enhance its palatability—the method was revealed to him, he contended, by a disembodied celestial voice—he began cooking it longer, with steam. Chiang Kai-shek, as an adult, doted on the more agreeable result and invested the physician with the Order of the Blue Star of China.

Dr. Miller, who lived to be ninety-seven, became known as the China Doctor, and his legerdemain has affectionately been chronicled by William Shurtleff, himself a towering figure in the soy-foods movement, who with his wife, Akiko Aoyagi, runs a Soyfoods Center at Lafayette, California. Probably the world's foremost contemporary soy-foods author and bibliographer, Shurtleff conducted four soy-milk seminars in the People's Republic in 1983—the very first Westerner ever invited to attend, let along preside over, such an assemblage.

Long before Andreas's early-morning walk in Shanghai, he had been apprised that the Chinese consumed 4 or 5 million tons of soy milk a year, but seeing was believing. And he was also aware that the soybean had long been known over there as the cow of China. He liked that. "You can get much better milk from a soybean than you can from a cow," he says. "It has no cholesterol and no lactose, and it's a hell of a lot simpler and cheaper and more convenient kind of milk to make than what you can end up with after obtaining a cow and housing it and feeding it and constantly having to be going out and pulling its teat."

20

There's something about the soybean that just seems to put a lot of people off. . . . Even the rats don't like us.

—DOA

TRUE believers in soybeans of the Andreas stripe—
"forever," as the *New York Times* once had it, "riding a bumpy road to widespread acceptance"—have
to put up with a lot. Two physicians affiliated with the
Division of Pediatric Gastroenterology and Clinical Nutrition of the Mount Sinai School of Medicine, who may never
have heard of Dr. Harry Miller, told the American Academy
of Pediatrics that as far as infants' diets were concerned, soy
milk was inferior not only to cow's milk but to mother's,
too. Why, they went on crushingly, for babies unable to
stomach either of the last two, soy milk was worse even than
a mouthful called "hydrolysate formulas containing predigested
proteins." They warned that "it is prudent to restrict the use
of products containing soybean protein to healthy, growing,
term infants."

Andreas, while refraining from going to the partisan lengths of some Buddhists in India, who assert that if children drink cow's milk they'll grow horns,* vigorously dissents from such critics, regardless of their formidable scientific credentials. He concedes that his aspirations for soy milk may be disappointingly analogous to Henry Ford's for automobile bodies made of soy-based plastics, which came to naught when it turned out petroleum-based ones were just as good and markedly less expensive.

Still, as Andreas likes to remind any audience he can corral, nobody gave margarine much of a chance against butter at the outset, and look what happened there! Soy milk can be transported dry, he argues, and most of cow's milk is merely water, and although he is used to dealing in astronomical figures, he hesitates to speculate how many millions of dollars or other currencies are spent transporting how many millions of tons of that kind of water— and often having to refrigerate it to boot—before it serves any discernible purpose. He is willing when the occasion arises, sensibly, to compromise. Back in 1981, hearing that school-lunch planners in Trinidad were looking for an innovative nutritional beverage, he dispatched an emissary there who soon came up with an acceptable beverage that, while it was heavily laced with soy-based protein concentrate, derived its liquidity from run-of-the-dairy skim milk.†

---

*"Do your own thing related to Soyfoods," Shurtleff and Aoyagi have written. "In this area, your imagination is the limit." But for all the concentration of their concerns, they are far from uncompromising fanatics, even though a biographical note in one of their joint literary ventures (*The Book of Tofu, The Book of Tempeh, The Book of Miso*, et al.) goes, "By constantly addressing the larger problems of world hunger, human suffering, and liberation, they hope to make their work relevant to people everywhere and a force for planetary renaissance." The Shurtleffs, whose dedicated path at last report had never yet, curiously, intersected Andreas's own much-trod one, sometimes contend modestly that they hope to do no more for the soybean than George Washington Carver did for the peanut or Johnny Appleseed for the apple.

†ADM has contributed soybean flour to be blended with rice flour and with both cow's milk and soy milk for a protein-rich infant formula developed in Taiwan.

Asked by one interviewer for a prognosis about the dietary future of the Soviet Union, where he had been happy to hear some twenty-five-million pounds of soybean protein were already being used annually as an additive to sausages, Andreas responded, "They should...build a network of plants to process wheat into hot and cold cereals; corn into meal, grits, starch, syrup, and other foods; soybeans into protein for chickens, cooking oil, margarine, and other foods for human consumption, including, of course, and by no means least of all, milk."

Andreas is too practical a businessman to fall prey for long to his own illusions. He noticed with interest that when some business associates in Japan—where soy-milk vending machines are common—bought a tract of land in the American South to build a soy-milk plant, they put their plans on hold when a market-research survey rendered a pessimistic verdict. When Andreas heard that some made-in-Japan dried soy milk was being sold in Detroit health-food stores (Henry Ford would doubtless have approved), he ordered a case of it to be shipped to Decatur. He confesses, however, that the beverage's prospects are dim—although he did tell his shareholders at their annual gathering in 1989, "Soy milk, if you want to look ahead twenty years, is a product that is sure to become a more important food"—until, he cautioned them, it is accorded prominent shelf space in nonspecialized groceries where health sometimes plays a secondary role to the pursuit of wealth.*

---

*Many of the American devotees of tofu, tempeh, miso, and other edible transformations of the soybean are patrons of health-food stores and restaurants (or are the proprietors of mom-and-pop businesses that cater to such establishments), whose menus feature delicacies with names like Tempeh Sloppy Joes, Strawberry Tofu Cheesecake, Ice Bean Sandwich, Soysage, and Soylami. More often nowadays, when the soybean is eaten by people, it is not so boldly labeled. If all the cans and cartons that contain soybeans were removed from supermarkets, the shelves would look looted. (Dog foods would have to go; many of them are approximately 10 percent soybean.) The presence of soybeans in—the list could be endless—Franco-American beef ravioli, Lipton's Lite-Lunch, Kroger Easy Dinner, Carnation Instant Breakfast, Duncan Hines pudding-recipe devil's-food cake mix, Pillsbury streusel-swirl dessert cake mix, and Chef Boyardee lasagna dinner—is rarely advertised. It is referred to, indeed, chiefly in the seldom-scanned small type that is employed to identify ingredients.

A study made by the UN's Food and Agriculture Organization disclosed, not to Andreas's surprise, that existing food-processing techniques had the capability of making all the comestibles needed by all the people on earth out of one variety of bean or another. Andreas—who is emphatically nonvegetarian and whose pro-soy crusades may have been hindered more than helped by some out-and-out unreconstructed vegetarians' reputations for, well, flakiness—has gone further. He believes that with a few suitable side dishes soybeans could turn the trick pretty much alone. (Asked one time if he knew of many Americans who subsisted exclusively, or largely, on soy-based foods, William Shurtleff replied, "As for the number of people in the USA in whose diet soy foods predominate, I would hope none.") In the United States, though, with processing equipment and distribution networks vastly superior to most of the rest of the globe's, the consumption of soy foods hasn't made much headway since 1938, when the Department of Agriculture put out a five-cent pamphlet titled "Soybeans for the Table," with recipes for Soybean Casserole, Soybean Soufflé, Salted Soybeans, and— it has yet to become a part of an ADM all-soy lunch—that venerable Chinese staple: Soybean Milk Soup.

Only 2 percent of the soybeans produced in the United States are used for humans' meals. Americans' paltry annual per-capita consumption of soybean products averages nine pounds—the equivalent in weight of a couple of small sacks of potatoes. Relatively few as they may be, those Americans who have embraced the soybean as a fundamental part of their diet are an outspoken tribe and are unflagging in their zealotry. Sometimes they get a boost from an unexpected source, as when Mimi Sheraton, the *Times'* restaurant critic, gave a rare four-star rating—it was surely coincidental that this was one of her last public judgments before she resigned from that job—to a Japanese restaurant whose carte included a "sunny and fragrant" soybean soup and also squid tentacles broiled with miso paste, iced bean-curd squares, raw fish with a paste made of aged soybeans, and dumplings of bean-curd sheet wrapped around meat.

Another writer, Richard Leviton, the editor of the now-defunct magazine *Soyfoods*—it had a circulation of seven thousand and ran features such as "Taking the Soy Venture Seriously"—frequently shared with his readers some of the tribulations they had resignedly accepted as their lot. Leviton attended a World Conference and Exposition on Soya Processing and Utilization held at Acapulco in November 1980. It was sponsored by the American Oil Chemists Society and the American Soybean Association, and it lasted a whole week. He reported glumly that during fifty-four morning plenary lectures only eight minutes were devoted to tofu (the curded end product of coagulated soy milk, after the whey has been discarded) and eight to soy sauce, and that of sixty-eight afternoon roundtable papers only eight dealt with direct human food use.

All told, tofu, which Leviton identified as the "bell-wether of American soy foods," was allocated only four-tenths of 1 percent of the audience's attention. And to make matters worse, at two banquets where the assemblage gorged itself on meat and potatoes, only two dishes were to his taste: shredded cooked soybeans in a vegetable taco, and white rice with a few green soybeans and carrots. "I detected a core lack of commitment to soy foods," he wrote.

ADM makes only a thousand tons a day—a drop in its mammoth production bucket—of soy foods destined for the stomachs of people who sometimes shy away from them out of fear they cause excess flatulence. (It is induced by the soluble sugar in soy flour.) Plant geneticists have moderated that social threat, but an embarrassing reputation is hard to live down. "There's something about the soybean that just seems to put a lot of people off," Andreas once said wistfully. "You know, if soybeans are in storage along with cereals, rats will always eat the soybeans last."* He paused and sighed. "Even the rats don't like us," he concluded in the resigned

---

*Recent studies have shown, for what it may be worth to humans, that a soybean diet reduces the incidence of breast cancer among female rats.

tones of a man who is convinced he will never again as long as he lives sink another five-foot putt.

Among ADM's many exhortatory tracts aimed at the heathens is one brochure extolling simulated meat products and illustrated with a mouth-watering photograph of what looks like a hamburger, nestled inside a bun and garnished with lettuce, tomato, onion, and—who would dare flout America's peculiar predilections?—ketchup. Solemnly asserts the accompanying text: "The soybean. In a world that's short on food, this little legume is as close to a 'miracle plant' as we're ever likely to see."

A tract issued by a Washington outfit called the Soy Protein Council—né Food Protein Council (its onetime chairman was Richard Burket, ADM's vice president and assistant to *its* chairman)—stressed analogs, "products resembling conventional foods in appearance, color, flavor, and texture...which represent the ultimate adaptation of soy protein." For *its* illustrations, it chose a family turkey-dinner scene that resembled a Norman Rockwell Thanksgiving cover for the *Saturday Evening Post* and a portrait of a trustworthy-looking gentleman at a desk with an American flag behind him along with the words: "Government officials must make policy and program decisions that can encourage the development of soy protein products for the savings in money and increase in nutrition that will accrue to the worldwide food system."

To that same end, ADM, in a rehabilitated Decatur high school building, has a Protein Specialties Division painstakingly engaged in research that it hopes might someday affect the human food chain. Alexander T. Bonkowski, its director of Meat, Poultry, and Seafood Applications, who came to the company in 1981 from Vienna Sausage, has roamed the earth seeking ways to, for example, enhance the firmness and elasticity of imitation salmon pâté. He is an expert on analogs. He has made them in South Africa to resemble *biltong*—dried beef jerky comprised of soy protein and kudu trimmings. For an ADM shareholders' buffet at their annual meeting, he came up with a savory facsimile of the Mexican stir-fried beef dish *fajitas*. (The accompanying literature mentioned TVP—the familiar old textured vegetable protein—as an ingredient, but even that sympathetic crowd shied away from the word *soybean*.) At a protein-utilization gathering in Singapore, Bonkowski served some made-in-Japan analogs: a fish paste called *kamaboko*, a diet "ham" (fewer than ninety-seven calories per hundred grams), and *kappa carageenan*, an isolated-soy-protein version of red kelp.

Bonkowski also delivered a scholarly paper titled "The Utilization of Soy Protein from Hot Dogs to Harmaki" (a sort of Japanese egg roll), which ADM was happy to have translated for some Russians who didn't want to miss out on anything. A slide show that he presented about prehistoric bipeds processing dinosaurs (it was a cartoon he'd produced earlier for the American Meat Institute) made such a hit that he has been thinking ever since of doing another on the subject of man's discovering the soybean—perhaps having it fall, like Newton's apple, on a bygone Chinese head. Bonkowski hopes someday, moreover, to be able to establish that isolated soy protein ("the cement that holds flavor," he says, "instead of its running out into the frying pan") is a microbial retardant—i.e., that it could lengthen the shelf life of refrigerated goods and thus radically change the meat and fish industries. Like Andreas, Bonkowski thinks big. "If this inhibition of microbial movement could be proved," he says, "it could rival the atomic bomb."

The trouble with getting people to eat more soybeans, Andreas has long grumbled, is that the meat and dairy lobbies have fostered all kinds of labeling laws for packages that contain them in more than minimal amounts—the theory evidently being that the mere mention of soybeans will turn people away—although they are not yet known to have tried to persuade the surgeon general to have the beans warned against like cigarettes.* The British, he is happy to reflect, are much more tolerant. "You can make a soybean meat pie and put it in the window of your establishment over there," he says, "and nobody will make a fuss about it."

In 1973, for $750,000—only $11,790 in cash, the rest a loan—ADM added to its ever-expanding family of subsidiaries a then-modest enterprise called British Arkady. By 1989, when it was showing an annual profit of $5 million and Andreas was turning down an offer to sell it for $100 million, Arkady had outposts in Ireland, Wales, France, Spain, Portugal, and West Germany (thus far, ADM had handled Eastern Europe directly from Decatur) and had a whole slew of subsidiaries of its own: Regular Tofu, Kwality Foods (sauces, mayonnaises, dips), Genice Foods (Ice Delight cones—vanilla-and-hazelnut or strawberry-and-hazelnut or vanilla-and-raspberry-ripple, all with carob coating), and Vegetarian Feasts. This last had been started in a modest way by a woman confined to a wheelchair with osteoarthritis who gave up meat and, put back on her feet by a combination of vegetarianism and cold showers, started marketing frozen dinners—among them a Stroganoff and a Chile Sin Carne composed mainly of textured vegetable protein.

Among British Arkady's myriad products—many of these unlike their American counterparts, actually visible on European supermarket shelves—are Sosmix, Sizzles, Soya Chunks, Smokeysnaps, So Good (a soy milk), and Vege Bangers, which to some who have sampled them have the true sawdusty taste of bona fide bangers. At last count, Arkady was making 30 million meatless sausages and 20 million meatless burgers a year. "My kids prefer this stuff to ordinary burgers," says Peter Fitch, the general manager of the health-foods

---

*Some soybean boosters, of course, believe the more mentions, the merrier. The Massachusetts makers of quasi–hot dogs called Tofu Pups are happy to list soybeans and soy oil as their two principal ingredients, along with spices, beet powder, liquid smoke flavoring, nutritional yeast, sea salt, paprika oil, and guar gum. According to the *Nutrition Action Healthletter,* "the Pups taste remarkably like the real thing, especially if you eat them with mustard, ketchup, or relish."

division of Haldane Foods, another Arkady subsidiary. "You never find any gristly bits that stick in your mouth." (Because there are some non-meat-eaters who are offended by anything that even reminds them of carnivorousness, Arkady offers meatless items in both meaty and nonmeaty guises.) Haldane not long ago achieved what Fitch proudly termed a breakthrough: a frozen cheeseburger that could be flipped while frying without making a mess, because the cheese had been folded inside the burger!

British Arkady, which Andreas has hailed as "perhaps the fastest-growing part of ADM," is proud, too, of doing its bit to save the world's dwindling supply of rain forests. Its Realeat division hands out a certificate attesting that the person who has devoured one of its Vegeburgers in lieu of a two-ounce burger made of beef has thereby saved twenty-five square feet of precious timberland.* (Realeat was heartened not long ago when a survey it made disclosed that 4.9 percent of the population of Great Britain eschewed real meat.) Andreas, who has been as pro–rain forest as the next man ever since his abortive joint Amazonian venture with D. K. Ludwig, has high hopes for Arkady's burgers. "The people over there may finally have hit on what we've been looking

---

*The back of each certificate contains a sort of lecture, or sermon:

> We're not asking you to send money anywhere, cut off packet tops, or pray for a better world. At Realeat we make it more possible for you to change the world by changing your own effect upon it. Today's level of meat and animal product consumption wreaks a heavy toll—on our environment, and often on our health.
>
> Many British Burgers may not contain meat from rain forests, but this Credit is still valid, since you are reducing the burden on our own land use too. Did you know that half of the European landmass is devoted to agriculture, and 70% of this is used to feed animals—not people? This costly and cruel process involves growing crops specifically to feed animals, and then taking a meagre return in the secondhand food that's left over after a lifetime's energy and waste disposal. Yes, it's a bum steer.
>
> Because it makes so little natural sense, the animal industry needs to be propped up with special laws and subsidies. These are estimated to cost the population of Europe over 50 Billion every year.
>
> And have you noticed how often meat and animal products seem to be associated with the serious hygiene and health problems developing in our food chain today?
>
> So don't send us £10. Eating sensibly is the most important contribution you can make.

for for years," he says. "Burger King and McDonald's are going to have to watch it. How can they not be worried about competition from a hamburger that tastes more like a hamburger than a hamburger?"

"But"—a nosy reporter for the magazine *Insights* inquired of him—"can you serve it up rare?"

"Who wants them rare?" Andreas was quoted as responding after a reflective pause. Then he added, implying a very modest appraisal of his own economic status, "Only the rich eat their meat rare."

In the United States today, vegetarians and other anti-establishment types—"aesthetics" as they are politely termed in ADM circles—are not consumer groups whose wish is anyone's command. Andreas sometimes seems sorry that they're not more powerful, considering how fond they are of emphasizing that if to much of the developed world the staple foods are bread, butter, meat, and milk, well, then, soybeans can be converted into reasonable and nourishing facsimiles of them all. "Consumers are fixed in their ways, and you have to go through fire and brimstone to change them," he says. "But I'll keep trying as long as I live. If I achieve anything important in my life, getting people onto a soy diet will be it."

So far, though, when it comes to Andreas's native land, soybeans have for the most part figured in human meals indirectly, when they have figured at all. The Burger King chain did announce in January 1986 that thenceforth much of its fried food would be prepared not with animal-based oils but rather, with a blend of 20 percent peanut oil and 80 percent soybean oil. (The word *hamsoyburger* has tried to creep into the English language, to describe a hamburger with an actual soy content, but has been largely, and praiseworthily, rebuffed.) More than four years later, McDonald's capitulated. It would soon be cooking its French fries, it declared, exclusively in vegetable oils—cottonseed and corn were those specified. ADM's common stock, which rarely fluctuated any single day by more than a quarter or an eighth of a point, leapt one whole point skyward.

American patrons of supermarkets and restaurants may not take the soybean as seriously as Andreas wishes they would, but American farmers do, though with the stomachs of chickens and hogs and cattle more on their minds than their own. The United States has lately been growing 2 billion bushels of the old bean a year, 800 million of which have become an export crop worth $5 billion—or as Andreas is quick to point out whenever the subject of balances of trade arises, more than exporters of jet aircraft receive for their extraterritorial endeavors. "The soybean is a massive economic institution in this world," he says. He once told Hubert Humphrey, in expanding on that theme, "Every dollar's worth of wheat or corn or soybeans not produced and hence not exported results in one dollar's worth of gold leaving the country."

Most Americans, though, are not farmers, and Andreas is gloomily aware of the majority's indifference to, and sometimes even deprecation of, *Glycine max*. Those of his countrymen who regard themselves as comics sometimes seem to take it as a joke. During one installment of *Wheel of Fortune* for example, when Pat Sajak—who often *is* funny—learned that a woman contestant grew corn and soybeans, first he asked her, "What do you do with soybeans?" and later—foolishly, considering what she'd just told him—"Have you ever seen a soybean?" It was as if she'd asked him if he'd ever met Vanna White.

People who traffic in soybeans do a lot with them. For sheer versatility and virtuosity, few plants, or any other of nature's gifts to mankind, can match them. Wherever one looks, one finds them: axle grease, beer and ale, wallboard, vitamins, dusting powder, putty, oilcloth, alcohol, varnish, bottle caps, caulking compounds, linoleum, cement, insecticides, nitroglycerin, a dust-buster for grain elevators—the list goes on and on. Back in 2838 B.C., Shen Nung catalogued over three hundred soybean-involved remedies for afflictions of the heart, liver, stomach, kidneys,and bowels. Much more recently, in her 1935 book, *The Soy Bean*, Elizabeth Bowdidge wrote: "It has been said, and it seems the truth, that a country growing the soya bean provides food for its people, its cattle, and its guns!"

In 1989, the *Soybean Digest* was glad to reveal that pages nine through twenty-four of its June/July issue were printed with soybean ink. Hundreds of American newspapers (not to mention the exhortatory tracts of Earth Day celebrants) had already abandoned old-fashioned petroleum-based ink for soy, which inhibited smudging and made color pages brighter and clearer. The *Kiplinger Agricultural Letter* had forecast that by 1992 every American newspaper would have switched. That could represent a use for the oil content of some 40 million bushels. A substantial amount, to be sure, but only one-two-hundred-and-fiftieth of the annual domestic output of soybean oil: 5 million tons, or forty pounds for every man, woman, and child in the country. In Decatur alone, ADM has nine soybean-oil production lines churning out 10 billion pounds a year of twenty-three items under 434 labels—only a few of these revealing their source, and all consigned, often in railroad-tank-car lots, to such readily identifiable recipients as Frito-Lay, Wesson, Fleischmann's, and Kentucky Fried Chicken.

Andreas once attempted to put some of this into a comprehensible perspective and, indeed, to give a partial explanation of how his company functions, while addressing a symposium at the Chicago Board of Trade:

> Although you have undoubtedly heard numerous stories about various products made from soybeans, I can assure you that none of the byproducts are of much consequence to the crusher except oil and meal. A crushing plant simply serves as a conduit through which soybeans move in their natural journey from farm to farm. Five-sixths of the weight of the bean is consumed right on the farm in the form of meal. They simply travel through the crushing plant for the purpose of having the oil extracted. They are then returned

to the farm in one form or another as a feed. In the economic sense it is only the oil that moves off the farm.

The merchandising department of a modern soybean operation includes four basic functions, which are usually managed by four individuals. First, and the most important functionary, is the merchandising supervisor, some of whose problems I will discuss later. The other three are the soybean buyer, the oil salesman, and the meal salesman.

The buyer is assigned the duty of buying soybeans day by day as the country appears willing to sell. He is not concerned with the flat price but is concerned with buying the beans at a proper relationship to the nearby future in Chicago. It is also his duty to pay attention to the quality and particularly to the origin of the beans from a freight standpoint. It is vitally important that the actual cash beans he buys have their origin at points convenient to the plant location where they will be crushed. Above all, it is his duty to see that there is an adequate supply of beans ahead of the plant to keep it running at capacity at all times.

The bean buyer has a corollary responsibility. That is to utilize as profitably as possible the company's warehousing facilities. Thus, if cash soybeans are selling at a substantial discount under the deferred future, he will make a greater effort to accumulate cash beans in excess of immediate crushing requirements so as to earn these warehousing charges. On the other hand, should cash beans be selling at a price above the deferred future less the cost of carrying the beans, he will probably be more inclined to let his warehouse space stay empty or use it for other purposes and buy the beans only as needed. Each time he makes a purchase he makes a corresponding sale of a future in the pit and his job is finished.

Another member of this team is the oil salesman. It is his duty to be prepared at all times to offer oil from the plant production to customers convenient to the plant. He tries to be prepared to quote a competitive price every day, regardless of the crushing margin at that time. He is particularly concerned with selling the oil to the proper destinations and for the proper shipping dates so that the entire production of the plant can be shipped regularly. The oil salesman has a responsibility to utilize his company's oil warehousing facilities. Thus, if there is a carrying charge in oil, that is, if the spot oil is selling at a substantial discount below the deferred futures, he will be inclined to hold his oil in his warehousing facilities so as to earn this carrying charge. On the other hand, if spot oil is selling at a price higher than the deferred future less cost of carrying, he will be inclined toward selling the oil as it is made, since there is no warehousing charge to be earned. After making a sale, he buys a like amount in the form of a futures contract and his task is complete. . . .

21

Waiting for [free trade] is like
keeping a porch light on
for Jimmy Hoffa.

—DOA

I N the dog-eat-dog world (who-eats-what-world might be
more accurate) in which Andreas labors, there are no
free rides. Soybean oil, for instance, has to compete
against other vegetable oils, most of which—corn, peanut, et
al.—ADM also produces. Its most recent rival of consequence is the upstart canola, a variety of rapeseed nurtured in
Canada (thus its name) that has already caught up with and
overtaken sunflower seed. Most rapeseed oils are rich in
erucic acid, which is bad for the heart. Canola contains very
little of that. Moreover, in a world increasingly dominated by
dietetic apprehensions, saturated fats have become as unpop-
ular indoors as the deer tick outside, and canola contains
only 6.8 percent of them. Sunflower seed's rating is an 11,
soy's—for all its protein glitter—a 15.

The March 1989 issue of the understandably partisan

Soybean Digest carried the worried headline "Is Canola Coming?" and estimated that by the year 2000 it might have taken root on 10 million United States acres—still measurably behind soybeans' 60 million, but patently to be reckoned with. Andreas was watching, too. ADM deals in all kinds of vegetable oils and did not want to miss the boat on this one. Starting in 1985, accordingly, it bought four canola-oil processing plants—one in Canada, one in North Dakota, and two in West Germany.

The American Soybean Association was less willing to welcome the newcomer, and for a while it argued against the Food and Drug Administration's granting it a "GRAS" rating— "generally recognized as safe." The ASA wanted food packages containing canola oil to be imprinted with the phrase— presumably scary enough to deter some prospective purchasers—"low-erucic rapeseed oil."

The American Soybean Association, with headquarters at St. Louis, was born in Camden, Indiana—initially, as the National Soybean Growers Association—in 1920. One of its progenitors was the agronomist William J. Morse, who has been called the Father of Soybeans in America, and who delivered himself in 1918 of the then-iconoclastic opinion that the soybean was "a very desirable article of human food." Morse added, "The large yield of seed, the excellent quality of forage, the ease of growing and harvesting the crop, its freedom from insect enemies and plant diseases, and the possibilities of the seed for the production of oil and meal and as a food all tend to give this crop a high potential importance and assure its greater agricultural development in America." Two varieties of soybean in the United States have been named the George Washington and the Morse.

Morse was born in 1884 and on getting a bachelor-of-science degree from Cornell, in 1907, went to work for the Bureau of Plant Industry of the Department of Agriculture. His immediate superior was Charles V. Piper, a pro-soybean man who soon had the apprentice cultivating soybeans on an experimental farm that Agriculture operated across the Potomac from the District of Columbia—a site that it later reluctantly yielded up so that the War Department could be Pentagonally encamped upon it. Morse and Piper were coauthors, in 1923, of *The Soybean,* which is still regarded as a classic in its field. "There can be little doubt that the soybean is destined to become one of the major American crops," they wrote, though at the time that was largely wishful thinking. Morse kept plugging away at what to many others seemed a hopeless enterprise. "We must keep this work going," he wrote, on his own, in 1927, "and place the soybean where it belongs— in the 'King' row with King Corn and King Cotton." Until his death, at seventy-five, in 1959, he was one of the most faithful of soybean consumers. Among his favorite dishes— an entrée that is not very widely served in Massachusetts, nor even at Decatur, Illinois—was Boston Baked Soybeans.

The American Soybean Association's major problem is that, unlike most agricultural or industrial groups, it has no single-minded constituency. Most of the five hundred thousand United States farmers who grow soybeans do not grow them exclusively. Thus the ASA's lobbyists and other spokesmen must be careful not to push too hard against the interests of organizations promoting say, milk or meat; its members may also raise cattle or hogs. Although member Andreas felt friendly enough toward the ASA to merge its interests with those of his other friend Tom Dewey, its goals and ADM's do not always jibe. Soybean farmers, after all, want to get the best price possible for their crops; soybean processors want to buy these cheap. Andreas was as pleased as any proponent of soybeans, though, by a report from the director of the ASA's office in China—one of eleven foreign outposts it maintains—following a weaning trial at Hangzhou, that the local government officials were high on soy. "Better animal nutrition using soymeal is the key to growth for commercial swine production in China," he wrote. "Not only will the four new six-hundred-sow farms help meet China's demand for pork, but they will also be models where more Chinese groups can see US soymeal at work."

The American Soybean Association had underwritten

those far-off trials with checkoff funds: levies it was author-ized by Congress (through a Soybean Promotion Research and Consumer Information Act) to collect from its members in the amount of one-half of 1 percent of the market price of each bushel they sell—some $60 million. (Checkoff money also enables the ASA to send emissaries it calls soy ambassa-dors to spread its gospel among schoolchildren and senior citizens.) Beef, dairy, and pork trade groups have similar checkoffs. So does the Malaysia Oil Palm Growers' Council, which for a while seemed to be occupying more of the ASA's time and expendable funds than all its overseas agents and domestic ambassadors put together.

The world's annual consumption of all kinds of oil fats comes to 70 million tons. The United States's 12.5 percent share of that is a billion-dollar business, and it has been affected, as Andreas has moved along from farm boy to supermarketer, by his countrymen's and -women's increasing preoccupation with environmentalism and health. There was much concern about the fat content of various foodstuffs using these oils, and whether the fats were saturated or unsaturated. By the spring of 1988, a Washington, D.C., nonprofit institution called the Center for Science in the Public Interest would be issuing a forty-five-page $5 pamphlet—its cover adorned with what appeared to be a two-decker hamburger dripping with goo—titled "Saturated Fat Attack." It said:

> After many years of research, debate, and delay, the medi-cal community generally agrees that the number one die-tary problem for most Americans is eating too much fat in general and too much saturated fat in particular. Saturated fat promotes heart disease, while too much of any kind of fat appears to promote cancer. The challenge now is to educate consumers to avoid such fats, and to persuade food processors to reduce fat levels in their products.

And later, getting more specific:

The words "palm" and "coconut" conjure up visions of idyllic islands, but the tropical oils made from these foods are highly saturated vegetable fats: palm oil (51 per cent saturated), coconut oil (92 per cent saturated), and palm kernel oil (86 per cent saturated). By comparison, beef fat is 52 per cent saturated, and lard is 41 per cent saturated. Palm, palm kernel, and coconut oils can be found in hundreds of products, ranging from cereals and coffee whiteners to frostings and frozen dinners. Tropical oils offer several advantages to food manufacturers. Because they are so highly saturated, these oils resist oxidation, rancidity, and spoilage. They are also often the cheapest fats on the market. Finally, some companies undoubtedly use tropical oils out of habit, having incorporated the fats into their recipes years ago, before the fats were linked to heart disease.

Starting in 1984, the Center tried to get the Food and Drug Administration to require that items containing these tropical oils have them identified on package labels. Politics got involved on, the pamphlet continued, a global scale:

> One reason for the broad support for the legislation is that many farm state legislators believe that more honest labeling of foods would encourage processors to switch from tropical oils, which are imported, to a domestically produced oil, such as corn or soy. The Soybean Association, which represents the huge soybean industry, strongly supports the legislation.

> The soybean industry's support for clearer labeling of tropical oils has, however, triggered stiff opposition from nations that export such oils to the United States, including Malaysia, (palm and palm kernel oils), the Philippines (coconut oil), and Indonesia (palm oil). Those nations (with the help of the well-known lobbying firm of Hill & Knowlton in Malaysia's case) have charged that better labeling would constitute an illegal trade barrier. The Philippines goes so far as to argue that the current Aquino government would fall if American foods were better labeled, because exports of coconut oil would decline.

The Malaysians could afford to hire a hard-hitting American spokesman. Their checkoff rate was 7.7 cents a bushel, and they had accumulated a war chest estimated by *Soybean Digest* at more than $14 million. The Center went on to list a slew of brand names that used the saturated fats, and how much went into each. Nabisco led all comers, with fifty-one citations, including Bonkers Chew chocolate candy, Chips n More coconut chocolate-chip cookies, Royal real cheesecake mix and cracker crust, and far more significantly, Fig Newtons, gingersnaps, and Ritz crackers.

In 1985, a wealthy Omaha, Nebraska, metal fabricator, Phil Sokoloff, who in 1966, at the age of forty-three, had survived a heart attack, got into the act, or sideshow. It was, for him, pretty much a solo performance. He formed a National Heart Savers Association, of which he was president and near as anyone could figure out, only member. He began taking out newspaper ads, some of them full-page ones, excoriating saturated fats, with challenging headlines like "The Poisoning of America!" He wanted his readers to boycott all products containing saturated fats; and to alleviate any doubts, he appended pictures of several of Nabisco's finest, including Barnum's animal crackers and Oreos. "Why do food companies care so little?" he lamented.

The Malaysians and their American flacks could hardly be expected to take that sort of thing without demurring. Four hundred thousand individuals out there work on producing oil fats from 4 million acres, and their efforts yield a $2.4 billion export income that represents more than 10 percent of the country's gross national product. Presently, Hill & Knowlton was buying full-page advertising space of its own, on behalf of its far-off client. "To the American People— The Facts About Palm Oil," one of them started off. It didn't mention Sokoloff by name, alluding, rather, to a "vested interest group [that] launched an extremely aggressive campaign to discredit imported edible oils, in particular palm oil. It has been insinuated that the consumption of palm oil could be detrimental to the cardiovascular health of the

American people. Indeed, subsequent advertisements have claimed that palm oil is poisoning America."

The ASA was treated more forthrightly:

> The Malaysian producers of palm oil have no objection whatsoever in accepting fair and nondiscriminating labeling legislation. In fact, on October 22, 1987, the Malaysian Oil Palm Growers' Council proposed to the president and senior executive officers of the American Soybean Association that both parties jointly undertake scientific research at various American research centers and then submit the results to the American Food and Drug Administration to establish without ambiguity whether consumption of palm oil would be detrimental to the cardiovascular health of the American people. This proposal was not accepted.
>
> We urge the American processors and consumers of palm oil not to be intimidated by scare tactics which are not based on scientific evidence.

Hill & Knowlton rounded up supportive statements from such as the American Council on Science and Health and the Wistar Institute of Anatomy and Biology, put out releases revealing that a study at the Institute of Medical Research at Kuala Lumpur had found that "the palm oil–enriched diet lowered both serum cholesterol and LDL (low-density lipoprotein) cholesterol levels of the twenty-seven volunteers who were fed a palm oil–enriched diet"; reminded all hands that American food processors often hydrogenated their soybean oil, in the course of which "a large percentage (25%–45%) of the natural polyunsaturated fatty acids are reduced to the modified *trans* monoene configuration and to modified *cis* monoenes, substances found naturally in only trace amounts"; and imported Dr. Augustine Ong, director general of the Palm Oil Research Institute of Malaysia, who let it be known at a press conference that among the virtues of the palm oil used in the United States was that the tocopherols and tocotrienols in it promote—or at least have done so in animal studies—"prostacyclin production, leading to a vasodilatory and antithrombotic state."

The American Soybean Association—without going to the trouble of trying to translate that from the original Malaysian—held a press conference of its own. "We will not be bullied," declared its president, James Lee Adams, a Camilla, Georgia, farmer, as his associates distributed a prepared statement:

> Alarmed by the power of US consumers, the palm indus-
> try is making a desperate effort to save its US market. A
> costly advertising campaign funded by foreign palm produc-
> ers and run by a Madison Avenue public relations agency is
> now under way. The campaign makes the same confusing,
> overstated claims the palm industry has used for two years.
> It cites unsubstantiated research to contradict dozens of
> nutritional studies done by this nation's leading institu-
> tions and others around the world.

But some of the difficulties the ASA encounters because so many of its members are engaged in so many activities not involving soybeans emerged when Adams was asked why, if his organization cared so much about health, it did not direct its criticism at, along with tropical oils, lard. He observed that many of his flock were also in the livestock business. "I don't think any organization would work against its own industry," he said.

Before long, all sorts of people got caught up in the controversy. A Texas correspondent who used the signature "Cholesterol Conscious" wrote to Andreas's friend Ann Landers that he and those close to him were scrutinizing labels and "when we see the dreaded words 'palm' or 'coconut' oil, we will put the product right back on the shelves." He went on, "Little people like us have a hard time getting the giants of industry to listen, but I believe when Ann Landers speaks, they will listen."

She spoke: "It is a well-known fact that saturated fats elevate the cholesterol level in the blood and an excess of cholesterol can clog the arteries and lead to a heart attack. The Keebler company recently announced it will no longer use animal fats and tropical oils in its products. Hooray for Keebler! Now how about the rest of you? Please show us you care!"

Miss Landers must be very widely read. Before long, another dozen companies—among them Nabisco and Procter and Gamble—had announced that they were in the process of reconstituting many of their offerings without tropical oils. By mid-March 1989, *Milling & Baking News* ran a dispatch from Kuala Lumpur: Malaysia's minister of Primary Industries, just back from a trip to the USA, had announced a "ceasefire in the war of words." The story said he had concluded that a continuation of the battle, much less an escalation, would cause great harm to both sides by frightening consumers away from foods containing *any* vegetable oils. He claimed that his American visit had accomplished a great deal to dispel misconceptions about palm oil among government and food officials. He said the campaign against palm oil was "a trade war disguised as a health issue." Noting that several major food manufacturers had decided not to use palm oil in various products, he said this would cost these companies millions because palm oil was cheaper. He said U.S. soybean producers were wrong to fear competition from Southeast Asia on account of enormous global demand for oils. He predicted that palm oil production would rise to 8 million tons by the end of this century from the current level of 5 million, but that palm oil would still account for only 15 to 20 percent of the edible-oil market.

Throughout the conflict, Andreas and ADM had done their best to keep aloof. As soybean farmers have a wide spread of interests, so does the company. There are few fats, saturated and un-, in which it has not at some time or other dabbled. Andreas was naturally sorry to see his friend Ross Johnson, then of Nabisco, taken to task, but he was not going to get involved any more than he customarily would in a duel for a farm-state congressional seat between a Democrat and a Republican. He did go so far as to grouse in a speech, at a time when the dispute was just building up steam, "The

World Bank poured hundreds of millions of dollars into Malaysia to create a palm-oil industry. Now Malaysia heavily subsidizes palm-oil production and dumps its surplus on world markets at half the price of other vegetable oils." He could have added, as he did on another occasion when the subject came up, "And people talk about free trade! There isn't any free trade anymore. And waiting for it to come is like keeping a porch light on for Jimmy Hoffa."

Later, asked what opinion if any he had about the one-man crusade of Phil Sokoloff, whose next big public move was to take out ads deploring the fat content of McDonald's hamburgers, Andreas answered, somewhat enigmatically, "I don't know anything about the man. It's probably a good thing I don't. If I did, I might have a new flock of enemies."

22

B Y 1978, just into his sixties, Andreas had become increasingly known as a man to be reckoned with. The
New York Times, for instance, gave him credit not
only for having high-powered connections with a couple of
Minnesota banking institutions (one of which administered a
trust Andreas had set up for Hubert Humphrey), but also for
being associated with more than half a dozen other impressive-
sounding financial entities that, as it happened, he had never
heard of. But the article's central point was valid: Andreas
was now moving surefootedly, and with long strides, in
big-business circles.

Still, the soil of his formative years was never far from
his thoughts. "I calculated the other day that the price of
land between Pittsburgh and Denver has dropped by about
six hundred billion dollars in twenty months," he said. (Low

crop prices were of course, one reason.) "If that happened to the New York Stock Exchange, that would be five hundred points off the Dow. People would be jumping out windows. But that is what has happened to the Midwest." One way to avoid that, he believed—he had by then become comfortable with large figures and could toss them around without blinking—would be to plant a billion trees. (Andreas is no more immune to inflation than any other businessman concerned with the economy. Several years later, his assessment of the near-suicidal damage to the Pittsburgh-to-Denver corridor reached a trillion dollars, and of trees to help repair it a trillion, too.)

Whatever the precise figures, to this day Andreas keeps reminding anyone who will listen that the nation's topsoil is disappearing astronomically, at the rate of close to eight tons per acre per year—6 billion tons' worth, or the equivalent of an inch of precious dirt for all the farmland of Alabama, Arizona, California, Connecticut, Delaware, Florida, Maine, Maryland, Massachusetts, New Hampshire, New Jersey, New York, Pennsylvania, and Vermont. To people who brought up the subject of nuclear weapons in his presence, he was apt to say—and his response had nothing to do with his closeness to Mikhail Gorbachev—that when it came to threats to the nation's survival, atom bombs were potentially no more catastrophic than the loss of topsoil. One reason for US recognition of Communist China, Andreas was arguing before Nixon betook himself there in 1972, was that Montana farmers' idle land was being blown away while just twelve miles to the north stable fields were waving with wheat destined to be exchanged for Chinese cash.

"The downfall of nearly every civilization in history," Andreas told Mike Carr of his home town's *Herald & Review*, "has been because they used up their topsoil and couldn't feed themselves and developed into a 'poor rich' society.... Let's face it. The state of Iowa has used half its topsoil in one hundred years, a greater disaster [he said another time] than the threat of an atom bomb. In another sixty years it will use the other half. There ought to be bells ringing all over America. There ought to be Paul Reveres going through the Eastern cities." Andreas pressed on to reveal, as he had earlier to Nelson Rockefeller and Hubert Humphrey, what Carr called his "visions":

> He would like to see a string of "vocational schools" throughout the Heartland, devoted solely to soil and water conservation. The whole project "would provide jobs for a million people for a generation, saving the topsoil.
> "If you have vocational schools that were built around tree farming, terracing of the soil... little dams, terraces, retaining walls, lots of people would get a great sense of achievement, a sense of pride, a sense of success.
> "... If you had fifty vocational schools in the Middle West, teach people how to do it, how to supervise it, you could have an enormous number of small businesses around the Middle West for the next twenty years, engaged in the process of surveying, and leveling the soil and damming up the subsurface water... and keeping it on the farm."

When he is echoing others' visionary words, Andreas likes to cite an ancient Vedic truth: "The earth is our mother, and we are all her children." He has one undeniable advantage over his Indian precursors: he can contemplate the earth, filially, from way on high. Approaching the Decatur airport one day, he beckoned for a companion to join him at a window—fasten-your-seat-belts be damned—to scrutinize some fields below. "The color's not too bad yet," Andreas muttered. "A good soaking would help, though." His eye roved to another area, where a cloud of dust trailed two crawling tractors. He frowned. "That *is* bad. Maybe they are planting a new crop. Maybe they had to because it was too dry for soybeans to come up." It was not a happy landing.

Earlier that ground-covering day, before a stopover at Shannon, Ireland—he likes to touch down there because the airport shops offer a mouth-watering choice of indigenous breads—he had mused, as he peered below, "It's interesting how small countries take better care of their land than we do. There are always a few American farmers who figure they can move if need be somewhere else, or their children can. The Irish, though, put hedgerows around their plots to conserve them, because they know they have nowhere else to go."

After another such aerial observation over another small country, Andreas remarked, "It's fantastic to see Israel. They've terraced every piece of land and have hung on to every drop of rain and have made it impossible for a grain of dust to blow away. That has to be done in the United States, too. If it isn't, our civilization will go by the boards, like all the rest of them."

What can one man—what can he—do about this? Well, there are always his Sunday-morning, soft-sell ADM television commercials. One commercial that Andreas especially liked had a farmer and his family standing by glumly while the land that could no longer sustain them was being auctioned off. "I remembered that sort of thing happening from the thirties," Andreas says. "I made them show that commercial three or four times."

"I've learned over the years that most politicians aren't interested in advice," Andreas says, "so I don't offer it. But if any of them ever asked me for any about redistributing the national wealth, I would say something like, 'Our farmers are entitled to money so they can keep their land. Most of them want to be able to turn over their land to the next generation. But the only way they can make money themselves is to mine their soil. So they should be given money to conserve it—to plant trees and bushes, that sort of thing.' But if I said it, would anybody listen? And if anybody listened, would anybody do anything about it?"

One person who was listening, and watching, was the columnist Michael Kinsley, who wrote in the *New Republic* and scattered newspapers how "Sunday morning is dominated by a mysterious company that is virtually unknown for anything *except* its public affairs commercials," although he did concede that Dwayne Andreas was known "for running a resort in Florida." Kinsley seemed to think it wrong—indeed, "offensive"—for a company to say nice things about itself in its own advertising, and his choices of chastising adjectives included "dishonest" and "cloying." Andreas did not personally respond—he was much too busy running an $8-billion global enterprise—but ADM's advertising agency, in a complaint to the *Washington Post*, did try to achieve some sort of adjectival balance by characterizing Kinsley as "malicious" and "juvenile."

Andreas has long been interested in discovering new raw materials, and finding new uses for old ones. If he was to be the Soybean King, what a realm to rule: there never seemed to be a limit to *Glycine max*'s adaptation. But *Zea mays* was no slouch, either.

One of corn's potential uses had been urged upon Andreas back in 1954 by Joseph Pew, four years before the Sun Oil man had inducted Dwayne into the Chemical Council fold. Petroleum products, of course, had made the Pews what they were, but this member of the clan seemed to be more interested in editing his *Farm Journal* than pumping gas. Pew, who knew about Andreas's Mennonite background, with its emphasis on self-reliance, liked to talk to the younger man, Dwayne recalled, about "the folly of farmers totally liquidating their horse population and thereby becoming completely dependent on foreign oil instead of home-grown oats as fuel."

Pew kept urging Andreas, as someone seeking to make ever better use of farm commodities, to investigate the potentialities of a replacement for, or at any rate additive to, petroleum-based gasoline: ethanol.

Ethanol—ethyl alcohol, a lead-free octane booster—first came to the attention of many American motorists during the gasoline crunch of the late 1970s, as an ingredient of the alternative fuel gasohol. Drivers lining up at pumps were more interested in getting their tanks filled, or sprinkled, than in the fact that the exhaust emissions of gasohol, which is 90 percent gasoline and 10 percent ethanol, were one-third lower in carbon monoxide than those of ordinary gas. Andreas was emphatically not among the uninformed; he has done his best to stimulate what he deems proper interest, with such challenging statements as "Do you know that more people die from carbon-monoxide poisoning than from drugs?"

However ignorant of or indifferent to the characteristics of their gas-tank intakes the general public might be, ethyl alcohol had been well-known to American farmers—and not merely Mennonites and other hippophiles—since the turn of the century, as another use for their corn and grains, and as a potentially indispensable and renewable asset when and if the world ran out of oil.* Ethanol can be made from potatoes, too, as farmers in Idaho have long been aware; indeed, they have seen to it that state-owned motor vehicles there must run on fuel containing at least 10 percent ethyl alcohol.

Then there is ethanol's rival methanol, a distillation from wood or coal or natural gas. While motor fuels containing 10 percent of either of the two additives tend to burn cleaner than unadulterated gasoline, to have a slightly higher oxygen content, and to throw off less toxic exhaust emissions, they also tend to be more expensive, and cars running on them get less mileage. Ethanol usually costs a bit more than methanol, but some of its partisans contend that the latter is more volatile, and a few have even resorted to expressing the hope that because of that unwelcome characteristic people driving with methanol in their tanks should take pains not to run into anybody.

In 1906, Congress passed a Denatured Alcohol Act, which exempted alcohol used for fuel from a $2.20-a-gallon tax on alcohol used for beverages. Secretary of Agriculture James Wilson told a House committee, while the bill was under consideration:

> In the future—it may be some time in the future—the time will certainly come when the world will have to look to agriculture for the production of its fuel, its light, and its motive power. It seems to me that through the medium of

---

*Andreas, in his own way a latter-day sharer of such apprehensions, once spent $25,000 having a well—a dry one—dug on some Decatur property he owned, to check out a neighborhood rumor that he might be sitting atop a gusher.

alcohol, agriculture can furnish in the most convenient form for the use of man this absolutely necessary source of supply.

During the First World War, with such newfangled machines as airplanes and tanks coming prominently on the scene and demanding motive power, Henry Ford was a conspicuous proponent of grain-alcohol fuels. Some of his automobiles had already been fitted out with adjustable carburetors. They could be accommodated at the owner's wish to either straight gasoline or blends.

In the early 1920s, Standard Oil of New Jersey experimented with a fuel a quarter of which consisted of war-surplus alcohol, but it was alleged to separate from gasoline and to make engines stall. A decade later, during the Depression, alcohol fuels once more claimed attention; now, they were looked to as an opportunity for impoverished farmers to derive some income from their surplus crops. The proliferation of the horseless carriage was a factor, too, of course: farmers were finding that they had diminishing remunerative use for the 30-odd million acres (with a potential production of 875 million bushels of corn) they'd long set aside to grow horse feed. One contemporary analysis of the scene concluded, "The acres that used to feed the horse would now feed the automobile."

With Prohibition in effect, naturally, Drys kept worrying about the likely diversion of farm produce from motor fuel to moonshine. Proponents of fuel alcohol countered that the stuff was not potable, except at grave personal risk. Some of the loudest outcries came from sources not thitherto suspected of occupying high moral ground—oil-company spokesmen who deplored the possibility of mixed fuels giving a leg up to bootleggers.

In 1937, a plant at Atchison, Kansas, began making a combination of alcohol and gasoline called Argol. That represented the only major attempt in the first half of the twentieth century to produce this kind of motor fuel on a commercial basis. The place turned out ten thousand gallons of ethanol a day, derived from four or five thousand bushels of corn or wheat. Argol was available for a while at some two thousand service stations in eight Midwest states, but only for two years. The public did not seem attracted to what *BusinessWeek* dismissed, unattractively, as "alky gas."

During the Second World War, ethyl alcohol made a comeback of sorts as a key ingredient of synthetic rubber. That important contribution to the Allied effort aside, Franklin D. Roosevelt's attitude toward ethanol seemed a trifle narrow-minded. The president wrote to a California state legislator (the American Petroleum Institute made sure it was widely circulated):

> While it is true that a number of foreign countries process agricultural materials for the production of alcohol as a motor fuel, it is equally true that the motor fuel economy of countries possessing no petroleum resources is very different from such economy in the United States. It has never been established in this country that the conversion of agricultural products into motor fuel is economically feasible or necessary for national defense.

Andreas got into ethanol in 1977, although he'd been what he called "a gasohol watcher" since his chemurgic chat about the future of fuels with Joe Pew twenty-three years earlier. When Illinois's Environmental Protection Agency suggested that ADM invest in a water-pollution control system for a fructose plant at Decatur, Andreas decided instead to spend the money turning the wastes generated from processing that corn into ethanol. Thirteen and a half million dollars later, he had himself a distillery capable of producing six million gallons—the contribution of two and a half million bushels of corn. But in 1978, as corn became scarcer and costlier at the same time that gasoline became more available and cheaper, ethanol couldn't be marketed for automotive purposes except at a substantial loss, and for a while ADM's venture into that field was described by some as "Dwayne's folly."

For Andreas, the initial absence of demand for gasohol

was only a temporary setback. There were other uses for his ocean of alcohol. The Smirnoff vodka people were happy to find a new source of supply for the white lightning—ADM's was 200 proof—they needed for their line of goods. (In Andreas's Decatur guesthouse, to this day, there are drinking glasses commemoratively imprinted "Ethyl Gasohol" and "Contents: Pure Alcohol.") But with his factory up and operating, he was ready for the shortages resulting from the 1979 revolution in Iran. A year later, there were gasohol pumps at nearly ten thousand United States service stations, mostly, to be sure, in the Midwestern corn belt.

In 1979, the federal excise tax on gasoline was nine cents a gallon. That year, Senator Dole of Kansas, who since the death of Tom Dewey was sometimes thought of as Andreas's Best Republican Friend (and whom all-time Best Democratic Friend Hubert Humphrey had once described to friend Dwayne as "the smartest Republican in the Senate"), was instrumental in getting Congress to reduce the tax on gasohol to three cents a gallon. That helped make it competitive with gasoline. So, at Dole's further urging, did a forty-cents-a-gallon tariff voted by Congress against gasohol imported from abroad—much of this from Andreas's old adversary Brazil. Although that didn't jibe with President Carter's views on free foreign trade, his administration didn't demur, in part, it was alleged, because it was an election year and Andreas had proposed building a $250 million ethanol plant in Iowa, a state the Democrats hoped very much would go their way. After Carter lost Iowa to Reagan, and lost the White House, too, the plant somehow never materialized.

There was criticism, much of it from Democratic politicians, of ethanol's tax break. Representative Charles Vanik, D., Ohio, called it "a steal for the benefit of one company." Senator Dole professed surprise. Why, he said, as a farm-state representative he'd been pro-gasohol back in the sixties, before he'd ever even met Dwayne Andreas, who, he would tell the *Wall Street Journal*, might have benefited from the tax exemption, "but not because of any action Bob Dole sneaked through Congress. I can't help it if anybody has a corner on the market. [ADM had its stamp on a good deal more than half of all the ethanol then in production.] He didn't get any corner on the market from anything I did."

As late as December 1985, Dole would be quoted by the *Washington Post* as saying, though by then he and Andreas had spent a good deal of time together at Bal Harbour and other sites, "I don't know anything about ADM." (Andreas has never professed not to know what line of work Dole was in.) And Andreas himself told the *Post* that the real beneficiaries of whatever special treatment was meted out to ethanol was for the benefit of farmers and the government. "For them, it's significant," he said. "For us, it's just a throughput." Raymond Price, who as a Richard Nixon speech writer, syndicated columnist, and president of the Economic Club acquired considerable expertise about the interrelationships of big business and politics, says, "Dwayne has a lot of friends who can do things. What Bob Dole does is what any farm-state senator would be a fool not to do."

"I'm not a political force," Andreas himself says. "I've never got Bob Dole to do anything. The people you have to persuade about anything are the farmers. They're the ones who have power. I'm not an evangelist. I'm involved in politics because of the business I'm in. Real cynics say that my operation is a toll bridge and that I'm the collector. I say that I'm a booster. Anyway, toll bridges are necessary. Our salvation is that we only make a nominal return on our investment."

It's not only real cynics who are fond of the toll-bridge analogy. When one new business associate asked Andreas, "What's the secret of your success?" the answer came back, "The trick is always to own the tollgate." His friend and ADM director John Daniels has said:

> Some years ago I heard DOA expound on his theory of the importance of the toll-taker. He harked back to the medieval days of movement on the Rhine, when all of the little castles along the river were originally built to extract a toll from every traveler. One of DOA's business theories

stresses the importance of knowing how and where to erect toll stations. A long time ago, for instance, he decided that moving the gigantic quantities of all types of agricultural products to the mills for processing and then moving the many different end products, both solid and liquid, to market is a terribly important part of the business and that it should be looked at as another profit center. DOA has taken ADM into barge, truck, and rail transportation in a massive way. In the agricultural-processing game, transportation is much too important a toll station to leave to others!

If you have to have an enemy, and you want
to win in politics, get for your enemy the
seven big oil companies and the five biggest
banks in the East. You'll never lose.

—DOA

MEANWHILE, according to some researchers at Purdue University, the development of ethanol had increased the annual income of American corn growers by a dime a bushel, or almost $900 million. And what was more, Andreas would tell a legislative conference in Washington, whatever tax benefits companies such as his might have accrued were emphatically deserved as "a national-security measure to make the United States independent of Persian Gulf oil."

It has never been easy for Andreas to maintain his political friendships and avoid censure therefor. If he let Bob Dole borrow one of his airplanes to fly to a speaking engagement, was that not carrying cronyism too far, Andreas's detractors charged, even when a Dole campaign committee reimbursed ADM for the courtesy? If the day after he had breakfast with the secretary of agriculture—they had talked principally, Dwayne insisted, about soil conservation—it was revealed that the government was going to allow an additional 30 million bushels of its hoarded corn to be channeled into ethanol production, was that not suspicious? Not at all, Andreas retorted; he had been allocated those 30 million only after agreeing that ADM would buy an additional 30 million at prices far above the market price.

The slings and arrows he constantly had to duck! The crosses to bear! Here was the magazine *Top Producer*, for example, quoting a cravenly anonymous agent of the gasoline industry: "ADM wraps itself in the American flag, God, motherhood, and farmers to sell ethanol at an outrageous advantage through government subsidies."

In 1980, Andreas had predicted in an amicable television interview with David Susskind—who that time around identified his guest as the "brilliant agriculturist"—that in ten years gasohol would replace half the crude oil being imported from the Gulf states. Andreas had brought along a couple of ears of corn, and as he was holding one of them up on camera, he felt constrained to explain that you couldn't operate a car by sticking it in a gas tank; there had to be a few intermediate steps. He also shared with watchers and listeners his reassuring conviction that "gasohol is good for the security of America." It almost went without saying that he had been using it himself. As over the years he had evangelically been chomping away on foodstuffs brimming with soy, so now was he filling up his Mercedes's unprotesting tank with a specially brewed admixture with a whopping 17 percent ethanol content.

Andreas did not lack for supporters in his crusade to win over the gas tanks of America. The Iowa Corn Promotion Board, the Illinois Corn Growers Association, and the Renewable Fuels Association arrayed themselves solidly behind him. But they, and even the National Corn Growers Association, had none of the clout—and the financial resources—of behemoths such as the American Petroleum Institute and the seven major oil companies that supported it. Why, Andreas's people had heard that one of the so-called Seven Sisters was going to plaster the pumps at its 250 stations in a single state with signs reading GUARANTEED NOT TO CONTAIN ANY ALCOHOL—as if that kind of gas could somehow precipitate drunk driving. (Some Mississippi stations were quick to remove their no-alcohol placards when regional corn growers threatened a retaliatory boycott.) And Andreas's alleged chumminess with Bob Dole had not deterred some gas stations in the senior senator from Kansas's very own state from flaunting NO ETHANOL signs—which in Andreas's view were as despicable as, say, WHITES ONLY.

"You know, Congress passed the legislation having to do with the search for renewable and alternative fuels, and the uses for excess crop production, well before ADM got into the act," Andreas says. "But the Seven Sisters can't very well attack Congress, so they have their Institute attack ADM and Dwayne Andreas, who weren't mentioned in the legislation. Oh well, if you have to have an enemy, and you want to win in politics, get for your enemy the seven big oil companies and the five biggest banks in the East. You'll never lose." Because Andreas feels that the National Association of Manufacturers and the Business Roundtable are pretty much dominated by the Seven Sisters and their close relatives, whose interests often conflict with agribusiness, he has kept ADM aloof from both organizations.

In 1978, Colorado, which Andreas had hardly ever visited, became one of his favorite American areas when it was the first state to attempt to reduce urban carbon-monoxide levels by requiring Denver drivers to use gasohol in winter, when their smog is at its worst. (One of the big oil companies with outlets there had gone on television, Andreas would tell friends, shaking his head at the ludicrousness of it, and warned its audience that if they filled up with gasohol, they shouldn't be surprised to have their mufflers fall off.) By the end of 1989, Albuquerque, Las Vegas, Phoenix, and Reno had followed suit. As 1990 got under way, Cedar Rapids buses were being converted to ethanol consumption. "What is good for Iowa is good for the whole USA," declared the city's bus department. "If ethanol replaces 20 percent of the current diesel-fuel market, it would require more than 2.24 billion gallons of corn-derived ethanol. This could help with the surplus of corn in the United States." Concurrently, Decatur's Mayor Anderson was paving the way for his municipal buses to switch.

Colorado had pushed its new rule through over the formidable objections of two dozen petroleum-industry protagonists who descended upon the state legislature. A few of them, according to a spirited organization called Coloradans for Clean Air, argued that maybe ethanol was acceptable for eight of ten cars, but if you were unlucky enough to own one of the other two, the most awful things could happen to you, like a head-on collision with your wife and kids in the car because of a clogged fuel filter. The oil companies soon came up with a regional group on their side, called the Consumers' Environmental Awareness Project, of which Barbara Charnes, executive director of Coloradans for Clean Air, remarked tartly, "It's like R. J. Reynolds sponsoring Lung Awareness Week."

By 1988, 325 million bushels of corn were being shunted into 825 million gallons of ethanol a year, although with corn prices once again relatively high and fuel prices low, it was not a profitable diversion. (Both presidential candidates endorsed alternative fuels, but then a candidate will endorse anything.) Andreas continued to be optimistic. A billion bushels was his estimate before the end of the century. Had not the Environmental Protection Agency decreed tough new fuel standards for all mass-transit buses by 1991, and for trucks by 1994? And by 1993 (when the six-cents-a-gallon reduction in federal taxes would come to an end unless Senator Dole or someone else engineered a continuation), would not all buses and rental cars in Los Angeles be compelled to switch to either ethanol or methanol? Had not scientists been looking into the possible use of ethanol in jet-plane fuels? And had not other technologists, moreover, refined conventional ethanol, plucking from it ethyl tertiary butyl ether, or ETBE, with lower volatility than its parent distillation and a greater tolerance of the water found in almost all fuels?

Andreas didn't have to wait for those distant dates for his ship, as it were, to come in. And where did it turn out to sail from, to his delight (and profit), but of all unlikely launching sites, Brazil! That country had traditionally imported petroleum as fuel for its motor vehicles—$10 billion worth annually by 1975, when oil prices were at their peak. Brazil took a radical step. What it lacked in petroleum resources it more than compensated for in sugarcane, and ethanol could be made from that. Moreover, São Paulo and Rio de Janeiro were becoming disagreeably polluted by exhausts; a shift in fuels could ameliorate that. So a new order of things was proclaimed.

By 1979, most of Brazil's vehicles were operating on fuel that was 22 percent ethanol, and some were being manufactured to accept a 100 percent dose. By 1989, five million Brazilian automobiles—50 percent of the country's total—ran entirely on ethanol. But then the price of petroleum went down, and the price of sugar rose. Sugarcane growers steered their crops toward the sweetener market. More cars were being refitted to gulp gasoline. The cities' air quality tumbled. Andreas paints a stark picture of what all that meant. "There were people dying on the streets," he says, "and children's noses were running something terrible, and the environmentalists were howling as only they can."

Petrobas, the Brazilian state agency in charge of automotive fuels procurement, heard them, too. It would have to keep providing acceptable, nonpolluting fuels, it concluded. If its sugarcane growers couldn't furnish them, Brazil would have to go elsewhere. It went, in the fall of 1989, to Archer Daniels Midland, with an initial request—more seemed almost certain to follow—for 100 million gallons of ethanol at $1.15 a gallon. It would take 40 million bushels of corn to produce that much.* ADM, not wishing to be accused of

---

*In Petrobas's eagerness and anxiety to appease the environmentalists, it also bought a batch of methanol, but the ship delivering it was prevented from unloading when some citizens complained that its formaldehyde content could lead to lung cancer.

monopolistic practices, thought it prudent to cut its chief domestic competitors in for a quarter of the order. "It was the biggest ethanol transaction in the history of the world," Andreas exulted. "There's never been anything like it. A wonderful redemption after all the screaming we had to put up with."

At home, now, too, Andreas had a forthright ally, the Department of Agriculture no less, which in a publication titled "Ethanol's Role in Clean Air" was saying: "With current technology, ethanol cannot be produced inexpensively enough to compete with gasoline or petroleum-based octane enhancers such as ETBE without subsidies. But air quality and other benefits may warrant subsidization until lower costs and higher oil prices enable ethanol to compete on its own."

Not altogether on its own. Dwayne Andreas would be in there fighting alongside it all the way. And apparently so also would, despite all the other things on his mind, the president of the United States. For on a visit to the University of Nebraska in the spring of 1989, George Bush's speech writers (when had any of their ilk last dared to defy the Seven Sisters?) had given him to declaim—Andreas could hardly have phrased it more ringingly himself—"Ethanol is a homegrown energy alternative. And that's good for national security—and that's good for our trade deficit. [That got applause.] And ethanol produces a fuel that burns cleaner. And that's good for our environment, just plain and simple— good for our environment. A source of energy that's clean, abundant, and made right here in the United States—three good reasons why ethanol and ETBE are fuels of the future."

Soon after being elected president, George Bush had opened his Oval Office door to the head of the National Corn Growers Association. Responding to a question from that eminence, the chief executive said that in order to help American farmers prosper he would support the consumption of ethanol and also—here was another conceivably massive use for corn to which Andreas heartily subscribed—of degradable plastics. If Bush had at that time specified *biode-gradable*, the White House visitor and his Decatur-based cohort would have been even happier, but they knew better than not to be grateful for small favors.

In 1975, an environmentalist in California named Ernest Callenbach had a novel published titled *Ecotopia*. It was set in the year 1999. The world its author envisioned was going to be cleaner and better because, among other reasons, the plastics its inhabitants depended on would be degradable—biodegradable, made from plants.

Callenbach, as it happened, didn't much care for any kind of plastics. He was addicted to things Japanese, and he thought the ideal raw material for the satisfaction of many human wants was wood. But he had grudgingly become reconciled to the prevalence, if not necessity, of certain items that seemed to cry to be fashioned from plastics: camera film, for instance, and shirt buttons.

There is no evidence that Andreas or anyone else who mattered at ADM ever read or heard of *Ecotopia* when it came out. However, they had also been thinking about degradability, and they were and would be interested readers of such studies as one by the National Oceanographic Society to the effect that the average one-square-mile stretch of Atlantic Ocean off the northeast coast of the United States contained forty-six thousand pieces of floating nondegradable plastic.* These were a particular bane to turtles, because of their resemblance to delectable jellyfish. An autopsy on one eleven-pound sea turtle revealed two pounds of indigestible plastic in its belly.

And what Western-world businessmen could help but sit up and take notice on being apprised of other relevant eye-bugging statistics: that, for example, 20 billion disposable

---

*Andreas and other advocates of degradability have attracted some rather special partisans, among them a Provincetown, Massachusetts, self-proclaimed environmentalist who collected three thousand plastic tampon applicators that had floated up onto his neighborhood beaches and converted them into a dress that he announced his hope of presenting to Nancy Reagan.

diapers and their guards were sold, soiled, and scuttled annually in the United States alone; and that plastics constituted considerably more than one-third of the over 150 million tons of trash with which Americans, every twelve months, were straining the capacities of their accessible landfills.

Andreas's interest in the potentiality—and potential profitability—of biodegradable plastics was sparked by his nephew and high-level employee Martin. In May 1987, Martin Andreas was watching the evening news on television when an item loomed up about how a regional Department of Agriculture laboratory at Peoria, Illinois—an outpost long familiar to ADM because it specialized in research on soybeans and corn—was conducting experiments into biodegradability involving the injection of cornstarch into plastics.

Early the next morning, Martin mentioned his glimpse to company president Jim Randall. They decided to embark on research of their own. Soon, their technical director, John Long, was heading overseas, in search of some extant technology that could be used to alter the composition of plastics without being so expensive as to be, whatever its environmental desirability, economically untenable. Almost at the outset of his quest, Long came upon a process that looked promising. ADM was quick to acquire the rights to it and filed suitable patents covering it in the United States, and for good protective measure, twenty-nine other countries.

As was its traditional wont, ADM did not propose getting into the making or marketing of any retail commodities. What it did do was to produce tiny pellets comprised of cornstarch and an oxydizing substance that the company dubbed PolyClean—this an ingredient whose composition is as guarded a secret as the legendary "formula" that purportedly makes Coca-Cola unique—which when combined with plastics theoretically causes them in due course to self-destruct, both in the air and below ground. *Photo*degradable plastics require prolonged exposure to sunlight to decompose. Once the biodegradable ones are buried, microorganisms introduced into them by the pellets feed on their starch contents, and they degenerate—in from six months to two years' time, some say; three to six years, according to others; hardly ever, to a few malcontents—into mere dust.* Although nobody has yet actually clocked the evolutionary process, it is widely believed that ordinary, untreated plastic bags may take a hundred years or more to disappear.

As Colorado had shown itself to be hospitable to ethanol, so again would that state be receptive to the novel PolyClean-stimulated plastics, the debut of which inspired *Vogue* magazine to burble: "The greatest vanishing act in the world has arrived." Indeed, when Martin Andreas flew to Denver to introduce shopping bags made from them to regional supermarket potentates, the mayor turned up in person and decreed that the city could thenceforth solidly be counted on the side of biodegradability.

Both Iowa and Illinois, corn-loving states from way back, would soon be climbing aboard the biodegradable bandwagon. The governor of Iowa announced at the beginning of 1989 his intention to propose that by 1991 all nondegradable plastic garbage bags be outlawed in his bailiwick. Next door

---

*Part of ADM's own explanation of its process goes: "ADM PolyClean contains components which permit both a biological and oxidative degradation. In the biological attack, microorganisms and/or enzymes digest away the starch and produce holes in the film where the starch granules were located. This decreases the strength of the film and increases the film's surface area allowing more oxygen to come into contact with the film. The oxidative component acts as a catalyst to produce oxygen free radicals. These free radicals are produced normally by UV light, but the PolyClean catalyst allows them to be produced even in darkness. These free radicals consume the antioxidants in the polyethylene and then react with carbon-carbon double bonds, which are another component of ADM PolyClean. The free radicals react with the unsaturated carbon bonds and create peroxides and hydroperoxides, which in turn decompose to create a free radical. Thus the reaction propagates itself. This is the same natural process which occurs in a vegetable oil that becomes rancid. With time the polyethylene molecules will be broken as they react with the free radicals. As the polyethylene molecules continue to be broken they will reach a low molecular weight, where they can be consumed by bacteria in the soil. Both the biodegradation of the starch component and the auto-oxidation processes will work independently, but together they lead to a synergistic effect under conditions such as a compost or soil burial. It is synergistic because the degradation of the starch increases the surface area of the plastic, and also its presence allows a population of bacteria to build up on the plastic. In conclusion, the use of Poly-Clean as an additive to polyethylene will provide a useful life for a polyethylene product, but cause the polyethylene to degrade upon disposal."

in Illinois, the city of Urbana inaugurated a yard-waste disposal program in which degradable collection bags would
play a prominent role.*

By the summer of 1988, moreover, there was another
formidable ally: the United States Navy had already declared
that even though the new tactic might cost $500 million, it
was determined to revamp its longtime dumping habits and
to spare the seas it patrolled from being daily desecrated, as
they so long had ingloriously been doing, by five tons of
nondegradable plastic refuse.†

Yet another powerful partisan materialized offshore. Mikhail
Gorbachev told Andreas at dinner one evening in 1988 that
he was "extremely intrigued" by the advent of biodegradability
and that the day was surely not too far away when ADM
would be exporting its novel technology to a welcoming
Soviet community.

The kind of attention that Andreas most likes to have
directed toward his business and himself was exemplified by
an item in the February 1989 issue of *Soybean Digest*, which
quoted an Iowa State University engineer as saying, all in one
heady sentence, "Certain products, such as biodegradable
plastics and ethanol, produce benefits to the environment
that won't be ignored."

But when it came to the biodegradables, Andreas's course
had by no means been all clear sailing. As in the case of

---

*Urbana would soon be rewarded for that good-neighborliness by being featured
in an ADM Sunday-morning TV commercial: "But what makes Urbana's operation
[picture of open rear of truck loaded with trash bags] even more remarkable are
these: trash bags made with a special cornstarch additive [closeup of stack of bags
on ground behind truck], which breaks down the plastic in just a matter of months.
As as result, these bags [close-up of one bulging bag with ADM faintly visible on it]
can be added directly to the compost pile, which has cut the cost of Urbana's
operation by 30 percent. While saving space and saving the environment [shot of two
youngsters filling bags with leaves in pastoral setting] at the same time. Composting
with these degradable bags [housewife raking leaves into single bag] could soon be
commonplace throughout America. For the sake of the environment [concluding
shot of tractor going off into the sunset], that day can't come fast enough."

†The decision was not altogether altruistic. The navy already had only until 1992
to comply with the provisions of Congress's Marine Plastic Pollution Research and
Control Act of 1987, according to the provisions of which all ships of all nations
would be forbidden to jettison any sort of plastic material within two hundred miles
of the United States coast.

ethanol when he had found himself at odds with the big gasoline companies and their articulate and well-endowed spokesmen, so were they now once again arrayed against him.

Mobil, Amoco, and Chevron were all heavily engaged in the packaging industry. Their much-trumpeted "degradable" plastics—photodegradable—were derived from petroleum. (Pressure from environmentalists and others persuaded Mobil to delete the word "degradable" from its Hefty trash bags.) Andreas has always been quick to point out, whenever he is caught up in a debate about the merits or demerits of rival plastic bags, that petroleum, markedly unlike corn, is nonrenewable. "You don't have to have a college degree to know that there is a limit to the earth's resources."—DOA. But then ADM functions in a capitalistic society, and Andreas would be surprised if any of its activities were not to encounter some spirited competition. As Martin Andreas has put it, "You can't expect an oil company to be happy with our technology."

There were skeptics, too, to be dealt with. Representatives of such well-meaning groups as the Environmental Defense Fund and the Coalition for Recyclable Waste contended not merely that there might be better ways of solving the plastic problem than disposing of it to begin with, but that entombed degradable plastics—bio- or photo- or whatever— would disintegrate, if they did at all, no faster than plain old unfiddled-with plastic. Some of the antidegradabilists argued further that plastics with built-in degradability were ipso facto weaker, and more likely to split open wherever they were dumped, than their run-of-the-mill counterparts; and that it didn't mean much to say plastics turned into dust when 90-odd percent of that ex-plastic would remain intrusively in the environment in its new but environmentally not much more acceptable guise.

To this last charge ADM, not surprisingly, stoutly demurred, asserting that talk about plastic dust was predicated on "the misconception that cornstarch-based degradable plastics consist merely of cornstarch blended into a plastic such as polyethylene," whereas its PolyClean had other significant features that "accelerate the normal oxidative processes that might take a hundred years or more to degrade the plastic. In practice, the biodegradable films made with this additive" —the Coca-Cola-like "secret" one—"will disintegrate in the presence of bacteria or fungi. The fragments of the film range in size from square millimeters to square centimeters. These fragments are simply intermediate products of the degradation process. Once the accelerated oxidation of the plastic begins, the fragments are broken down to simple paraffins (waxes), which serve as a food source for microorganisms. In the end, the plastic is converted either to carbon dioxide and water or to biomass."

In the end, though beleaguered by the oil companies and others about *proving* that biodegradable plastics would disintegrate into soil once interred, ADM, after all its talk about the important difference between photo- and biodegradability, dropped the "bio" from all its pronouncements on the subject and reverted to the use of mere unembellished "degradable."

Who can predict the future of any sort of degradability? Beyond trash bags, grocery sacks, and diapers, many other uses have been visualized. ADM commissioned a North Carolina factory, for instance, to fabricate eight thousand one-gallon jugs, not to do anything more with them than to ascertain how they'd fare as milk containers. They seemed to hold, and hold up, well. Meanwhile, Andreas and his confreres were pressing forward on all fronts. The few dozen shareholders who betook themselves to Decatur for ADM's annual meeting in the fall of 1989 were proffered red-white-and-blue plastic bags bearing the patriotic legend USING AMERICA'S ABUNDANCE TO MEET THE WORLD'S NEEDS. That "abundance" stood for corn; the National Corn Growers Association has estimated that degradable plastics could become an agreeable disposition for up to 300 million bushels of *Zea mays* a year.

All told, plastics and ethanol together might enable ADM to boost by a billion bushels annually the nation's newer uses of corn. (Andreas is probably the only CEO ever to have concluded an address to a gathering of Wall Street security analysts by urging one and all to take home a plastic bag inscribed "Corn for a cleaner environment.") For those more than twenty thousand shareholders who couldn't make it to the meeting, their annual report for 1989, brimming with good news about all manner of corporate progress, was mailed out tucked into a plastic wrapper embellished with a phrase the company had not long before trademarked: ENVIRONMENT FRIENDLY.

24

IN 1986, two years after Andreas met Gorbachev, Dwayne's son Michael tried to appraise his father's business relationship with the Soviet Union. "Dad's role with the Russians is on a different scale from the rest of us at ADM," he said. "We trade with them—they're tough, but they pay their bills—but his relation with them is political and philanthropic. He doesn't like nuclear bombs, and he doesn't like to see farmers going broke. The biggest hobby he's developed in the last ten years is a much broader sense of responsibility than ever for the national interest. He thinks that if we just keep feeding the Russians instead of embargoing them, they won't be over here dropping bombs."

Andreas *père* has said, for his part, "My interest in the Soviet Union doesn't especially relate to their doing business with ADM. It's that *any* business they do with the United

States is important to our farm economy. The American wheat and corn and soybean growers regard people like me as their avenue to the rest of the globe."

By that time, Andreas's interest in the Soviet Union and its leader had gone far beyond business. Wishing to dissociate himself from the gloomy prophecies of many so-called experts that Gorbachev wasn't getting anywhere with his newfangled notions and that his regime might well be just a passing phase, the Decatur man began more and more frequently to make his own opinions known. In May of 1986, for instance, Andreas accepted an invitation to join some foreign-policy pundits at a Washington, D.C., symposium put on by the Center for Strategic and International Studies. After politely disclaiming any authority in their field, he proceeded to say:

> I am here to tell you gentlemen today that I have had a lot of conversations with Gorbachev and many of his lieutenants. They are smart, able, conservative people. They seem to know what they are doing and to have made changes that are absolutely irreversible. If Gorbachev disappeared tomorrow, we probably have a man like Ryzhkov, who reminds you of any conservative businessman manager that you know in America. And he would go straight ahead with the policies that are already put in place. For a matter of fact, he could not reverse the policies in the Soviet Union, in my opinion, without a new Stalin. And a new Stalin in this day and age is impossible to come by. In order to have a Stalin *they* would have to have an enemy.

By 1989, Andreas had flown in and out of Moscow more times than he could keep track of. *Fortune* was dubbing him "an old Russian hand." He felt sorry for other travelers who, not given to arising as early as he was, probably missed the sight of the early-morning sun striking the Kremlin's golden domes. "At that moment, you can't help thinking about all those old buildings," he once remarked, half-chidingly, to a relatively late sleeper.

It was agreeable to have access to the inner sanctums of the Kremlin when that seemed desirable. Says Andreas:

In conversations I've had with Gorbachev, he's made it clear that it's in his own interest to reorganize the Soviet economy and that to do that he has to cut down on defense spending. He also wants to make progress in human rights. But he's got to proceed at his own pace. Anybody who's spent any time with him feels that he's the kind of fellow you can do business with. It's clear further that his mission is to correct a lot of Stalin's mistakes—if he can do that within the framework of Lenin's teachings. Lenin and Marx left a lot of room for market-oriented free enterprise.

I think that Gorbachev has assembled a pretty good team, and that the ideological resistance to him there has been overemphasized. Management is his main problem. His glasnost was, among other things, an invitation to debate, and as soon as he got some of that, the Western world began crying, "Dissidence!" But he said to me once, "I have to have debate. If I didn't have a Boris Yeltsin to disagree with me, I'd have to create one." That's like what Hubert Humphrey used to say: "The most important thing is to pick your enemies."

I was saying to Gorbachev once, "You know, the West has already adopted five of the ten points in the *Communist Manifesto.*" He laughed. But he agreed.

Since that concurrence of views, Andreas, to emphasize his point, enunciated them in a 1988 appearance before the Chicago Council on Foreign Relations, whose members may never theretofore have heard Karl Marx's ten commandments declaimed, were self-annotated:

Point One—abolition of private land. Well, Gorbachev has just about nullified that provision by offering fifty-year leases renewable to one hundred, which is almost the same as owning and paying taxes.

Two—progressive, graduated income tax. Every capitalist country has that.

Three—abolition of the right of inheritance. In some

western countries, inheritance taxes are so high that Marx's principle is almost in effect.

Four—confiscation of property of emigrants and rebels. Thank God that hasn't hit us yet.

Five—centralization of credit through a national bank. Many capitalist countries have nationalized banks, and U.S. credit policies are set by the Federal Reserve.

Six—state control of communication and transport. We do it through regulation; other western governments own the airwaves, the railroads, and the airlines.

Seven—central planning and state ownership of production. That applies in part to much of the west. Replace "regulation" for "ownership," and it's common to most countries we call capitalist.

Points Eight and Nine [having to do, broadly, with integrating industry and agriculture] are in complicated jargon and fortunately don't apply.

Point Ten—free education for all children in public schools. That's universal today.

Ten points that define the communist program—and six of them are regularly found in countries we call "capitalist."

Some other Andreas pronouncements from that Chicago podium:

Economic principles often take a backseat to political considerations. And that sometimes makes the world a more dangerous place—a place in which ideology takes precedence over common sense.

Two centuries ago, Alexander Hamilton supported trade with a hostile Great Britain this way: "The spirit of commerce has a tendency to ... extinguish those inflammable humors which so often have kindled into wars."

Today, that pragmatic, nonideological viewpoint is held

by none other than the General Secretary of the Communist Party of the USSR.

Mikhail Gorbachev approaches political issues with the sensibilities of a businessman. His country's politicians and ideologues have made a mess of the Soviet economy, and he knows that only perestroika and glasnost—restructuring and openness—can save it.

Gorbachev has encouraged greater religious liberty and is pushing a new law on freedom of conscience. He invited church leaders to the Kremlin. He peppers speeches and private conversations with phrases like "Thank God" and "God willing," quotes from the Bible, and cites stories about Jesus. In short, he's taking the "godless" out of "godless Communism."*

Agriculture is a priority. The farm sector eats up to a third of Soviet investment resources, and 15 percent of their budget goes for food subsidies. But a fourth of all farm output comes from the 3 percent of farmland given over to private plots.

The Soviets are learning from that; they are moving away from state farms to encourage private farming, cooperatives, leasing land to family farmers. They've consolidated their agricultural ministries and sent almost fifty-thousand bureaucrats packing.

Cooperatives now have equal status with state enterprises, with no restrictions on their size and few limits as to what businesses they can enter. The Soviets expect the new cooperative movement to become an important source of jobs and production.

Already, there are over fifteen-thousand cooperatives employing over 150,000 people. They operate restaurants, gas stations, and a host of other businesses. In Moscow alone, cooperatives are growing at the phenomenal rate of three hundred a month.

I wonder if the Soviets fully realize the enormous poten-

---

*That was enough to make the tindery Pat Buchanan explode. The Soviets had just pulled out of Afghanistan, and referring to the "aspirant to Armand Hammer's place as favorite capitalist poodle at Gorbachev's feet," the columnist mentioned Andreas's "insights into the warm, wonderful man he has come to know," quoted his reflections on God and godlessness ("Shall we gather at the river?" Buchanan intoned, his sarcasm approaching a crescendo), and concluded, "Perhaps Andreas can one day give his speech at the Kabul Chamber of Commerce."

tial economic power they've unleashed by allowing cooperatives and individual enterprise.

When the Soviets ran into economic trouble, they turned to businessmen to get them out of it—for Gorbachev and his people think and act like businessmen. But our business people are basically frozen out of policymaking.

The Soviet Union, once the model ideological state, is becoming a pragmatic, business-oriented government. And the U.S., once the model business society, puts politics and ideology over economic self-interest.

When the President met with General Secretary Gorbachev in the Kremlin, it seemed as if half of official Washington was there. But our secretary of commerce wasn't invited along. An example of how we ignore our business interests.

On one of Andreas's business trips to Moscow, though, Reagan's secretary of commerce, Malcolm Baldrige, did get to tag along.

By the spring of 1989, the sixteen-year-old preparations of the US-USSR Trade and Economic Council were approaching results. It had not been all easy going, even after the thaw between the two nations had begun to set in. At a meeting of the group in Washington to which a Soviet delegation 170 strong had trooped, an American still in a cold-war frame of mind took out after Andreas's counterpart on the Council, Vladislav Malkevich, chairman of the USSR Chamber of Commerce and Industry, demanding to know how he dared have in his party a man who everybody knew had been a KGB operative.

"Vladislav had a perfectly satisfactory response," Andreas said afterward. "He said something like, 'Well, he's been retired from the KGB for ten or fifteen years, and he's a good man, and we wish we had more like him.' But I didn't think that was quite enough. So I got up and said, 'We have a kind of precedent for that sort of thing over here. The former head of the CIA is now president of the United States.' That seemed to take care of that."

But it didn't altogether take care of Andreas's good friend

and golfing partner, the incumbent secretary of commerce, Robert Mosbacher, who when his turn came to speak splashed cold water far and wide by saying—for all anyone knew, with the blessing of the White House—"It is frankly difficult for me to commit wholeheartedly to a new era of trade with the Soviet Union while Soviet efforts to acquire proscribed Western technology continue."

Malkevich said when Mosbacher was finished that "emotionally, I did not get a very good feeling." Andreas, who has long contended that there are few developments in technology or any other aspect of business or industry that are or deserve to be secret, confined himself to the gentle rejoinder that "the purpose of these meetings is to find out what's on the minds of public officials, and we heard it."

Mosbacher later backtracked and made a point of letting Andreas know that President Bush had read and concurred with some of Dwayne's thoughts on bipartisan relations; but the following January when it came time for the United States to start negotiating a new commercial treaty with the Soviet Union, some observers of the Washington scene were not surprised to learn that the secretary of commerce had been bypassed, as leader of the talks for his side, in favor of US Trade Representative Carla Hills.

On a far more consequential level—partly because Andreas and James Giffen, who was devoting himself virtually full-time to Council affairs, had persuaded Gorbachev and his people to simplify a longstanding and hopelessly bogged-down bureaucratic system in which every industry was beholden to a separate government ministry—the Soviet Union was showing itself increasingly receptive toward joint ventures. True, being the shrewd capitalists Andreas kept saying they were at heart, the Russians insisted that in any forthcoming collaboration there would have to be a 51–49 percent split of ownership, in their favor.

That division of spoils, assuming there were to be any to share, had not deterred foreign entrepreneurs from wanting a piece of the unfamiliar action. Starting in 1987, when the not-quite-fifty-fifty ownership ratio was proclaimed, more than two hundred ventures began to move off drawing boards. Pepsi-Cola, of course, had been in Russia all along, balancing its accounts with the host country—rubles having nothing to commend them to foreign exchange—through Smirnoff vodka sales in the USA. Now there were many emerging hands across the sea and the Urals proferring such as pizzas, sanitary napkins, tank-car heaters, and Baskin-Robbins ice creams. Here was an incipient deal between Aeroflot and Marriott for an enormous flight kitchen at Moscow's Sheremetyevo 2 airport; there, a projected 100-acre entertainment complex on which a Canadian syndicate planned to erect, among other titillations, a miniature-golf course and a roller coaster. The Baptist World Alliance disclosed its intention to send over— just what would be the reciprocity was not made entirely clear—one hundred thousand Bibles. And as the final decade of the twentieth century approached, Muscovites, so historically resistant to would-be alien conquerors, were invaded by and quickly surrendered to McDonald's omnipotent fast-food legions.

Armand Hammer—who had earlier deplored the "fathomless complications of doing business with the Soviets" and said, "Every arrangement made in Moscow is tangled with as many obstacles and complications as an octopus has limbs"—was, naturally, not to be left out. This time, he had a big petroleum operation under way in cahoots with some Italians and Japanese. But then he died. One knowledgeable American had meanwhile observed:

> How could Hammer not be in the hunt? Lenin is still God over there, and Hammer's cachet derives in part from his having at least met him and probably shaken hands, which is more than Gorbachev or any other contemporary Soviet leader can claim. Sure, Armand has easy access to the Soviet brass, but so now do guys like Dwayne Andreas and Jim Giffen, who can get to see Gorbachev or, say, Dobrynin if they think they need to. With Hammer, it's different. He'll run into Dobrynin somewhere, and the

Russian will casually mention that they're releasing some dissident. That'll be all it takes for Armand to instruct his pilots to rev up their engines. Then he'll ask Dobrynin, "Do you mind if I take him out on my plane?" By the time the plane lands at London or Paris or wherever the press has been alerted to meet it, the idea will somehow have got around that Hammer sprang the guy all by himself. I guess that's one difference between Hammer and Andreas. Hell, most people, if they've heard of Dwayne at all, don't even know he *has* a plane.

By the spring of 1988, after countless rounds of negotiation—Giffen for a while all but commuted between New York and Moscow—the Americans and Russians serving on the US-USSR Trade and Economic Council had put together a one-hundred-page agreement spelling out their mutual accep-tance of procedures governing new joint ventures—in such areas as accounting, labor, insurance, taxes, and repatriation of profits. They even made sure to agree on Sweden as a neutral site for the arbitration of irreconcilable disputes.

The next step was to announce the formation of—all along, precise equality had been de rigueur in their delibera-tions and operations—of a Soviet Foreign Economic Consor-tium and an American Trade Consortium. There not yet being, of course, any nongovernmental businesses on the Russian side, its consortium was made up of nineteen "production associations," under a board of directors consisting of those associations' chairmen and representatives of six powerful agencies: the State Foreign Economic Commission, the Ministry of Foreign Economic Relations, the Ministry of Finance, Vnesheconombank, Gosplan, and Minneftekhimprom.

The American group had six members: ADM, Chevron, Eastman Kodak, RJR Nabisco, Johnson & Johnson, and—tying all the loose ends together—Giffen's merchant bank, The Mercator Corporation. There was one last-minute defection: the Ford Motor Company. Ford had a Soviet connection going back to the 1930s, when it had helped the Soviets build automobile assembly plants; now, sixty years later, it was going to turn out cars there on its own. But it apparently was too uncertain of the likelihood of getting any profits out in hard currency, and so it backed off.

Andreas was disappointed, but not especially surprised. "Look, at the start of all this there was only a fifty-fifty chance we'd get on with the Russians," he said, "and that, mind you, on top of a fifty-fifty chance we could get on with one another."

What was formally known as a General Trade Agreement was signed at nine-thirty A.M. of March 30, 1989, in the Maly Zal—Small Hall—of the Kremlin. It was, Giffen proudly revealed, "the first private agreement to have been concluded in this historic location." Close to one hundred men and women crowded into the chamber, which measured roughly twenty by forty feet and featured two rather plain chandeliers, a hovering portrait of Lenin, and a T-shaped table with a green cloth surface. Along one side of the table were four green upholstered chairs. On it were two small flags, some pens, and a pair of red leather folders containing copies of the agreement, which some of the Americans present acclaimed as a "precedent-setting breakthrough" and a "milestone," and their Soviet counterparts, not to be outdone, as "exceptionally important" and "truly unique."

While two television cameras recorded it all, Vladimir Drovosekov, the chairman of the home-country consortium, said, "We Soviets are very different people now." The signing, accomplished with a great flourish of swapped pens, took only a few seconds and was followed by much applause and an exchange of toasts all around. (Fruit juices only; to try to curtail drunkenness, Moscow drinking places couldn't serve anything stronger before two P.M.) Dwayne Andreas, standing behind the signatories—for the Russians Drovosekov and his deputy, Yuri Scherbina; for the Americans, Giffen and Robert Carbonell, the CEO of the Del Monte Foods Division of RJR Nabisco—beamed.

It was surmised at that bubbling-over time that during the next ten or fifteen years the members of the American group might put up to $10 billion into Soviet enterprises: Eastman Kodak in floppy discs and blood analyzers, Johnson & Johnson in a variety of health-care products, RJR Nabisco in Camel cigarettes and Ritz crackers. Chevron was to play a special role. It would be drilling for oil in the Soviet Union, selling its output abroad, and swapping some of the hard currency proceeds it earned for the rubles its partners amassed inside Russia.

Andreas was less concerned than a few of his compatriots about who got paid in what. "The simple fact of history," he said, "is that most American companies never repatriate funds. Profits are far more likely to be reinvested in expansion and growth in the country when they are earned. In fact, profitable enterprises attract more capital from the parent company—to build more plants and to expand capacity." He was glad to be able to pass along such sentiments during a two-and-a-half-hour session the Americans had with Prime Minister Ryzhkov. (Gorbachev was preoccupied with a trip to Cuba.) "I was delighted to hear him say that the Soviet Union's number one production priority is now food," Andreas says. "We also learned that the Russians have begun converting defense plants to civilian use. One former atomic-energy installation, the prime minister told us, is now making dairy equipment and is known as Milkman No. 1. And an aircraft plant is making macaroni machinery. Swords into ploughshares."

As for ADM's own venture over there, "The Russians wanted a soybean-processing plant in the western part of the country," Andreas says, "but soy won't grow there. Much too far north. I had to explain to them that you don't put a dam where there's no river. The only logical place for soy cultivation is way out east, around Vladivostok." He and his ADM associates concluded that it would make more sense, and make greater profits (whether or not repatriated), to concentrate on an indigenous food crop and to drive from it the largest possible added value. Building a plant to convert local barley into malt looked propitious for a time. ADM had some newfangled malting technology that hadn't yet been tried out anywhere on earth, and Andreas liked the idea of giving the USSR the first serious whack at it. When his vice president in charge of international affairs, John Reed, who came to ADM from Continental Grain in 1982, heard about that possibility, he told a friend, "With Dwayne, it's not merely a matter of doing something that's never been done before but doing it bigger and better."

At one point, Andreas outlined his thinking in a memo to his people at Decatur:

> I want to summarize the conclusion we have reached from all of our studies from the Polotsk soybean concentrate-isolate project. We have come to the conclusion that the project is commercially not viable. The reasons are very clear. First, soybean meal can be bought on the world market with indirect and direct subsidies of from $10 to $30 a ton. Vegetable oils are available at subsidies of up to 7¢ a pound. Under these subsidies, to pay world-market prices for soybeans and sell meal, oil, concentrate, and isolate at competitive prices could only be done by absorbing losses of as much as $20 to $40 a ton. Further, it is possible to make the isolate and concentrate in the United States, where the only suitable beans are available, at a far lower cost than moving them to Polotsk.
>
> For these reasons, ADM has decided to use its capital for other purposes, such as wheat, corn, and barley processing, and perhaps other things like vegetable-oil refining.
>
> However, we have been told that, despite the fact that this would not be a commercially viable investment, the Soviet Union would like to have such a plant for public-policy purposes. If this is the case, ADM, wanting to cooperate with the objectives of the Soviet Union, would make the following proposal.
>
> We would provide all the technology, supervision, training for people in the Western plants, help start up and run the plant, which would be owned 100% by the Soviet Union. All we would want for these services would be:

1. To provide the concentrate, isolate, meal, and oil at world-market prices, to build up the market during the time of construction.

2. We would like to have an option over five years to purchase 50 percent interest in the plant at its cost, should world-market conditions in the meantime adjust or Soviet policies could be put in place to make it reasonably profitable.

3. We would want to be paid our out-of-pocket costs of supervision, training, and so forth, but the technology under these circumstances would come to the Soviet Union at a nominal charge.

Please give this consideration.

In the course of that precedent-shattering trip to Moscow in the spring of 1989, Andreas did some window-shopping of a sort. In accordance with an agreement signed in 1972, the United States government had started to build, at a cost of $95 million, an eight-story embassy building in the capital. It would dominate the center of a sprawling complex consisting of more than a hundred apartments occupied by U.S. diplomats and their families, and for their collective benefit, a bowling alley, a swimming pool, a gymnasium, a cafeteria, a barbershop, a mail room, two squash-and-racquetball courts, and an underground garage. The USSR offered to facilitate matters by providing the needed prefabricated concrete for the main building. It was nearly finished when, in 1985, Washington abruptly ordered construction halted; listening devices had been detected embedded in the concrete. Someone estimated that it would take $80 million to eliminate them, if indeed that were possible at all.

So what was to be done with the empty edifice? Andreas had a ready answer. He knew that as the consortium's activities burgeoned, the Americans would need more and more office space. He proposed to buy the building from the State Department.

Andreas had made his offer sight unseen. In Moscow for the signing ceremony, he had an hour or so to spare, hopped into an available Chaika limousine, and was driven over to the site. A guide who offered to show him around the occupied parts of the enclave—all components except the unfinished building were in high gear—said its occupants called it the Fortress.

The eight-story centerpiece lacked both a roof and, the guide said, interior partitions. Andreas wanted to see it up close. He said he wasn't worried about bugs. "I'm bugged in everything I do," he said cheerfully. "In New York, probably. Certainly in Washington. I don't worry about bugs. I only worry about the ones I don't know about."

He headed toward a gap in a fence around the tainted building. "My theory is, 'Don't ask,' " he said, striding briskly forward. Before he had progressed four feet, a man in a sentry booth hopped out and stopped him. His plane had been able to fly into Sheremetyevo 2 unescorted. But that was one thing, and entering a vacant American building was another.

Andreas was still ready to buy. He more or less asked Washington to name its own price. The federal government, which was running up an annual deficit of $150 billion or so, hemmed and hawed for a year—the Reagan administration deftly passing the buck to the Bush—before turning him down and announcing that it planned to tear it down and build an entirely new building for, according to the best estimates, half a billion dollars.

25

We have one thing going for us—the hundreds and thousands of bakers who get their flour at eight in the morning and produce bread at nine from what twenty-four hours earlier was wheat in a freight car. Knowing that that happens every day is why we can sleep nights.

—DOA

ANDREAS is hardly a self-denying individual, but he has made Archer Daniels Midland a corporation notable for its austere ways. The company stands high on *Fortune*'s ranking of sales-per-employee, with a more than three-quarters-of-a-million dollar score; and considering its size, it has a relatively small headquarters complement—only about four hundred people in its upper echelons. It takes special pride in such accomplishments as that in 1988 its bushels-of-corn-ground-per-employee came to a robust 189,063. "We're not layered with a lot of management types," one of them says. "We don't seem to have a purchasing department at all. You don't have to go through a lot of people to get what you want. People have a lot of authority, and there isn't much second-guessing. If you're right, you're right. And if you're wrong, you're wrong. Of course, in a business where a quarter of a cent's price change on a bushel of beans can involve hundreds of thousands of dollars of profit or loss, it helps to be right more often than wrong."

When Andreas took over ADM in 1966, though its gross sales then were only in the $200 million category, it had a public-relations staff twenty-seven strong. He did away with it. In 1990, with gross sales over the $8 billion mark (a large figure; larger by a cool billion, for instance, than the total sales of the one hundred biggest black-owned companies in the United States), ADM had a public-relations staff consisting entirely of Vice President Richard Burket and his secretary. It did not surprise one journalist acquainted with ADM's bare-bones ways that when he sent Burket some questions about the company, he received his own letter back, with replies scribbled on it in that high-level spokesman's own hand, along with the explanatory scrawl "Judy's out sick."

Still, as ADM grew bigger, it could afford to do bigger things. To process all its commodities required vast amounts of steam and electricity, and to generate these, vast amounts of fuel—at Decatur alone, three thousand tons a day. In 1984, President Jim Randall heard about some innovative Swedish technology for a cogeneration plant that could burn all kinds of fuel—even garbage, even tires—and yet produce clean steam with hardly any smokestack emissions, 90 percent of the sulfur dioxide in them being magically eliminated. ADM spent $180 million building an initial such plant—it received the 1988 Energy Conservation Award of the American Society of Mechanical Engineers—and has since invested in four more.

Andreas has had it in mind ever since to train a movie camera on one of his immobile, puffless smokestacks—as if he were making an Andy Warhol kind of film—for twenty-four hours, nonstop, and perhaps to use a slice of this graphic nothingness for one of his Sunday-morning TV commercials. "We have the biggest private power plant extant," Andreas says proudly, "and it's the most satisfying sight I've ever seen. We took the lead out of gasoline and saved kids from lead poisoning, and we put ethanol into gas and saved old folks from carbon-monoxide poisoning, and now we've found the answer to acid rain. Why, you could call it the eighth wonder of the world."

In June 1988, long before anybody even dreamed the Berlin Wall might come tumbling down, ADM was pleased to play host to a joint tour of its first cogeneration plant taken by a group of visitors from both West and East Germany. (While the wall was still being pounded into souvenirs, ADM opened an East Berlin office.) Never much of a winter sportsman himself—arising at dawn on a Midwest farm tended to make him avoid low temperatures whenever possible, and he has been a cold-weather pilgrim to Florida since his teens— Andreas has been thinking of using the mountains of slag from his plants (mostly calcium sulfate) to create a ski slope for his fellow citizens in Decatur.

By 1989, the value of the common stock of the company that one newsmagazine was calling a "megagrocer" had increased by two-thirds in twelve months, thus adding a hundred million or so dollars to Andreas's paper worth. The corporation continued to grow at a fast clip, though with circumspection. One company that ADM took over had a Chicago office with a staff of 125 doing work that the new owners calculated could be done just as well by far fewer. When ADM had finished its shakedown, only 2 of the 125 remained.

There were all those recently acquired peanut plants to keep track of. Then there was the Tabor Grain Company, merely a $33 million acquisition, to be sure, but one that brought into the widening fold the singularly stoical Burnell Kraft, a man who goes to Moscow much more often than Andreas, to talk to the foreign-trade people there at Exportkhleb. While at home, Kraft gladly accepts phone calls at three in the morning from business associates, like a broker in Rotterdam wondering how much ADM would wish to charge the Soviet agency, right that moment, for, say, half a million bushels of corn. It may take two hours of spirited haggling to arrive at a deal. After one such protracted predawn negotiation, Kraft, who has an understanding wife, remarked, "For all their friendship, the Russians won't give you one cent more per ton than the cheapest price quoted anywhere on earth."

Kraft has a high opinion, not surprisingly, of Andreas's own far flung trading skills. "I think Dwayne is more international than anybody I know," he says. "Also, he perceives things as they are and not as they are presented. He's apt to say, when somebody starts carrying on about the complexities of foreign trade, 'For anyone who's a prospective buyer, a soybean grown in Argentina is the same as one grown in America or anywhere else.'"

One major step in ADM's near-nonstop expansion dated from 1983, when Andreas bought a 45 percent stake—subsequently raising it to 50—in the venerable Hamburg trading firm Alfred C. Toepfer International, a colossus with offices in fifty countries and an $8 billion gross sales figure of its own, from its annual handling of some 30 million tons of assorted commodities. (The other half of Toepfer went to eleven cooperatives on several continents, among them Agway, Land O'Lakes, United Cooperatives of Ontario, Union Nationale des Coopérative Agricoles de Céréales, and DSV Silo und VerwaltungsGesellschaft MBH.) The cooperatives have the right to cast the deciding vote in the event they cannot agree with ADM on a proposed course of action. Granting them this edge enables Toepfer to conduct its business as a non–United States entity, which suits ADM fine, because it facilitates some aspects of engaging in international trade.

The German company's chairman in 1983 was Dr. Alfred C. Toepfer, then eighty-eight, who was generally conceded to be the dean of European grain merchants. Andreas had met him more than thirty years earlier, when Dwayne was at Cargill, and had told him then, with the brashness of youth, "I may be the only man in captivity who can run your business when you retire." And now it had come to pass. Dr. Toepfer joined the ADM board—Dwayne's son, Michael, reciprocally joining *his*—and despite his age and near stone deafness began faithfully to travel to the United States four times a year for directors' meetings. In 1988, however, the by then nonagenarian concurred with Andreas that he had earned the right to take it easier—though he was still walking his three miles daily—and to settle for the role of director emeritus.

One of Andreas's most-used phrases is the old standby "Knowledge is power." The periodic reports he gets from his Toepfer associates contribute substantially to his share of both. A single routine memorandum reporting on a Hamburg get-together may contain, among myriad other data, references to Turkey's probable wheat exports, South Korea's corn sales, the barley situation in Saudi Arabia, the status of soybean-crushing in Argentina and Brazil, and the impact of the reduced availability of citrus pellets on Thailand's tapioca quota.

As was the case in England with its British Arkady, so, at home, did ADM come to have subsidiary companies with subsidiaries of their own. (By 1990, Andreas had long since abandoned any intention of even laying eyes on everything in his domain; Jim Randall and his deputies took care of that.) ADM Milling's twenty mills make it the second-largest wheat-flour miller in the world. (ConAgra is first.) From its headquarters at Shawnee Mission, Kansas, Joe Hale's offshoot also operates three dry corn mills, three rice ones, two sorghum, and one bulgur. Musing one time about ADM Milling, Andreas said, "We're the counterpin between the farmer and the consumer. In the continuous jungle warfare characteristic of our industry, we have one thing going for us—the hundreds and thousands of bakers who get their flour at eight in the morning and produce bread at nine from what twenty-four hours earlier was wheat in a freight car. Knowing that that happens every day is why we can sleep nights."

As Archer Daniels Midland's hardest-selling outlet, ADM Milling dispenses free nutritional-information kits containing recipes for cream-cheese muffin puffs and lemon-butter angel-hair pasta; uplifting health hints such as "When the brain begins to make more serotonin, as it does when the carbohydrates are eaten, negative feelings are eased; anger is modulated, worrisome problems seem to shrink in magnitude, the edge is taken off anxiety"; and such nuggets of knowledge as that Americans eat an average of twenty-two and a half pounds of pizza a year and that during the Civil War the Capitol in Washington, pressed into service as a bakery, daily produced sixteen thousand loaves of bread.

This subsidiary's subsidiary—ADM Arkady, at Olathe, Kansas, just outside Kansas City—boasts a state-of-the-art research laboratory and, according to a wide-eyed report in *Milling & Baking News*, a state-of-the-art line of ingredients including—whoever said making bread was simple?—"dough conditioners, enzyme systems, emulsifiers, protein supplements, enrichment products, icing stabilizers, yeast foods, baking powders, mold inhibitors, mixes and bases, release agents, flavors and custom blends, as well as new product formulations."

Archer Daniels Midland has attained its robust proportions in spite of handicaps Andreas has not managed to overcome. To outsiders, it sometimes seems that the federal government has been rather nice, all in all, to ADM, giving its customer, the oil companies tax breaks on ethanol production, for instance, helping fructose operations by maintaining tariffs on imported sugar, and aiding soybean business through price supports. (The petroleum industry, by Andreas's rough calculation, has been spending about $5 million annually to spread the word that ethanol production is subsidized. Of course it is. So is the petroleum industry, which can afford to spread volumes of words inasmuch as since 1916, according to less partial calculations, it has enjoyed federal subsidies in the amount of about $125 billion.) But the Defense Department has declined to support soybeans in one consequential way at its disposal, so far barring the incorporation of soy additives into its hamburgers; there is apparently too much apprehension about angry congressmen, or mothers, crying, "Adulterated beef!" (Back in the 1970s, Andreas had Anwar Sadat just about persuaded to put soy flour into *his* army's bread and to use textured vegetable protein as a meat substitute, but public antipathy prevailed there, too—even after successful tests were made out on the desert, where no refrigeration was available nor was needed.) "Dealing with any government anywhere," Andreas says, "is like being in a ring with three prizefighters and trying to make sure you don't get hit, even by mistake, by any of them."

As ADM prospered in spite of having to keep its guard up, there was, inevitably, talk of takeovers. Any such attempt would have involved heavyweight action. The company has consistently been so long (more than $1 billion in cash reserves and so short (a mere $700 million) in debts that any prospective interloper would have a flock of Andreases to contend with—enough of these on the board, for instance, so that when at annual meetings directors' names are respectfully intoned, theirs are carefully separated, lest they seem too formidable a clump.

Even so, every so often inquiries come in. "When I get a call about a takeover," Andreas says, "I usually say something like, 'I guess we're worth about seven billion, but if you really want to buy the outfit, it'll cost you at least twelve. And then of course you'd have to learn to run it. If you're still interested, come around and bring your checkbook.' They never seem to call back."*

---

*Purvis Tabor, whose grain company Andreas would take over, purchased ten thousand shares of ADM stock, which was then selling at $11. He bought it for his grandchildren, but when word got around, rumors briefly circulated that ADM was up for sale. Andreas wasn't displeased; the stock, of which he owned considerably more than the Tabor offspring, went up $2 a share.

Don't ever make the mistake of
assuming governments are rational.

—DOA

I N view of all the time he has spent with and all the
money he has contributed to high-level members of the
political establishment, Andreas sometimes seems to
have a singularly unflattering impression of how they go
about their work. "Don't ever make the mistake of assuming
governments are rational," he says, for instance. Thus it
came as something of a surprise to people acquainted with
his modus operandi when it was revealed early in 1989 that a
couple of FBI agents who had perpetrated a sting upon the
Chicago Board of Trade had spent the previous two years
being trained to carry out their deceptions, at the federal
government's request, by none other than yet one more
Archer Daniels Midland subdivision—ADM Investor Services, Inc.

Chicago has two giant trading pits—the Mercantile Exchange and the Board of Trade, where Andreas first bought a seat in 1957. The place was like a club then, and the $288 the seat cost him was analogous to membership dues. In 1970, Andreas sold the seat, for $33,000, to his son. For a while in the heady inflationary years that followed, a seat was traded for as much as $500,000. Michael still owns his.

The Mercantile Exchange, which had its own disguised G-men but not ones bearing the ADM imprimatur, deals in the likes of Swiss-franc and yen futures. (Futures, of course, are commitments to buy or sell a specific amount of something at a specific price within a specific time frame.) The Board of Trade's futures cover assorted grains, and a trinity of soybean items—meal, oil, and the unprocessed beans themselves—passing all these back and forth, without actually laying hands on any of them, in carload lots. In August 1977, Treasury bonds joined the fray.

Fortunes have been made and lost by trafficking in soybean futures; the price per bushel fluctuated in the 1970s from $3.25 to $12.90. (Soybeans were known in American financial circles as "the Cinderella crop" in 1971 and as "the markets' miracle legume" in 1978.) In 1977, almost 8 million soybean contracts, each representing five thousand bushels, were swapped at the Board of Trade, with every swing of one penny in the price per bushel representing a $50 profit or loss on every contract. That was the year in which the Hunt brothers of Texas—Nelson Bunker and W. Herbert—along with other members of their family, tried to corner the soybean market. They acquired control of some 23 million bushels, worth around $135 million (the limit for any person or group of speculators was supposed to be 3 million bushels), before they were forced to cut out their tomfoolery and were fined $500,000 by the Commodity Futures Trading Commission.

Founded in 1848 for the purpose of stabilizing grain prices and protecting them—not altogether successfully, obviously—against wild speculation, the Board of Trade, ensconced on La Salle Street, Chicago's counterpart of Wall, was to become one of the largest futures markets on earth.

Its members, who rarely sit down at work, hold thirty-five hundred seats. In the course of a normal year, jostling each other in the organized pandemonium that characterizes their peculiar niche in the national economy, they pass back and forth 100 million contracts in grain futures, each standing for five thousand bushels. ADM Investor Services owns ten seats and has ten associate memberships, and its representatives on the bustling floor consider any business day a lackluster one if at least a million pounds of soybeans haven't, figuratively, passed through their hands.

In 1986, Washington got tipped off to some alleged hanky-panky going on in Illinois. Brokers on the Chicago exchanges, the FBI was informed, were using their clients' funds to trade for themselves, or were overcharging their customers on purchases, or undercrediting them on sales.* Even the FBI's celebrated expertise didn't qualify its operatives for getting into that line of business unassisted. So it came to ADM, presumably with Andreas's acquiescence, for edification and enlightenment.

It would later be suggested that ADM had acceded to the request in part because it wanted to pay back some Board of Trade people who in 1985 had accused it of rigging soy-oil prices. A Business Conduct Committee, made up of other traders, had summoned Michael Andreas to a meeting then, and when on the advice of lawyers in Decatur he refused to show up (he said he'd be glad to discuss the matter with the Commodity Futures people in Washington but not with the locals), the company was fined twenty-five thousand dollars and young Andreas a like amount for his recalcitrance. Even-

---

*Explained the *Soybean Digest* to its readers: "...one type of illegal trading is bucket trading, allowing traders to dump losses on to customers and split profits with another trader. Say one trader receives an order to purchase 50 contracts of soybeans. Instead of immediately placing the order, he signals his friend to buy the same amount. After a short time, the market moves up and the trader executes the original order at the higher price, probably buying from his friend. But the order is actually filled with contracts purchased by his friend at the lower price. The two traders split the price difference. If the market goes lower, the original trader can use his purchase to bail out his friend, while the customer pays the higher price. Much of the alleged cheating involves nickels and dimes on orders. But on thousands of orders, it can add up to big bucks."

tually the fine against ADM was rescinded, but Michael was stuck with his. "I was kind of proud," he said afterward. "It was the biggest fine up to then ever."

Certainly Andreas *père* had no particular love for the prevailing system. It grieves him that according to the Board of Trade's archaic rules, the actual soybeans and corn its traders dicker for—though not the soymeal and soy oil— must be delivered exclusively at Chicago or Toledo, where facilities for processing them are, at best, severely limited. "It's absolutely obsolete," he has told the magazine *Chicago Enterprise.* Another time, he said that Chicago had "become more of a gambling town than a hedging center, and that's too bad." As for the G-men and their undercover activities, "All they did was to ask us to plant a couple of guys in our company. What kind of a citizen would decline to do that?"

That was about as much as he cared to say on the record about the matter, then and since.

What the two agents did was to assume identities and create fake résumés (Washington carefully seeing to it that in case anybody tried to check up on their backgrounds, the schools and universities they put down were alerted to substantiate their claims), and at a cost to the taxpayers of $1 million or so, they bought two seats on the Board of Trade and played the role of big spenders to the hilt: posh apartments, luxury cars, generous entertainment. Many of the legitimate traders belonged to a fancy health club. "Richard Carlson" and "Michael McLoughlin" were welcomed as the right sort there. Unlike their fellow traders, though, they sported fountain pens and finger rings that were actually microphones, and (except, presumably, when they stripped at the health club) they had recorders strapped to their backs.

The mischief-making the G-men uncovered, Michael Andreas later contended, was partly the result of the Board's opening its floor to the sort of people who dealt in financial instruments. "The grain pits were always full of old-timers who knew each other and didn't screw each other," he says.

"But when you get into Treasury bonds and the like, you have two hundred guys out there who are just leasing their seats and are strangers and don't care whom they abuse. Why, there was one guy who wore a wig and a mustache, and if his trades weren't working out, he'd just disappear."

When the truth about the FBI moles leaked out (one of them disappeared fast himself, not even bothering to pick up four thousand dollars he'd won in a football-game-score lottery), ADM came in for a good bit of criticism. A petition was circulated at the exchange to suspend ADM Investor Services from floor privileges on the grounds that it had violated a Board of Trade rule: "It shall be an offense against the association to engage in any act which may be detrimental to the interest or welfare of the association." Eventually, on the basis of what "Carlson" and "McLoughlin" had observed and recorded, indictments were obtained against forty-six brokers and traders, and the Board set up a new in-house watchdog: a Commission on Ethics and Integrity.

Dwayne Andreas told Reuters that if the "antiquated" and "provincial" Chicago Board of Trade would just loosen up and let the soybeans relevant to its contracts be delivered "on the Illinois River, the Mississippi River, or in Duluth, where you could do something with them, this could not have happened." And in a speech he prepared but couldn't give because of a higher-priority engagement in Moscow, he delivered himself of some further reflections—unconventional, if not downright daring, for an executive of his stripe:

> Much of the deterioration in the ethical standards of business is encouraged by the American press. For instance, the *Wall Street Journal,* if you examined their writings of the last three years, comes up always on the side of the crook. They are on the side of the crook in the Chicago Board of Trade; they are on the side of the crooks in the New York investment-banking business who have made billions on insider trading; they are on the side of the petroleum companies who earn millions of dollars on their rights and continue to pollute the air...

Had Andreas actually delivered the speech, he decided later, he would not have used the nasty word "crook."

Always ready and eager to merge his diverse interests, when CEO Andreas and Chairman's Assistant Richard Burket arrived in Moscow in October 1989 for an eight-day-long US-USSR Trade and Economic Council fair at the Krasnaya Presnya Embankment, they had in tow not merely Happy Rockefeller, whom they stationed at an ADM booth that dispensed hot dogs and cold cuts fashioned from fortified soy isolate to VIPs (Joan Godbey, their all-soy lunch chef de cuisine from Decatur, was on hand to prepare them), but also, for all comers, ten thousand packages of Protoveg's Burgamix, courtesy of British Arkady's Direct Foods subsidiary, of Barrow-on-Soar, Leicestershire. The novel giveaways precipitated a near stampede. Pinned to each souvenir was a Russian translation of the instructions printed on the packet, among them "Burgamix is a complete Savoury Premix requiring only the addition of water to give a mixture which can be easily formed into rissole or burga shapes for immediate use or for chilling/freezing. Being based on Textured Vegetable Protein, Burgamix has more dietary fibre than ordinary burgas and, of course, contains no animal fat."

Until an hour or so before the exposition was declared open, the thousand American businessmen on hand from 150 companies, including, naturally, the six members of Andreas's Trade Consortium, had no idea whether or not President Gorbachev would be putting in an appearance. Then Andreas got a phone call; Gorbachev was on his way, and could the ribbon-cutting ceremony be delayed so he could participate? He arrived accompanied by Prime Minister Ryzhkov, and the two of them spent an hour and a half touring the exhibits: a General Motors Cadillac, some Band-Aids, a Caterpillar tractor, blue jeans, stuffed dogs, an IBM microchip, a videotape touting California almonds, some Estée Lauder cosmetics, and a toy called, in more or less English, a Powermaster Autobot Leader Transformer. And where they stopped, Andreas was pleased to say afterward, it wasn't just for chitchat. "They got right into the guts of what these people"—Q-tips and Ritz crackers were also on display—"were really doing," he declared.

At the ADM booth, Gorbachev politely forwent a chance to make history of sorts by becoming the first Soviet leader ever to bite into a soyburger received from the hand of a Rockefeller. He did appear to be listening attentively, however, when Andreas shared with him one of the American's favorite statistical nuggets: twenty-eight times as many people could be fed per acre planted to soybeans than by the meat resulting from the same acreage's output of grain passing through cattle. Andreas also had a letter from George Bush to share, in which the US president said he was "prepared to work with Congress to open the way to extending most-favored-nation status" to the Soviet Union" (i.e., by rescinding its 1974 Jackson-Vanik Act) and added, "It is time to begin to think anew. Positive changes are evolving in relations between our two countries."

Then the Russians and their party repaired to a private room for another ninety minutes, now to commune more intimately with a dozen American big businessmen—in, reported *Tass*, "a constructive and candid manner"—about joint ventures, trade, and other mutual concerns. When Andreas was subsequently asked about what noneconomic endeavors Gorbachev had said the two nations might fruitfully collaborate, he identified them as nuclear proliferation, global warming, and space exploration. And while Gorbachev didn't sample his meatless burger (ADM hoped this critter could ultimately become known as "vegeburger" but for the time being was using "Veggie Burger"), he did ask to have two hundred tons' worth of its basic ingredient shipped over for the delectation of those of his compatriots who hadn't made it to the exposition. By mid-1990, a Café Grill in Moscow was dispensing four thousand of the novel burgers every day. When Andreas got the news, he exclaimed, "I told Gorbachev that this was going to be the most important food development of the century!"

*   *   *

Meanwhile, Andreas was doing his level best to spread the gospel about vegeburgers in his hard-to-convert homeland. (ADM has trademarked the words "Vege Burger" in Great Britain, the USSR, and the EEC.) He himself was feasting on them for dinner, he wanted his friends to know, three times a week. In view of his previously confessed addiction to catfish as a favored entrée, it was becoming hard to visualize him supping on much else. (ADM's board member Robert Strauss, for his loyal part, though a born-and-bred scion of meat-eatin' Texas, was going around proclaiming a new breed of soy-derived sausage the actual superior of something merely carved from a steer.) The cartes-du-jour menus at Andreas's Florida enclave, old Sea View hands liked to joke, hadn't been changed since pre-Castro Cuba. When Andreas brought his ADM directors down to Florida for a warm-weather board meeting in January 1990, however, they were greeted by a sign posted outside the main dining room, proclaiming the availability of vegetable burgers—"Good for you," it was annotated—at a bargain five-dollar price.

During the directors' formal deliberations, Andreas told them that the vegeburger was going to prove to be "the most important agricultural development of the twentieth century," and that they should be on the lookout for commercials touting its historic evolution on the Sunday-morning "decision-making" television programs on which ADM liked to advertise. At lunch immediately after that solemn session, when Andreas ordered one of the new specials and addressed himself to it with a blend of gusto and reverence, quite a few of the other directors—who, to be sure, had been treated the evening before to heaps of the finest gray caviar Gorbachev could (Jackson-Vanik be hanged) ship out—were quick to follow suit. A notable exception was Dwayne's brother Lowell, who, with the defiance so characteristic of younger siblings the world over, ordered stone crabs.

Back in Decatur, concurrently, the vegeburger had become the pièce de résistance of the ADM all-soy repast. It did not appear to bother Andreas that while he was presiding over a lunch for four bemused engineers from Blagoveshchensk, out near the Soviet-Chinese border ("I've never known anyone eating one of these who didn't think he was eating good meat," the host assured the guests), he was the only one present who accepted a waitress's proffer of seconds.

27

I guess when you come right down to it, if there's one thing I've learned in all these years, it's that if we ever really want to feed the world, we can.

—DOA

O F the ten decades of the rapidly evolving twentieth century, the very first was the only one Dwayne Andreas missed. On the threshold of the very last, he could hardly wait to see what would happen next. The year 1992 was especially in his thoughts about economic affairs, as indeed it was in many of his contemporaries', for it was then that Europe was scheduled to embark on a no-holds-barred common market, the limits of which in Andreas's far-flung view might well stretch—as his friends in the Soviet Union became even more involved in trade with the West—all the way east to Vladivostok. He had already forecast that by the time that conceivably epochal year rolled around ADM would have as much as 25 percent of all its equity invested in both West European and East European ventures; and he had a bona fide Andreas, his nephew, Allen, hunkered down abroad, prepared at the hint of a deal to hop from his base at Rotterdam to Barcelona, Budapest, or Brest-Litovsk.

Andreas had professed all along not to be worried about reports suggesting that Mikhail Gorbachev might not figure prominently in the affairs of that terminal decade. In a November 1989 speech in Washington, Andreas said:

> Our media are having a field day predicting Gorbachev's imminent downfall because he has not been able to improve the standard of living in three or four short years. My feeling is that they're all wrong, and he's going to last a long time. He is learning, as all political people in America have learned long ago, that when you are an officer in an open democracy, the principal adversary is the press. First, you need and must have freedom of the press, but secondly you need a little freedom from the press. That's the learning experience that Gorbachev is going through....I see Gorbachev as the messiah of reform. His reforms to date are largely irreversible because they are a rational, pragmatic response to fundamental political and economic needs of his country. Any successor to Gorbachev will have to follow policies very much like the ones now being implemented. They are based on common sense, not ideology.

In Andreas's risk-taking line of business it is considered prudent always to hedge. Thus, he was glad to have a chance, in mid-1989, to become aquainted with President Gorbachev's most celebrated critic, Boris Yeltsin. Andreas met him at a Council on Foreign Relations lunch given in the Russian dissident's honor by David Rockefeller. Yeltsin was on a tight schedule during his stay in the United States, the arrangements for which had largely been made by the Russian expert Grace Warnecke, who was just then starting up her own advisory enterprise, called Sovus, to help American businessmen cope with some of the complexities of dealing with their Russian counterparts. Mrs. Warnecke—whose own knowledgeability and fluency stemmed from her childhood,

when her father, George Kennan, was United States ambassador to Moscow—happened to remark to Andreas that Yeltsin
might have to forego an appearance at the University of
Florida, in Miami, because of transportation and accommodation difficulties.

Andreas promptly offered to put one of his planes at
the visitor's disposal, and while he was at it, to offer to
put him up at Sea View. On learning further that Yeltsin
hoped to fit the Houston Space Center into his tight
agenda, Andreas assured her that would be no problem:
The plane would be available to speed him there and
back—and as for his being appropriately received, a single
phone call to Bob Strauss, Andreas well knew, could arrange for just about anything short of secession to be done
in Texas.

Yeltsin spent two days in Florida. Alongside the Sea View
swimming pool, in front of Andreas's two-phone cabana, he
and his host had several long talks, in the course of which
Andreas got the impression that his guest's impatience with
the course of progress in the Soviet Union might in the long
run prove to be more of a help to Gorbachev—because it gave
him clear insight into how others were thinking—than a
hindrance.

"Gorbachev and Yeltsin are on good terms," Andreas told
an audience a year later. "They have a liaison where they talk
back and forth to each other all the time. Since they're
leading different groups, they have to occasionally insult
each other, like our politicians do. I saw that happen with
Humphrey and Nixon when they were the best of friends.
And you have the same thing going on there... You'll see,
as time goes on, Yeltsin and Gorbachev will be on the same
side, bickering. The difference between them is that Yeltsin
is more radical: he's a populist, he wants to go much faster.
That's easy to do when you're an advocate. It's not so easy
to do when you're running the show. Gorbachev told me in
Minneapolis just the other day, 'Yeltsin wants to go faster. I
think I'll just turn the economy of that republic over to

him and let him go to it.' That's a wonderful solution for Gorbachev."

And however eccentrically Yeltsin was alleged to have conducted himself during that American sojourn, during the Florida phase of it his only departure from the regional norm was to wonder whether there was a Russian Orthodox church around with a Sunday service he could attend. The Andreases found one in Coral Gables, and Dwayne and Inez were happy to escort him there in their stretch Rolls-Royce and observe his devotions.

Andreas did not happen to bump into Yeltsin in the spring of 1990 when the American betook himself once again to Moscow for a US-USSR Trade and Economic Council session on the eve of Gorbachev's summit meeting with President Bush; but the ADM man did manage a two-hour tête-à-tête over there with the Soviet president. (On that jaunt, Andreas took along Bush's older brother, Prescott, whose perestroikan mission was to design a golf course outside Moscow, but who was frustrated by the complaints of mushroom hunters about his approach to digging vis-à-vis theirs.) "Gorbachev came over at a Council dinner and sat down," Andreas said, "and he said, 'Dwayne, all the things we talked about five years ago are coming to fruition, and the next few days [the days in Washington] will be the most important in history for my economic program.'" In this get-together, Andreas went on, they discussed chickens and privately owned farms and freedom of the press and freedom of religion. "When you're talking to Gorbachev, there's never any small talk," Andreas says. "It's always about how to solve a problem."

In Washington, the following week, Andreas went to both state dinners, one at the White House and one at the Soviet Embassy (the other American businessmen invited to the latter were Armand Hammer and Donald Kendall), but he skipped an Embassy lunch, which, as he later explained, was "for movie stars and Henry Kissinger and the likes of that." When Gorbachev descended upon Minneapolis for a meeting with one-hundred–odd American businessmen, Andreas was very much in evidence. At Gorbachev's request, he had arranged the gathering, at the Radisson Plaza Hotel, assisted by Minnesota's governor Rudy Perpich and Cargill's Whitney MacMillan; and it was Andreas who introduced the visitor to, among other luminaries, representatives of the National American Wholesale Grocers Association, the National Milk Producers Federation, the American Association of Soy Producers, the National Pork Producers Association, the National Turkey Federation, and the Minnesota Vikings. (Lowell and Michael Andreas were also lucky enough to make the list.) President Gorbachev, after Andreas presented him to the august assemblage, was gracious enough to say that the US-USSR Trade and Economic Council had "contributed very substantially to the development of a new cooperative approach that led to the political decision" to sign a bilateral trade pact; and to refer to his friend Andreas as "an anchor for our relations."

Andreas, for his part, said of Gorbachev, "He has stayed the course, even though it has become an obstacle course," that the Soviet leader could "make it possible for us to save the capitalistic system" from, among other obstacles, debt and depression; and that the guest of honor "has given our nation freedom from fear."

When Andreas turned seventy, in 1988, some people naturally began asking him when he was going to retire. (Those close to him knew better. And indeed at its midyear meeting in 1990, his board of directors were so confident he'd go on running the company that they raised his salary to $2.5 million.) His response one time was:

> How could I ever even think of retiring? Just look at all I have to do. Why, by 1995, the Chinese will be needing to import something like five million tons of cooking oil a year, and the Russians fifteen million tons of soymeal simply for [he is as aware as the next megagrocer of the incongruity of the words' oft-used meaning] chicken feed. You know, one-third of all the business in the world is my kind of business. The longer you're in it, the more things

you see that need to be done. When you see them and you see that they're not being done, you get very uneasy, and the next thing you know, you're trying to do them yourself.

Look—it takes a new flour mill every week somewhere on earth just to feed the new mouths. And then along come the politicians and tell the farmers not to grow more grain! Every port city in the world—Dakar, Buenos Aires, Shanghai, you name it—is developing chicken farms, and chickens eat, eat, eat. Every night if you're like me, you go to bed knowing that when you wake up, there'll be another few million chickens and pigs eating and eating and another few million people looking for a piece of bread. That's what needles you, especially when you know that we *can* feed the world. When I get to thinking like that, I remember something I once read about Tolstoy, about how he worked terribly hard to get himself a bike, and then couldn't stand it because not everybody had a bike, and so he started a program to get everybody else bikes.

Now, if I were somehow in charge of feeding the world and had unlimited funds at my disposal, I would see to it that all people extant, as the underpinning of their daily food requirement, would get a bowl of porridge made up of wheat, soybeans, and corn. That would cost only twenty-five cents a portion. Throw in a few greens, for vitamins, and some cassava, for starch, and there you'd be. And for those lucky enough to have access to bread I'd mandate the inclusion in it of soy protein, which would improve its nutritive value by two hundred percent.

Let's say that there are at least five hundred million people alive who don't now live as human beings should. Well, for a mere one hundred and twenty-five million dollars a day I could feed them all. That's only fifty billion a year. We could knock fifty billion off the USA defense budget, and the Pentagon would still have around three hundred billion left for *its* purposes. The human race can't go on solving its problems with billions of dollars for weapons.

You know, years ago the idea of feeding grain to animals had merit. People feeding them also fertilized their land with the manure. But today, with other fertilizers, animals are a luxury. If you accept that as a premise, then you come to a number of conclusions, one being that the trend will have to be to make food for human beings out of feed. Anyway, to provide enough meat for everybody alive today, you'd have to have so many animals on the planet you couldn't live on it yourself. I guess when you come right down to it, if there's one thing I've learned in all these years, it's that if we ever really want to feed the world, we can.

EPILOGUE

How things can change over the years! A postcard sent from
St. Paul, Minnesota, to Mankata at the start of 1954 was
addressed to "Mr. Duane (*sic*) Andreas, the skunk who wants
to trade with Russia!," and among the unflattering sentiments expressed was, "It would serve you greedy men right if
some Korean veteran or POW came down there and blew your
demoralized heads off for even suggesting that we trade with
those Communist Devils!"

Andreas is as fond of clichés as any corporate CEO. Early
in 1991, by which time he was long since accustomed to
trading not only with those reconstituted ogres but all over
the globe, one of his favorite phrases remained "Knowledge is
power." A business associate at Decatur, casting humility to
the winds, said not long ago, "Routine memos we get from
our Toepfer people in Europe—such as 'Who would have

believed three years ago that it would be possible to sell Philippine coconut extractions to Korea!'—help explain why Dwayne and his ADM people seem to know so much more than anybody else in the world including governments."

There were more and more matters for him to keep informed about. At home, the company was doing its environmental bit by using scrapped automobile tires as fuel for its state-of-the-art boilers, and using the energy they unleashed to facilitate the production of biochemicals—amino and citric acids, penicillin, threonine, tryptophan, lysine, and others. (A good number of these fitted logically enough into the ADM scheme of things, being derived from the dextrose content of corn.) Then, too, there was the problem, at a time when other large companies were struggling to stay afloat, of determining where to invest ADM's surplus cash, a tidy billion or so. Andreas has long had a low opinion of going into debt, because he doesn't like paying interest. His explanation is a typical farmer's one: "It ain't the horse; it's the oats it eats."

ADM was unlikely to suffer unduly from a recession or depression. "Our business is mainly in cooking oil, margarine, chicken feed, bread, and sweeteners," Andreas says, "and during recessions bread and margarine consumption usually rises, at the same time that the cost of some of our raw materials goes down. In the end, though, the big thing in our favor is that we've never got involved in anything that's a luxury."

As for the Middle East crisis, a rise in the cost of oil and, therefore, of conventional gasoline could only help the sales of fuels containing ethanol. At one of his most recent shareholders' gatherings, Andreas felt impelled to jocularly remind the shareholders that while he had nothing personal against ethanol's longtime rival methanol, the latter was, more or less, wood alcohol, and that if they drank it they'd soon be dead. Ethanol, on the other hand, was practically indistinguishable from vodka, and drinking *it* would merely make them happy. There was no evidence that any stockholder rushed to the parking lot with a siphon or ladle.

Meanwhile, Andreas was increasingly striving to promote soybean offshoots for human consumption. ADM's 1991 Sunday-morning television commercials—each approved after careful scrutiny by Andreas himself—touted succulent-looking dishes any rightminded American would presumably choose over Mom's apple pie. To his delight, some two hundred and fifty grocery stores in the Midwest were stocking soy-based products. And he had finally hit upon what he judged to be the appropriate name for his meatless hamburgers. "Vegeburgers," his nomenclatural advisers had persuaded him, sounded too generic. So he and they had thrown in their lot with "Harvest Burgers," and they hoped the new name would reap suitable rewards.

More consequentially, Andreas professed not to be fazed by the much-publicized tribulations of his friend Mikhail Gorbachev. Andreas has a low opinion of the press, which, having no interest in a political career, he has never hesitated to air. "Farmers are always reading insulting pieces, almost daily, in the Eastern press," he told the board of directors of Harvest States, a big Midwestern cooperative; and to another audience he declared, "No Eastern newspaper has an educated agricultural writer." When it came to Gorbachev, his indictments were more sweeping. During the height of the Persian Gulf crisis, Andreas told an acquaintance, "In spite of all the things we read in our notoriously inaccurate press—reports usually based on fringe information—Gorbachev's very solidly in. You read stories every week about how he's going to be pushed out, but every time something comes up for a vote in the Supreme Soviet—except in the case of his choice for a vice-president—they vote for him. And Gorbachev and Boris Yeltsin have a liaison where they talk back and forth to each other. But since they're leading different groups, just like our politicians do, they occasionally have to insult each other."

Toward the end of 1990, his seventy-third birthday looking not too far off, at a stage of life when most corporate executives either had retired or were seriously contemplating such a step, Andreas seemed busier than ever. He hadn't found time to learn much more about a new organization called the International Agribusiness Association than that he'd agreed to become its president-elect. Concurrently, he treated himself to three newfangled electronic chess sets—one for each of his principal residences. He had played some chess, as a boy, with his older brothers—especially with Osborn, the intellectual of the tribe, who was a concert pianist and read Joseph Conrad and Henry James—but in later years had always been too busy to pursue the challenging conflict. Now, though, he could indulge in a match without having to arrange for some other human to sit across the board. A friend hearing about the multiple purchases couldn't help surmising that this signified Andreas's intention of finally calling it quits, and wondered when that might come to be. Andreas's response was thoroughly in character. "Not till I outsmart all three sons of bitches!" he said.

APPENDIX

*Excerpts from a November 1, 1989, speech by Dwayne
Andreas in Washington, D.C., at a forum on East-West
relations conducted by the Brookings Institute:*

I first met President Gorbachev in 1984 before he was promot-
ed to general chairman. I perceived him right then and there to be
an *extremist;* that is, a man in possession of *extreme common
sense.* A pragmatic and practical gentleman.

This is before, you understand, he became general secretary.

He said then he would try to make socialism work better by
borrowing a few things from market-oriented countries. He indicated that he would unleash market forces and the forces of supply
and demand and authorize private farming, which he had already
recommended to the Politburo three times and had been rejected.
He would plan for the organization of cooperatives to conduct the
business of millions of farmers and workers. I perceived that he was

thinking of an economy something like the democratic socialist economies of Western Europe. That's what his role model is, in my opinion. That will take time—when you have to correct past mistakes, things usually get worse before they get better.

Here is one reason I think he will stay: We have to keep in mind something we already know—*"Man does not live by bread alone."* He has given the Soviet citizens some important freedoms. FREEDOM TO *FARM*, OF THE *PRESS*, TO *WORSHIP*, TO *TRAVEL*, AND NOW FREEDOM TO *VOTE*. These freedoms have revived *HOPE*. Whole populations have been known to live on *HOPE* for decades. I expect them to give him a few more years to *turn things around*.

It reminds me of our Great Depression, which I remember very, very well. Most of our citizens thought capitalism had failed, and we had lost faith in our system in the depths of the Depression. When Roosevelt was elected, his first year was busy adopting features of socialism to make capitalism work better—quite a number of them. And then for years journalists predicted Roosevelt's demise. Every time there was an election, he got a bigger majority. [Or so Andreas liked to believe.] The reason they predicted it was because unemployment and depression persisted for several years after Roosevelt began to apply new policies. But Roosevelt revived *HOPE* and survived until improvements were manifest. He did a lot of it by just promising freedom from fear.

I think Gorbachev has some of the same problems to go through that Roosevelt did.

I believe our national policies should be firmly based *in our own self-interest*. That's the way *other nations* operate, including the *SOVIETS*. And from every conceivable standpoint—*national security, economic, and political*—I believe it is *very much* in our national self-interest to *normalize* relations with the East.

If I'm right, we should be rushing to *sign agreements* with Gorbachev.

But if I'm wrong and Gorbachev is headed for a fall, then we'd better sign those agreements *even faster, and try to lock them in (while this window of time is open)* into *arms* and *trade* deals that are not likely to be reversed.

We need normal relations with the Soviets, not to help Gorbachev or to help Russia dig *itself* out of the hole *it's* in. We need them to help us and to dig *ourselves* out of the hole *we are in*.

Gorbachev is throwing us a lifeline. He says we both ought to stop the arms race that's *wrecking our economies.* He traveled extensively in the West. Maybe he saw capitalism and decided it was worth saving. One of his comrades made this comment to me: *"Capitalism stinks,* but I love to get a whiff of it."

Saving our place in the capitalist system requires getting the monkey of runaway defense spending off our back. Only Gorbachev has the power to make that possible—Gorbachev and President Bush. Because we are not likely to do any unilateral disarming.

The *New York Times* columnist, *William Safire,* who is anything but a dove when it comes to the Soviets, *recently wrote*—I want to quote him exactly: "As the percentage of Soviet GNP spent for *arms* is forced down, ours *is sure to drop, too*—say from just *under 7 percent of our GNP* to *4 percent.* That saves $150 billion, *the size of our current deficit."* That's what our President Bush and Gorbachev have on the table.

Forbes October 30 edition says: "Defense spending will decline steadily," and "Armed Services manpower and Defense Department jobs will fall by 750,000."

The October 29 *Chicago Tribune* editorializes: "President Bush and Congress should look at compromises that would include the *dirty words—taxes* and *defense cuts."*

What they all fail to mention, and what most people forget, is that the savings would be far greater. The *$150 billion* that Safire refers to is just *deficit spending,* a onetime appropriation, but it is financed by *government borrowing* from *foreign lenders.* A far cry from the good old days when we borrowed from ourselves and didn't worry.

My father once told me that you can figure the true cost of a loan by dividing any interest rate into *seventy-two.* That will tell you how long it takes the lender to double his money at your expense with *compound interest. Try it*—it is a simple formula. *It works.* Compound interest is what we pay because our government is committed to borrow the money for all interest payments *as far ahead as the eye can see.*

Accordingly, when the Treasury funds a $150 billion deficit with *9 percent bonds,* compound interest doubles it *every eight years.* Now follow me. Doubling in eight years. One hundred and fifty billion dollars spent this year. In eight years, that is $300 billion; in sixteen years that is $600 billion; and in twenty-four years, that is $1.2 trillion—$12 hundred billion.

It reminds me of another bit of advice I got from my father. In my early life I remember I wanted to buy a $20 horse: "Son," he said, "it's not the cost of the horse—it's the oats it eats."

It makes you wonder why we permit Congress to mandate deficit spending without also appropriating money to cover future interest charges on that spending. The original appropriation, the $150 billion, is just the tip of the iceberg.

That's why thirty-six cents of each income-tax dollar goes for interest on the public debt.

It is no secret that about a third of our military budget is earmarked for the defense of Japan and Western Europe. They spend a lot less on arms and a lot more on production than we do. The result is that we're losing the war that counts—the war for *economic independence.*

That is why someone recently said the Cold War is over and Japan won.

If we persist in living it up, pouring dollars abroad which come back like homing pigeons to buy American assets with our self-depreciated dollar, we, of course, will ultimately become a colony again.

Over the past seven years, our budget and trade deficits have *spun out of control.* Our cumulative foreign debt is *$700 billion,* and it's climbing. Ten years ago they owed us $500 billion, the biggest transfer of wealth in the history of the world by far.

There's an old Chinese proverb that says, "If you don't *change* direction, you'll get where you're headed." We're headed for runaway inflation. If we don't change our direction, we'll wind up like three other very rich countries—*Argentina, Brazil,* and *Australia*—whistling in the graveyard of inflation while our debt snowballs.

Australia's huge external debt just led Moody's to downgrade their bonds. As a result, they've got interest rates that are way up in double digits. That's what's in store for us, a few years down the road, if *we don't get our house in order.*

I believe it was Alan Greenspan who predicted: If we can get rid of the budget deficit, long-term interest rates will fall to *4 percent.* That would knock about *$150 billion* off of our interest costs, *cut $50 billion* off the interest costs of the Third World, and make it possible for them to be customers and *buy from us again.*

This is a formula that would save the capitalist system from self-destruction.

Normalizing relations with the Soviets can help us *cut military spending* and *balance the budget*. And it can help us improve our *trade balance* by exporting to the East—the *last untapped markets* in the developed world.

So the vital question today is, *who will get the business* that any future Soviet regime will do with the West?

Our trade rivals right now are beating us to these markets. They are way ahead of us.

When Gorbachev talks of a *"common European home,"* he's really referring to a *post-1992 EEC alliance* with the Soviets, a common *market* stretching from London to Vladivostok, encompassing a *fourth of the globe, a fifth of the world's population, and half the world's GNP.*

It's already taking shape.

I don't think it's generally understood here in America just how fast the *Europeans* are moving to secure their strategic *economic interests* in the East.

The EEC has signed trade deals with Poland, Hungary, and Czechoslovakia, and it's going to conclude a treaty with the *Soviets in just a few weeks*. They have already negotiated. They are in a rush—negotiations with the Hungarians began in March, and a complete and comprehensive treaty was signed in September, with unheard of speed.

Poland and Hungary have whispered that they would like to be members of the Common Market. The EFTA group have already gone to Moscow and said we would like to be party to the trade agreement with the EEC.

Seventeen Latin American countries have signed trade treaties with the Soviets.

In an *amazingly* short period of time, the eastern countries have boosted their trade with the EEC by 20 percent *or more*, and the Soviets now do more trade with market-oriented countries than they do with their so-called satellites, who used to do almost all of it.

The Japanese aren't looking on trade with the Soviets and Chinese as a spectator sport, either.

They now do about $6 billion in business with the Soviets—

twice what we do. But if you disregard the agricultural commodities and refer to value-added products, the Japanese are doing twelve times as much business with the Soviets as we are. If you combine Japan's finances and productive capacity with the raw materials of the Soviet Union, you might come up with a program that will satisfy the Soviets' hunger for consumer goods—without us.

Unless we move quickly to normalize economic relations with the Soviets and China, we will find ourselves a second-rate power with a *Third World debt* and a deteriorating living standard.

But we come to the table with some serious handicaps—the legacy of years of politicizing our business relations and antagonizing customers. We've used trade as a weapon to force the Soviets to behave, with predictable results.

Fifteen years ago, when we passed the Jackson-Vanik legislation to get the Soviets to increase emigration, they just responded by shutting their doors even tighter.

We slapped an embargo on grain exports. They just bought their grain elsewhere. We not only lost billions in direct and indirect cost, but gave up huge chunks of market share *permanently* to Brazil, Canada, Argentina, and the EEC.

To President Reagan's everlasting credit, he healed this self-inflicted wound one month after his inauguration.

We banned exports of one hundred thousand different items of goods and services—almost all of which the Soviets can buy freely from many other places in the world. Trying to control technology exports in this world is like trying to catch water in a sieve. We've found that out the hard way.

We have made a botch of it, causing hundreds of companies to do business through foreign affiliates or lose out to foreign companies entirely.

One former cabinet member, whom I consider to be one of the most enlightened, estimated to me that these policies have cut $15 billion a year off of our export capabilities in recent years.

There are plenty of other examples of how our Cold War politics inflicts damage on our own economic interests while other countries put their own economic self-interest first.

We could be doing tens of billions of dollars in two-way trade, creating sales and jobs for both countries. Instead, our trade in 1988 was only $3.2 billion, most of it in US agriculture exports. If you subtract them, we did less trade with the Soviet Union than we did *with Haiti.* Less than we did with Trinidad.

In order to export to the Eastern bloc, we'll have to open our doors to their goods and offer most-favored-nation status to the Soviet Union as quickly as possible. No one expects them to sell much here, but granting access to our markets will encourage them to buy more from us. You can't do business when you have a "KEEP OUT" sign over the door. The insult alone is enough to send a potential customer elsewhere to spend his money.

The EEC commissioners have just recommended an open-door policy to eastern imports. Last week they declared free trade with Poland! Under these circumstances, who do you expect to buy from?

Today, when national security is defined in terms of economic and financial strength, we've got to wipe out our trade deficit. *Self-interest demands expansion* of our trade with the Soviets, and for that matter, with China, too, and *I believe this administration will help do that.* I believe they will help open doors.

President Bush has wide experience and is extraordinarily familiar with international trade and economics. His team—Secretaries Baker, Cheney, and Yeutter, and Mr. Scowcroft—are all very knowledgeable about the international scene and its impact on our economy. I believe they will act to strengthen our economic relations with the Soviets. They are a strong team. They work together, and I believe they will get results.

They have already made great strides in arms control and in bilateral and regional issues. I'm sure they know you can't construct a solid house of political and military agreements without a strong foundation of economic and trade agreements.

Let me briefly mention some important steps that ought to be taken right now:

One, let's get rid of laws that stand in the way of expanded US-Soviet trade. Conditions have changed. The Cold War is over. Cold War *laws* must have change, too.

With emigration from the Soviet Union far above our most urgent requests and a liberalized emigration law in the works, Jackson-Vanik should be a prime candidate for review.

So, too, are statutes that restrict Export-Import Bank financing and impose export-licensing restrictions. Most-favored-nation treatment to the Soviets right now is clearly in our best interest.

Two, align our trade laws with changing world political and economic realities. Among other things, we need to spell out the meaning of "strategic" interests and the principle of contract sanctity so other countries can trust our contracts once again.

Three, we should codify our export-licensing procedures. Today, they are expensive, time-consuming impediments to commerce. Licensing should no longer be a political football kicked from one department to another—nor a mechanism to sabotage trade.

Most controlled items could be placed on automatic general license at *no risk to national security,* and we need to do that as soon as possible.

Four, we must begin serious negotiations on new US-Soviet trade and tax treaties, right now. We are late with this negotiation.

They would provide guarantees against expropriation and accommodate changes in the Soviets' foreign economic practices, such as joint ventures. Substantially all other countries protect their businesses in the USSR by treaty, and we should, too.

Five, we should offer Ex-Im credits and guarantees, as well as OPIC guarantees.

The Soviets have more credit offered to them from our Western European allies than they are willing to use, and they've got a top credit rating. But very often, in commercial transactions, credit is part of the price. Usually it's the seller who uses credit as a means of inducing the buyer to buy. Eight thousand companies in Russia who have never done foreign business before are now authorized to negotiate with foreigners. Sellers will occasionally find credit profitable and a means to induce a sale.

Six, we need to use export-enhancement programs and CCC credits when necessary to keep the US competitive in the world's agricultural markets. We have to sell at world market prices, or we won't sell at all. No buyer will pay us more for wheat, corn, or vegetable oil than our competitors charge.

This is a must. We'll never close our trade deficit unless we export more of our farm products. And we can't export more unless our government uses the same tools and devices other governments are using and treats this customer like we expect to be treated and like we treat others—the golden rule.

Seven, I'd also suggest that it is very much in our national interest to have the Soviets in *GATT*, the *IMF*, and the *World Bank*.

The closer they are tied to international trade and financial institutions, the greater the stake they'll have in preserving the international economic system. We're far better off binding them to international agreements than looking on from the outside while they cut bilateral deals with other countries.

The Soviets will have to make some basic changes in order to qualify for full membership in these institutions—such as further moves toward a market economy and a viable program for ultimate ruble convertibility.

They have indicated their intention to do this, but it will take some time. They surely can be accorded observer status *right now*. There are many precedents for that. And it is in our interest that they make the adjustments needed to qualify.

These seven points represent a clear trade policy that advances our economic and national security interests. And every single proposal I have made is *already the established policy of our trading partners*.

We've finally reached a point where most of us recognize that the US and the Soviet Union have nothing to fight about. Our common interests far outweigh our differences. Cooperation is an economic and *national security imperative for both our countries*.

Gone are the days when the US was the capitalist devil, and the USSR was the evil empire. Today we both recognize that our real enemies are the common enemies of mankind: *nuclear proliferation, chemical weapons, deterioration of the environment, depletion of the earth's energy supplies, world hunger, and tragic loss of the world's topsoil*.

The other day in our meeting with President Gorbachev someone asked him, if the military problems are resolved, what other thing could we cooperate on in the near future? His answer was nuclear proliferation, global warming, and space exploration.

Those enemies can be conquered and world peace secured through economic cooperation and trade. In my experience, international trade is one of mankind's most necessary and ennobling activities—the essential building block of peace and prosperity.

The historian Arnold Toynbee once wrote: "Our Age will be remembered not for its horrifying crimes or astonishing inventions, but because it is the first generation since the dawn of history in which mankind has dared to believe it is practical to make the benefits of civilization available to the whole human race."

I *believe he was right*—and that *normal trade* and commercial *relations* with the Soviets will bring us closer *to that goal.*

INDEX